IMAGES
of America

SUWANNEE COUNTY

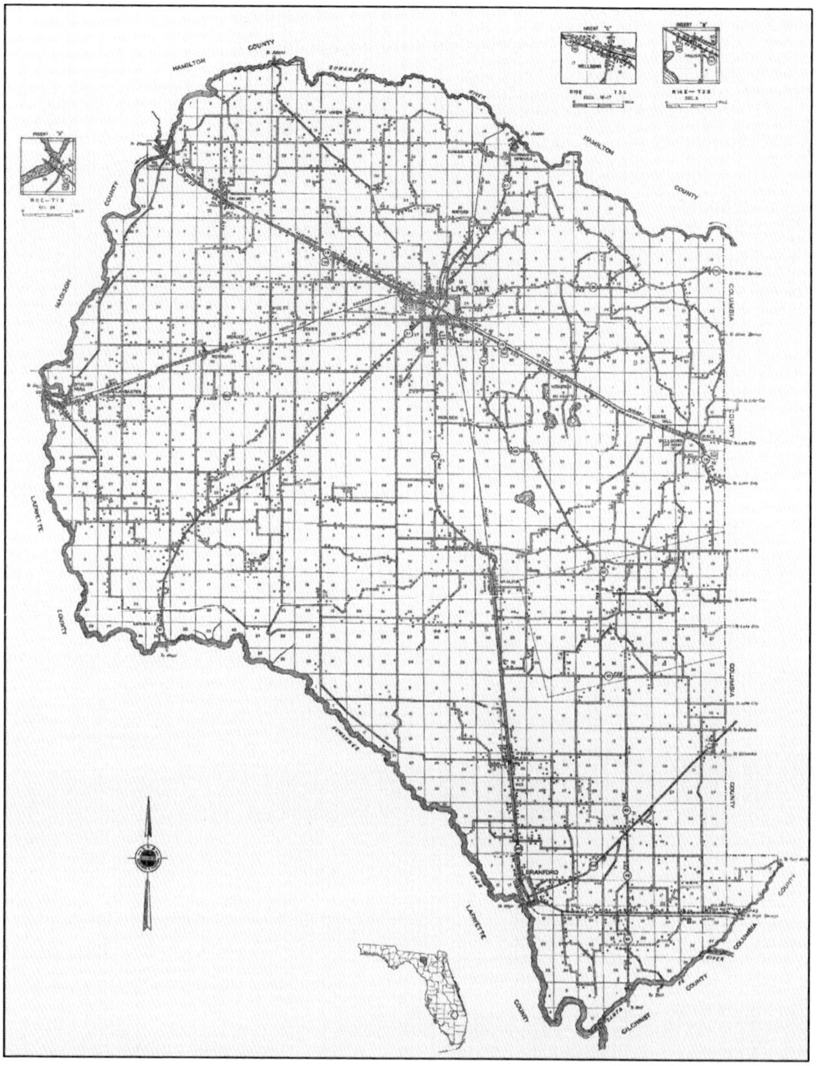

This 1946 map shows the famed Suwannee River running along the north, west, and south borders of Suwannee County. The county seat is Live Oak, situated near the top center with numerous roads leading into it. The town of Branford lies near the southern tip of Suwannee County, just a few miles north of the junction of the Santa Fe River and Suwannee River. Some of the other communities shown here are now little more than names on a sign and a few scattered houses. The numerous isolated homes throughout the county testify to the rural nature of Suwannee County; a majority of the population was, and still is, found in a rural setting. (David Phinney.)

On the Cover: Because the Suwannee River borders the county on three sides, it was only natural that many ferries would spring up prior to the expansion of railroads and invention of automobiles. For many years, the ferries charged fees based upon the number of people, animals, and wagons crossing the river. One of those many ferries was Irvine's Ferry, near Luraville, named for Col. Washington Lafayette Irvine, its operator. This photograph shows Irvine's Ferry in or around 1882; the young man fourth from left appears to be wearing a Confederate uniform. Local tradition states that the man holding the ferry pole is Washington Irvine. (Suwannee County Clerk of the Court.)

IMAGES
of America

SUWANNEE COUNTY

Eric Musgrove
foreword by Randy S. Torrance

ARCADIA
PUBLISHING

ISBN 978-0-7385-8821-6

Published by Arcadia Publishing
Charleston, South Carolina

Printed in the United States of America

Library of Congress Control Number: 2011929611

For all general information, please contact Arcadia Publishing:
Telephone 843-853-2070
Fax 843-853-0044
E-mail sales@arcadiapublishing.com
For customer service and orders:
Toll-Free 1-888-313-2665

Visit us on the Internet at www.arcadiapublishing.com

To my family, who has put up with my countless hours of work,
and to all those who have inspired me to preserve our history

Contents

Foreword

"A Pictorial History owes much to its predecessors."

This pictorial collection is only a glimpse, a brief look into the life and landscape of a community that has been home to tribes of Indians, farmers, storekeepers, and innkeepers and today is home to more than 40,000 residents.

Suwannee County is intended to introduce you to those who found the delights of living in the Suwannee Valley years before we did and to arouse your curiosity about what happened here in days gone by.

As Jerry Clower, the famous country comedian, said, "Every story I tell is *almost* true." The stories and events recorded in this book are all true. The people are real. The events really happened. The places really do exist.

Within these pages, you will find random slices of the lives and times of some people, places, and events, pieces of a larger story snatched up and patched together and crafted into photographs in a form that passes for history.

As the curator and executive director of the Suwannee County Historical Museum, much of my job is based around these random slices of history. While these slices all come from the same fruit, they are sometimes bittersweet in taste: tastes of reflection, as demonstrated during the reunion of Civil War veterans in 1909; tastes of joyous occasions, such as the dedication of the Hal Adams Bridge in 1947; and tastes of devastation, as reflected in the flood of 1964. It is through these slices of history that our future is shaped and molded.

You can look for some unity and harmony in these slices of history—a collection of random photographs and anecdotes of Suwannee County—and you might find it. These slices represent the people and events of a people that developed and maintained a way of life on a portion of the surface of earth along the banks of the Suwannee River, an area of 2,000 square miles. But beyond that, these are only slices of lives and times.

—Randy S. Torrance
Executive Director/Curator
Suwannee County Historical Museum
Live Oak, Florida

ACKNOWLEDGMENTS

It is difficult to write an acknowledgment because I will, without doubt, forget someone's contributions; nevertheless, I would be remiss if I did not thank the many who have assisted me. First of all, I wish to thank those who lived in prior years who had the foresight to preserve old pictures, diaries, and records, detailing Suwannee County's early years. No doubt I would have much less to work with without them.

Secondly, I must thank all of those who have spent their time, money, and efforts in continuing to preserve Suwannee County's photographic history over the years. Most notably are the late Carol Herring of the Suwannee County Historical Museum; her successor, Randy Torrance; the Suwannee County Historical Commission; the Suwannee County Clerk of the Court; Steve Sharpless (formerly of the Suwannee County Maintenance Department and now enjoying a well-earned retirement); Susie Baxter; Kenneth Thrower; Thomas and Glenda Musgrove; and Millie Griswold of the Advent Christian Village Archives.

I also wish to thank Lindsay Carter and Caitrin Cunningham, my editors at Arcadia Publishing, for their tireless devotion to their profession and for holding the hand of a publishing company newcomer as he asked questions, made mistakes, and slowly learned the art of professional publishing. Without them, this book would not exist.

Finally, thanks to my wife, Sarah, and our children, Alex and Abby, for their love and encouragement during the long hours of research, scanning, and writing. I would be nothing without them. To all of you, I say, "Thank you!"

Unless otherwise noted, the photographs in this work are courtesy of the Suwannee County Historical Museum. Many other photographs are courtesy of the Suwannee County Clerk of the Court (SCCC) and the Advent Christian Village Archives (ACV Archives).

INTRODUCTION

Almost everyone in America, and indeed many throughout the world, know the first line of the song "Old Folks at Home," and most refer to the song by that first line: "Way down upon the Swanee River." That famous river begins in the Okefenokee Swamp of South Georgia and meanders its way some 266 miles before emptying into the Gulf of Mexico. Nestled halfway between those points is Suwannee County, established by an act of the Florida Legislature on December 21, 1858, and bordered on three sides by the famous river of song, which gave the county its name.

First inhabited by indigenous peoples, the county was claimed by fierce warriors called the Timucua when the Spanish explored the territory in the first half of the 16th century. A knight of Panfilo de Narvaez's 1528 expedition became the first recorded victim of drowning on the Suwannee River when he foolishly rushed into the dark waters. And 11 years later, Hernando de Soto's expedition crossed through the territory that is now Suwannee County, fighting and severely defeating the Timucua near the village of Napituca. Little was done for the next 50 years, until the Spanish established several missions in the area, but they were abandoned or destroyed by the beginning of the 18th century, leaving the territory in the hands of native peoples who were later called the Seminoles.

The Spanish eventually ceded Florida to Great Britain in 1763, at the end of the Seven Years' War (called the French and Indian War by Americans), but regained it in 1783, after the American Revolution. It was during this second Spanish period that the first permanent settlers of European descent moved into what is now Suwannee County. They were soon joined by others, and by the time Florida became a state in 1845, there were several hundred men, women, and children eking out an existence in the area. By 1836, with the arrival of steamboats upon the Suwannee River, these settlers had sporadic access to better goods from far away. The expulsion of the Seminole Indians from the Suwannee River area sped growth, eventually resulting in the creation of Suwannee County in 1858.

Unfortunately, war clouded the horizon, and some 15 percent of Suwannee County's adult male population marched off to serve the Confederate States of America during the Civil War. Railroads had entered the county just before the Civil War, when the Pensacola & Georgia Railroad was constructed eastward from Tallahassee toward Jacksonville, with the competing Florida, Atlantic & Gulf Railroad expanded westward from Jacksonville until they met at nearby Lake City. This railroad provided transportation for troops and food as the Civil War quickly engulfed the nation. This link was so vital, in fact, that Union troops landed at Jacksonville with orders to destroy the railroad bridge over the Suwannee River at Columbus, a community in the northwest corner of Suwannee County. This attempt led to the battle of Olustee, Florida's largest Civil War battle. A second railroad was constructed from the hamlet of Live Oak northward into Georgia, being completed only months before the demise of the Confederacy. At the close of the Civil War, Suwannee County was a poor and struggling county, much like the rest of the South. Although the county had not seen the physical devastation of other parts of the Confederacy, great economic changes occurred with the loss of some $15 million worth of slaves, who suddenly were free. The situation in the South allowed Northern businessmen to enter into the market, and Suwannee County was no different. Among those who came South for a new start were John and Nancy Parshley, who built a home and various businesses in the community of Live Oak.

The abundance of natural resources allowed entrepreneurs to make large fortunes in turpentine, lumber, and cotton during the last decades of the 19th century. The increase in railroad service throughout the county made it possible for those men (and one or two women) to ship their products to the rest of the United States, and it served as a means to bring in even more settlers. The central location of Live Oak in regards to these railroads and related businesses meant that it became the county seat in 1868, replacing the community of Houston, which stood only a few miles to the east.

During the rest of the 19th century, many steamboats traveled the length of the river as far as White Springs, until the *City of Hawkinsville* ended its days alongside a pier on the lower Suwannee in 1923, replaced by the railroad and automobiles. Numerous railroads continued to expand into Suwannee County, and many well-known Florida short lines made their home here, including the Live Oak, Perry & Gulf (the "Loping Gopher"), the Florida Railway, and many logging railroads. For the most part, these railroads have been replaced by road transportation.

The beginning of the 20th century saw Suwannee County, and particularly Live Oak, at its heyday, with numerous residents enjoying a well-to-do life from logging, turpentine, cotton, and manufacturing. Live Oak was the fifth largest city, and largest inland city, in all of Florida, with a variety of entertainment and business open to its population; the natural springs at Suwannee Springs and Dowling Park, for instance, brought travelers from around the world to bathe in the sulphur waters there. Unfortunately, this period of time was relatively short-lived, and soon, South Florida growth, coupled with the decimation of the cotton crop in 1915, doomed Suwannee County's commercial rise.

Suwannee County faced World War I and the Great Depression with great anxiety over the future, but World War II brought the beginning of revival for the county, as more businesses once again began to move into the area. The focus upon agricultural interests has remained strong since then, and people have been drawn to the laid back, rural atmosphere of this county and its abundant natural resources. The residents of Suwannee County have faced trouble before, and will no doubt face it again, but the indomitable spirit of its people will continue to endure. This book is a testament to their will.

One

Early Years and Prosperity

Suwannee County was created by an act of the Florida Legislature on December 21, 1858, with the county seat designated as "the house of William Hines." Soon, the seat was moved to the community of Houston in the northeastern portion of the county. The first census in 1860 showed merely 2,303 people, one-third of whom were enslaved. The Civil War saw part of this population go off to war, while the rest floundered about without them, stifling growth for several years.

At the close of the Civil War, businessmen such as Ohioan John Parshley moved to Suwannee County to make a fortune. Looking to the vast stands of virgin timber for a profit, Parshley and others built up Live Oak from the tiny hamlet it had been at the end of the Civil War. The completion of a north-south railroad junction through Live Oak to Lawton, Georgia (now DuPont), as the Civil War ended was a major factor in the growth of Live Oak; for several years, it was the only railroad into Florida. This, coupled with the various nearby natural resources of timber, turpentine, cotton, and mineral springs, led to Live Oak and all of Suwannee County growing exponentially.

By the 1905 state census, Live Oak was the largest inland city and fifth largest city overall in Florida, following Jacksonville, Pensacola, Tampa, and Key West. Numerous sawmills, cotton mills, manufacturing plants, and other businesses thrived in the city limits, and its residents had access to nearly everything commercially available to Americans. As befitted such a community, many new (mainly brick) buildings were constructed, replacing the first-generation wooden structures that had outlived their usefulness. Settlers continued to arrive in the outlying areas of Suwannee County, benefiting from the cheap land, abundant timber stands, and the possibility of growing rich from cotton and other crops.

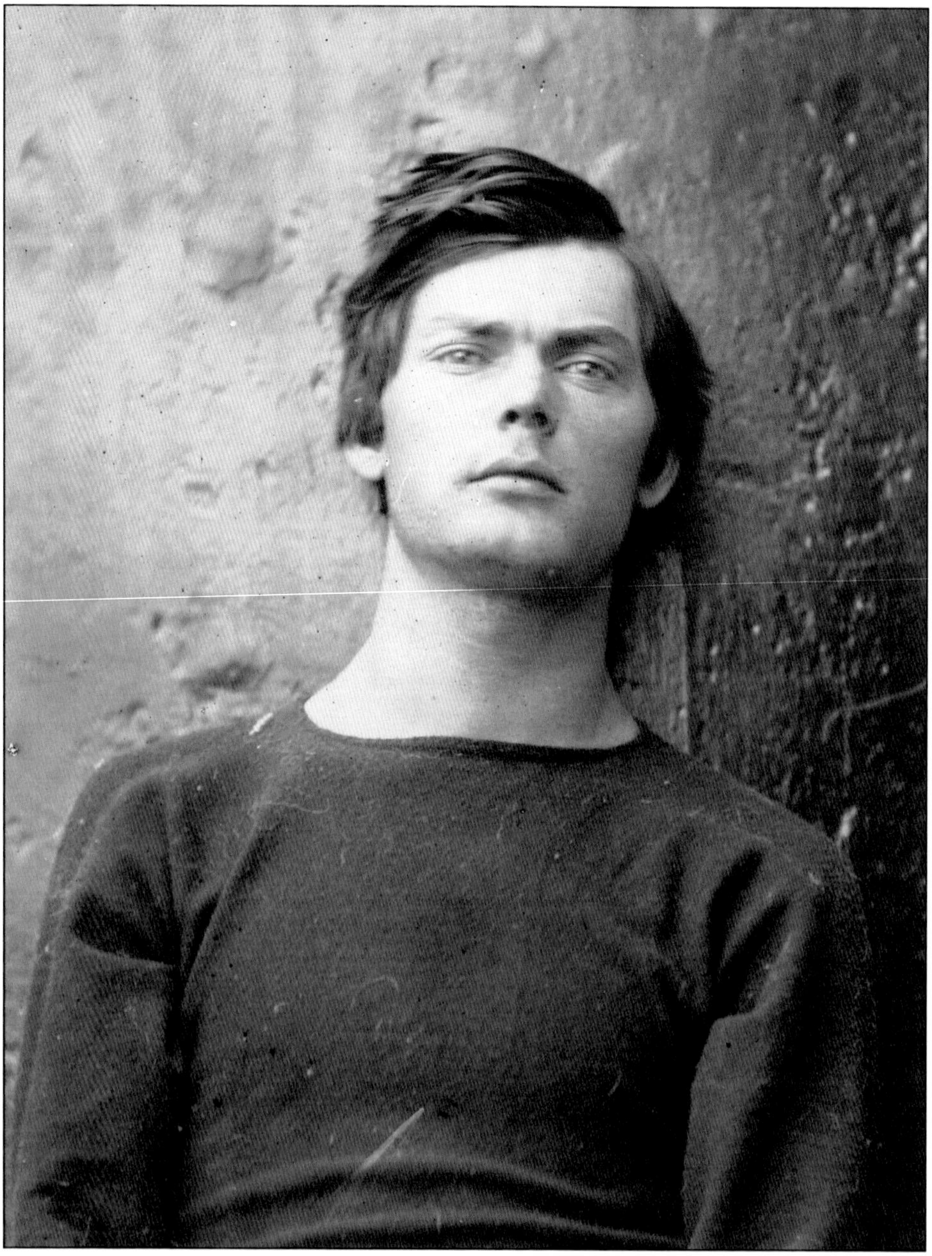

In 1859, Baptist minister George C. Powell and his family moved to Suwannee County from Georgia. Son Lewis Thornton Powell enlisted in the Hamilton Blues of the Confederate army in 1861 at the age of 17. Fighting through the Peninsular Campaign, Lewis was wounded and captured at Gettysburg in 1863 but escaped and joined Mosby's Rangers. In April 1865, Powell was part of the conspiracy to kill Pres. Abraham Lincoln, wounding Secretary of State William Seward and four others at the same time that John Wilkes Booth was in Ford's Theater, shooting Lincoln. Seward was only saved because bandages from an earlier carriage accident deflected Powell's knife. Fleeing the scene, Powell returned to the scene of the conspirators' meetings at the exact time Federal troops arrived to arrest those inside. This photograph shows Powell during his 1865 trial. (SCCC.)

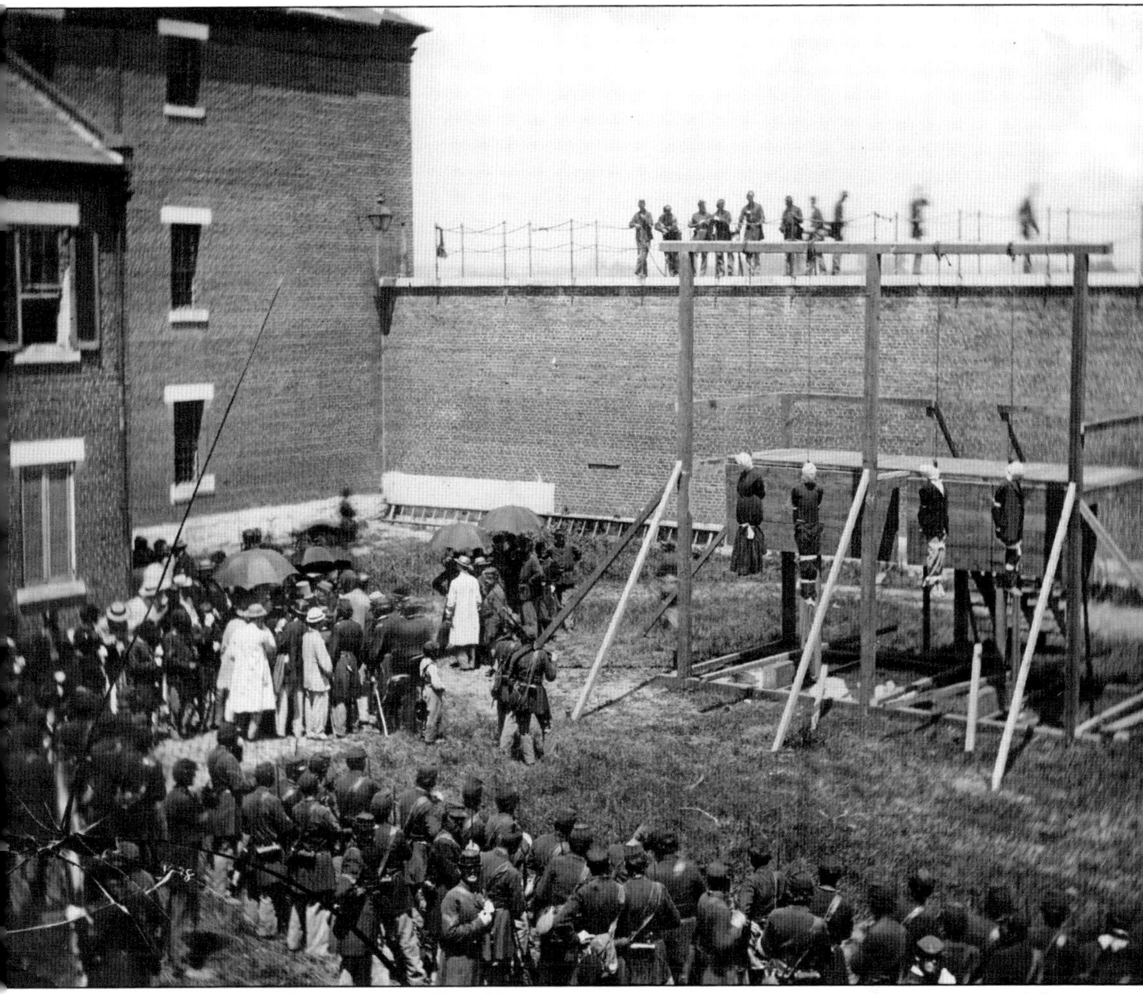

The trial of Lewis Thornton Powell and his surviving coconspirators was a news sensation. After a short trial, Powell, Mary Surratt, David Herold, and George Atzerodt were found guilty of conspiring to kill President Lincoln and sentenced to death. On July 7, 1865, the four were hanged in Washington, DC, with Powell remaining dignified to the end. This photograph shows the four conspirators shortly after the hanging; Powell is second from left, next to Mary Surratt, the first woman executed by the federal government. Lewis's father was unable to arrive in Washington until after his son was dead. Later, Powell's body would be buried in the family cemetery in what is now Seminole County. In an ironic twist, the skull of Lewis Thornton Powell was discovered in a Native American collection in the Smithsonian Institution in 1994 and finally buried with the rest of his remains. (SCCC.)

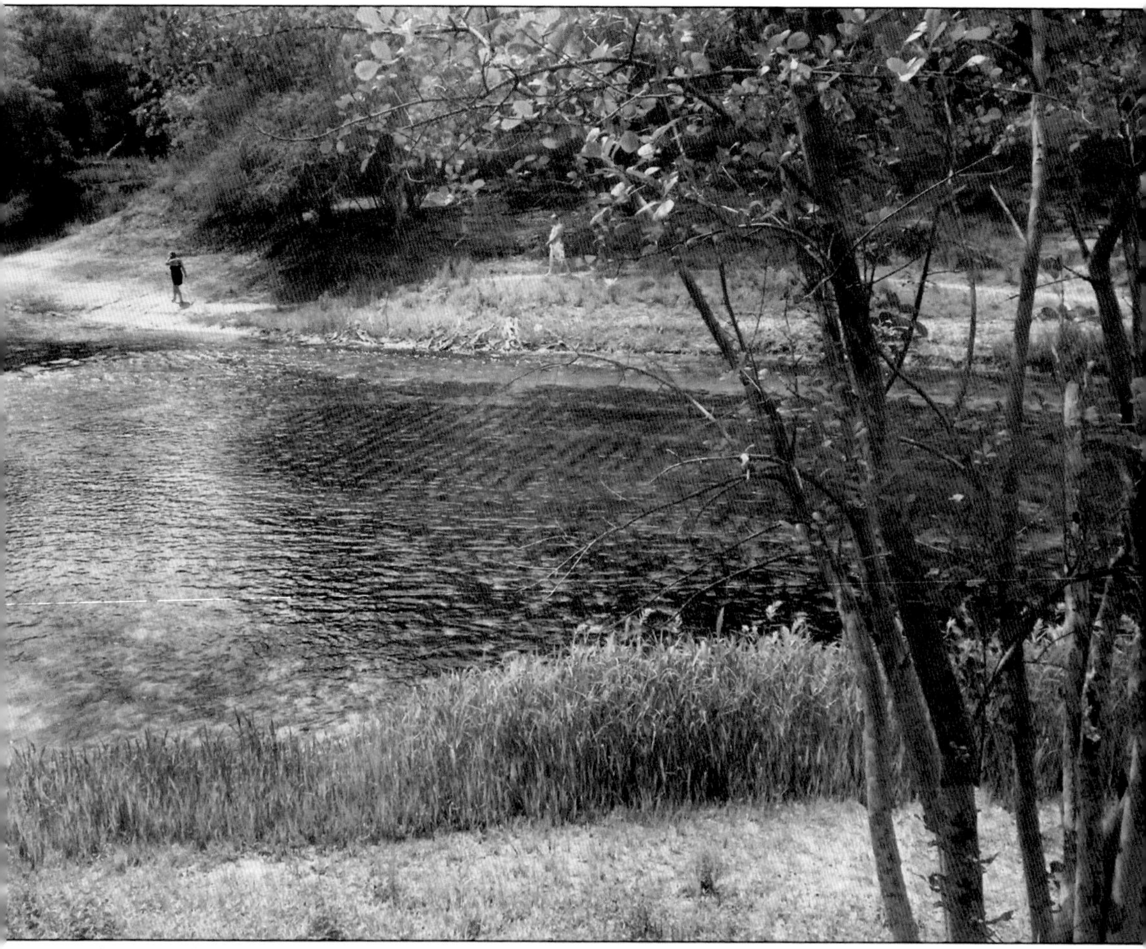

The steamboat *Madison*, built by Capt. James Tucker in 1855, was one of many that operated on the Suwannee River before railroads and paved roads supplanted them. Operating it as a floating general store, Tucker would take *Madison* as far up the Suwannee as he dared, blowing a whistle that could be heard 10 miles away; this would inform the settlers that it was trading time. Bartering locally produced goods such as deer skins, cotton, and hogs for luxuries such as ironware and fancy furniture, Captain Tucker would remain at each stop until trading was complete, then move on to the next stop. When the Civil War erupted, Captain Tucker converted *Madison* into a warship, capturing several Federal boats at the mouth of the Suwannee River before he and his men were ordered to Virginia. *Madison* was scuttled in Troy Springs, where its remains lie today. (Author.)

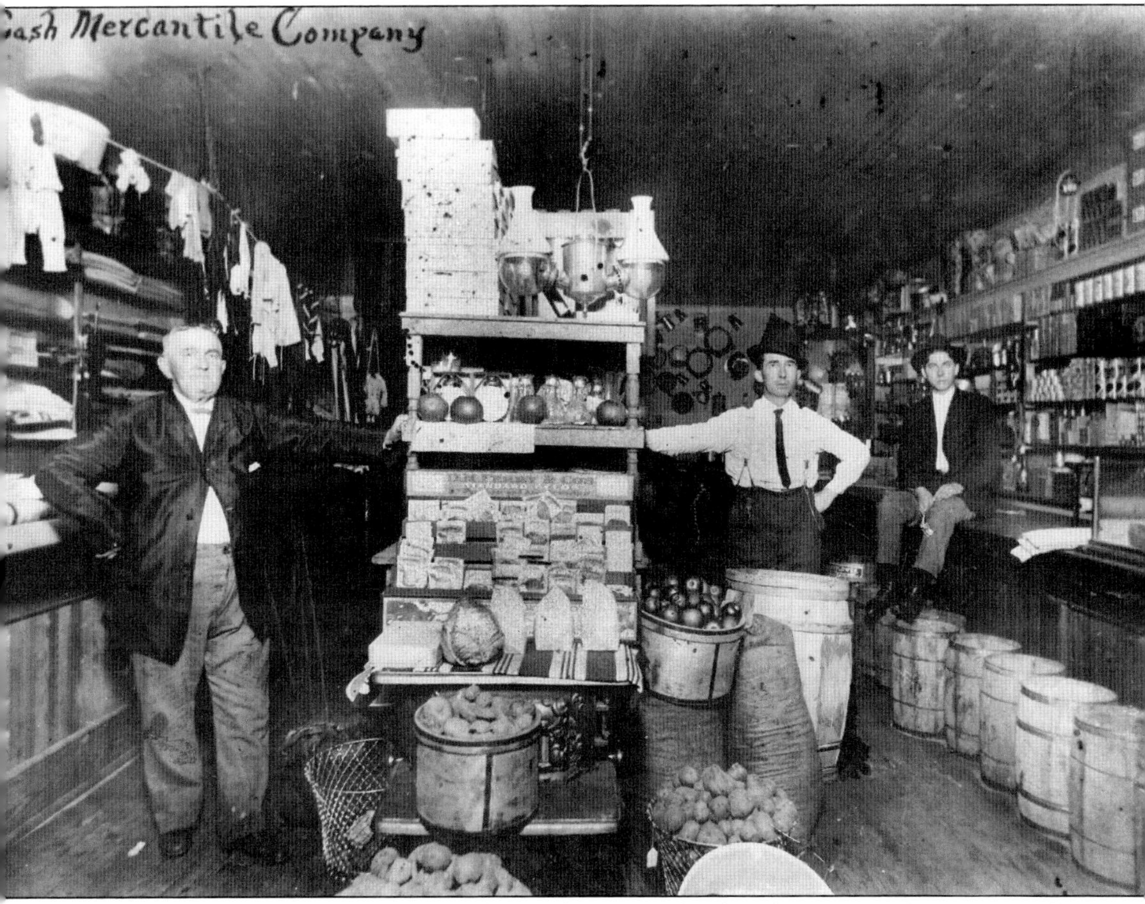

The town of Wellborn was established near the eastern border of Suwannee County in 1860. Wellborn was named after Louis Wellborn Dubose, a civil engineer who surveyed the right-of-way of the Pensacola & Georgia Railroad through Suwannee County, and in appreciation of his work, he was given 182 acres near the community that now bears his name. Wellborn supplemented and then supplanted the earlier community of Little River, established a mile south of Wellborn by early settler George McClellan in 1830. By the last quarter of the 19th century, Wellborn was well-established with several businesses, including cotton gins, general merchandise, gristmills, boardinghouses, saloons, drugstores, blacksmiths, coopers, shoemakers, sawmills, millinery stores, and livery stables. This photograph, taken around 1880, shows Wellborn's Cash Mercantile Company; the building still stands today. From left to right are A.D. Hemming, Paul Hemming, and Elmer Mosley. (ACV Archives.)

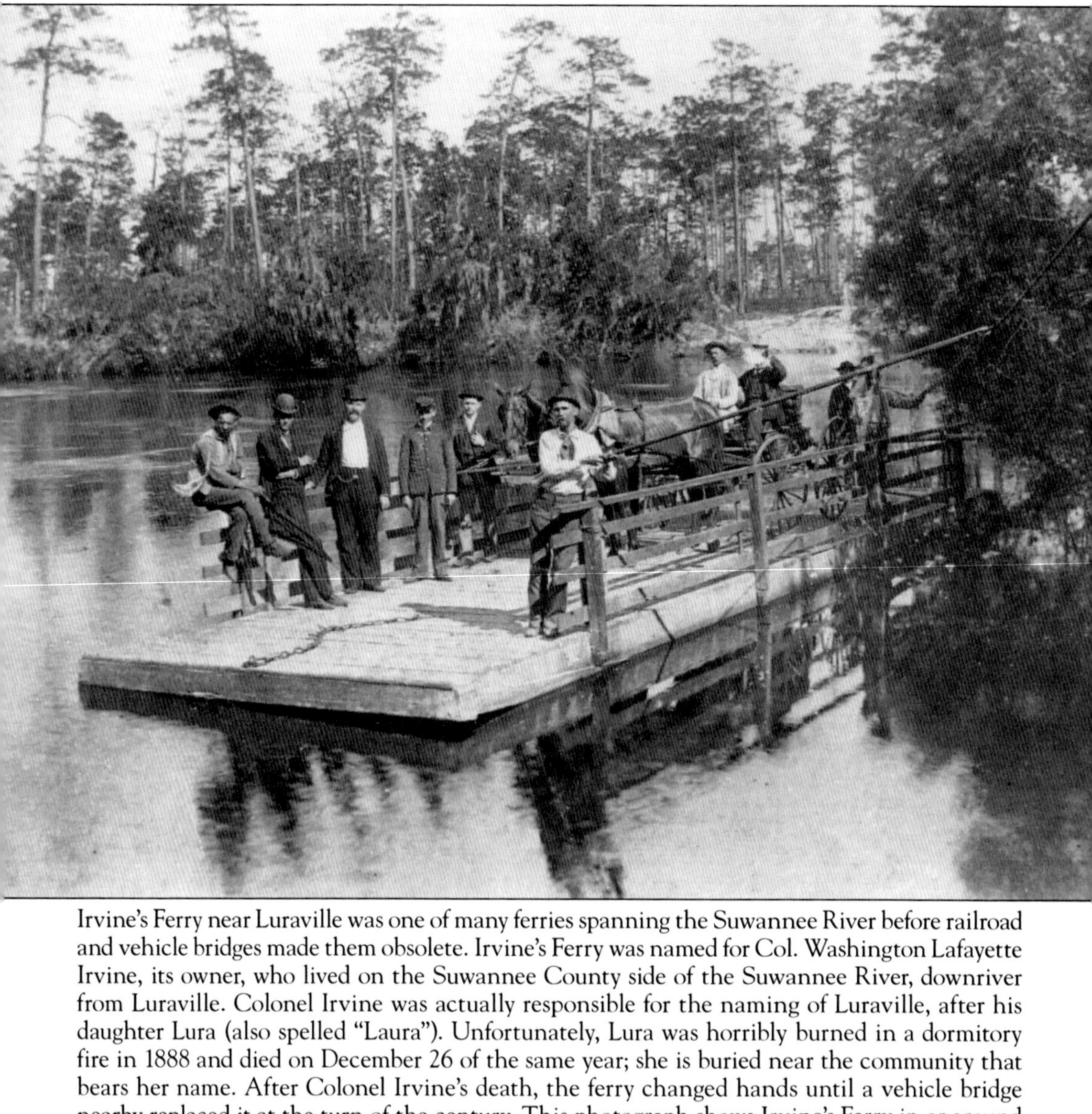

Irvine's Ferry near Luraville was one of many ferries spanning the Suwannee River before railroad and vehicle bridges made them obsolete. Irvine's Ferry was named for Col. Washington Lafayette Irvine, its owner, who lived on the Suwannee County side of the Suwannee River, downriver from Luraville. Colonel Irvine was actually responsible for the naming of Luraville, after his daughter Lura (also spelled "Laura"). Unfortunately, Lura was horribly burned in a dormitory fire in 1888 and died on December 26 of the same year; she is buried near the community that bears her name. After Colonel Irvine's death, the ferry changed hands until a vehicle bridge nearby replaced it at the turn of the century. This photograph shows Irvine's Ferry in or around 1882; it is also the cover photograph. The young man fourth from left appears to be wearing a Confederate uniform. (SCCC.)

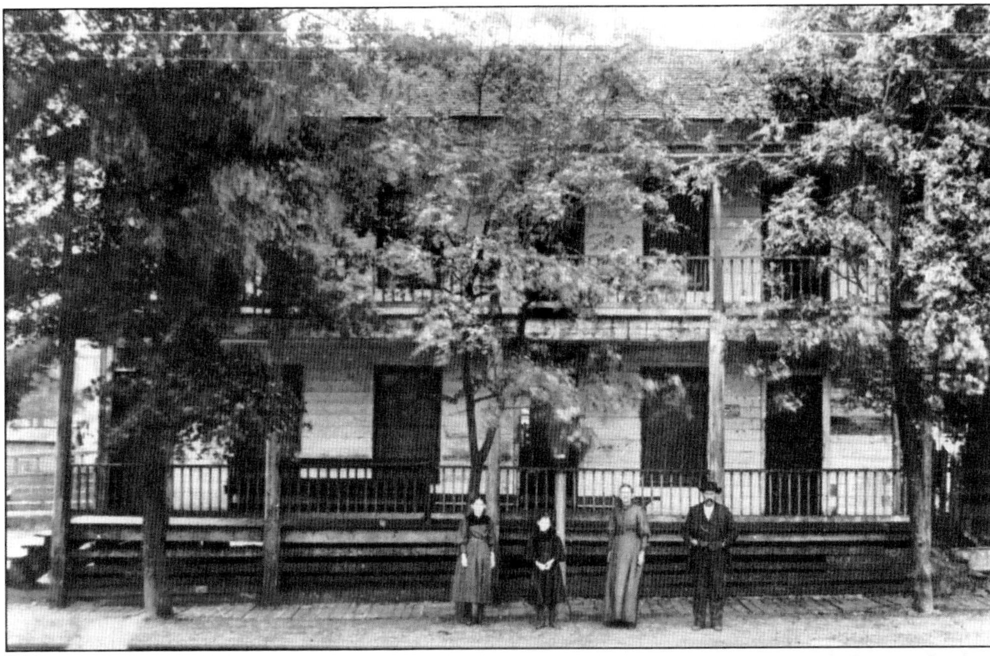

Built around 1875, the Live Oak House was a well-known landmark in Live Oak during the late 19th and early 20th centuries. Situated on the south side of the east-west-running railroads, it was suitably located for travelers. The hotel burned down in 1915, taking several other buildings with it. This picture, taken between 1893 and 1895, shows the Live Oak House with, from left to right, Ruby and Lula Gamble, their mother, Carrie Taylor Gamble, and her husband, Wesley Gamble.

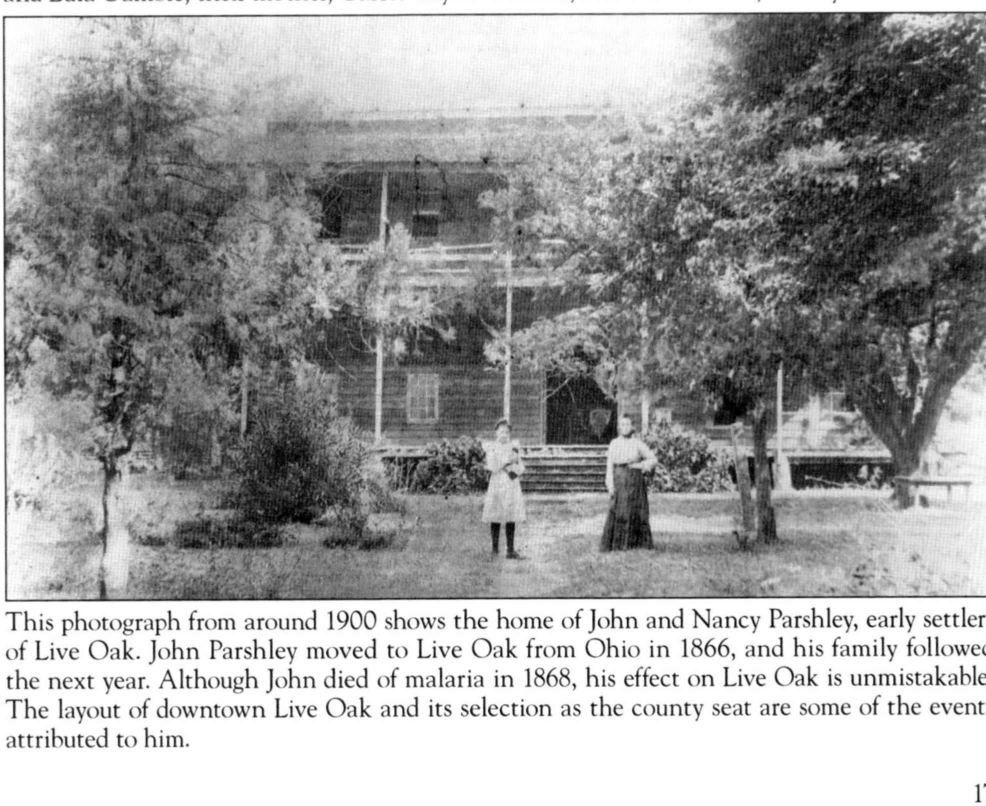

This photograph from around 1900 shows the home of John and Nancy Parshley, early settlers of Live Oak. John Parshley moved to Live Oak from Ohio in 1866, and his family followed the next year. Although John died of malaria in 1868, his effect on Live Oak is unmistakable. The layout of downtown Live Oak and its selection as the county seat are some of the events attributed to him.

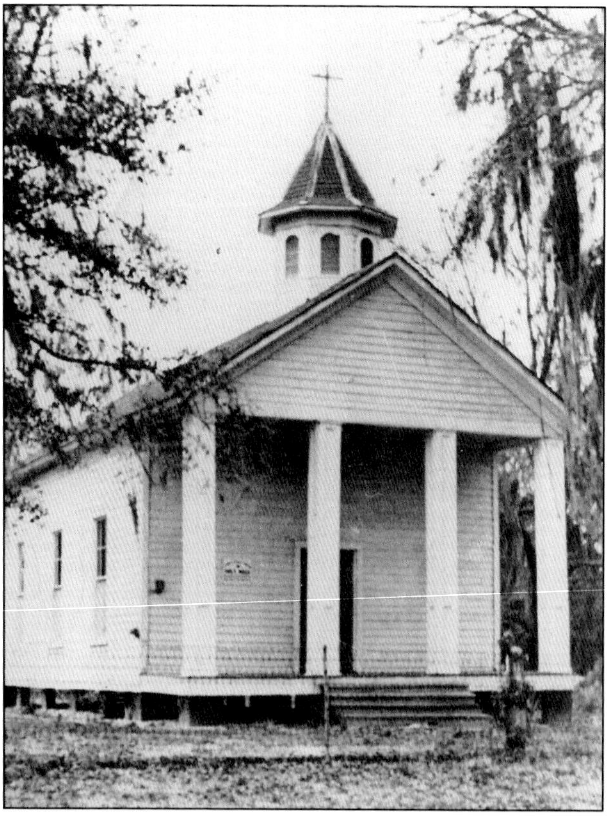

Churches have always been an important part of Suwannee County. This photograph shows the old Presbyterian church that was originally on Ohio Avenue in Live Oak. In later years, it was moved to neighboring Pine Avenue and sold to the Roman Catholic church, which operated it for many years in the same location. According to the description of the photograph, this was taken in 1880.

Among the many philanthropic endeavors of Nancy Parshley was the donation of land for the first public school building in Live Oak. This photograph from about 1889 shows the first school building erected on the land now owned by the First Baptist Church. It was replaced by a brick structure in 1905; that building, too, was torn down in the 1990s and replaced by the current church structure.

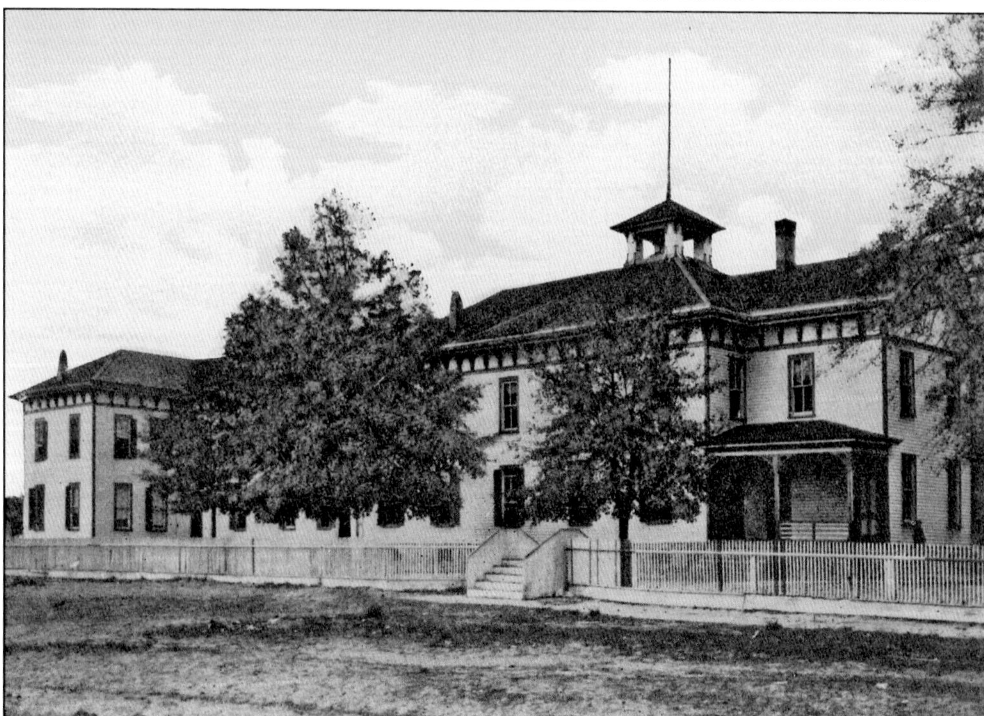

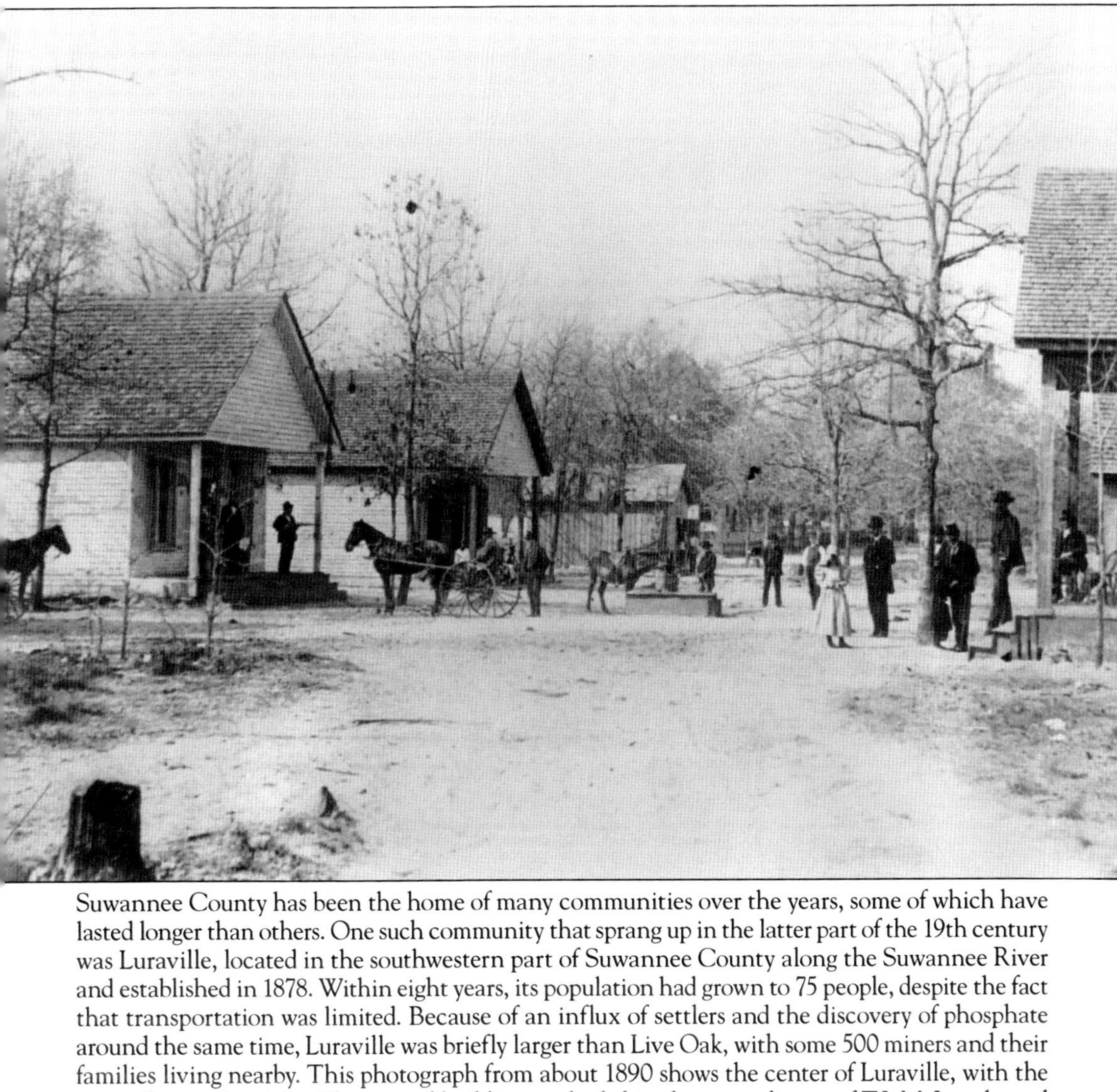

Suwannee County has been the home of many communities over the years, some of which have lasted longer than others. One such community that sprang up in the latter part of the 19th century was Luraville, located in the southwestern part of Suwannee County along the Suwannee River and established in 1878. Within eight years, its population had grown to 75 people, despite the fact that transportation was limited. Because of an influx of settlers and the discovery of phosphate around the same time, Luraville was briefly larger than Live Oak, with some 500 miners and their families living nearby. This photograph from about 1890 shows the center of Luraville, with the post office to the right. The second building to the left is the general store of T.I. McIntosh, and the third building on the left is the blacksmith shop. (ACV Archives.)

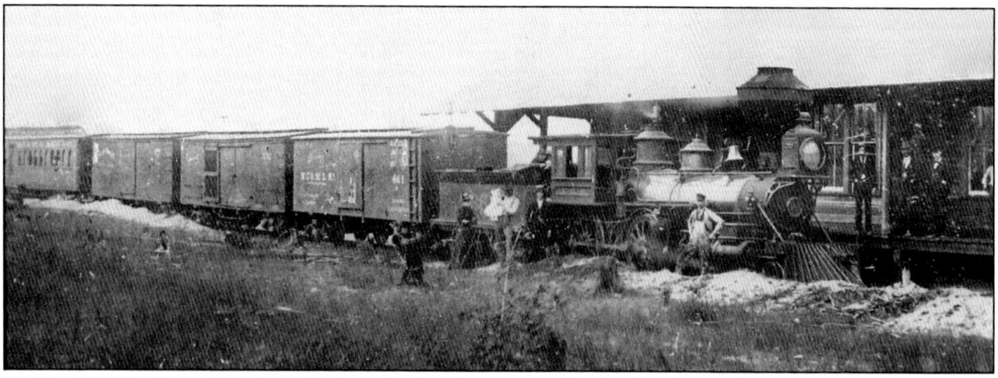

The discovery of phosphate caused a brief explosion in Luraville's growth, necessitating depot service for the many railroads that sprang up to access the precious natural resource. The depot of the Live Oak & Gulf Railway (not to be confused with the Live Oak, Perry & Gulf Railroad) is seen here in Luraville around 1896. A Jim Crow segregated passenger car brings up the rear.

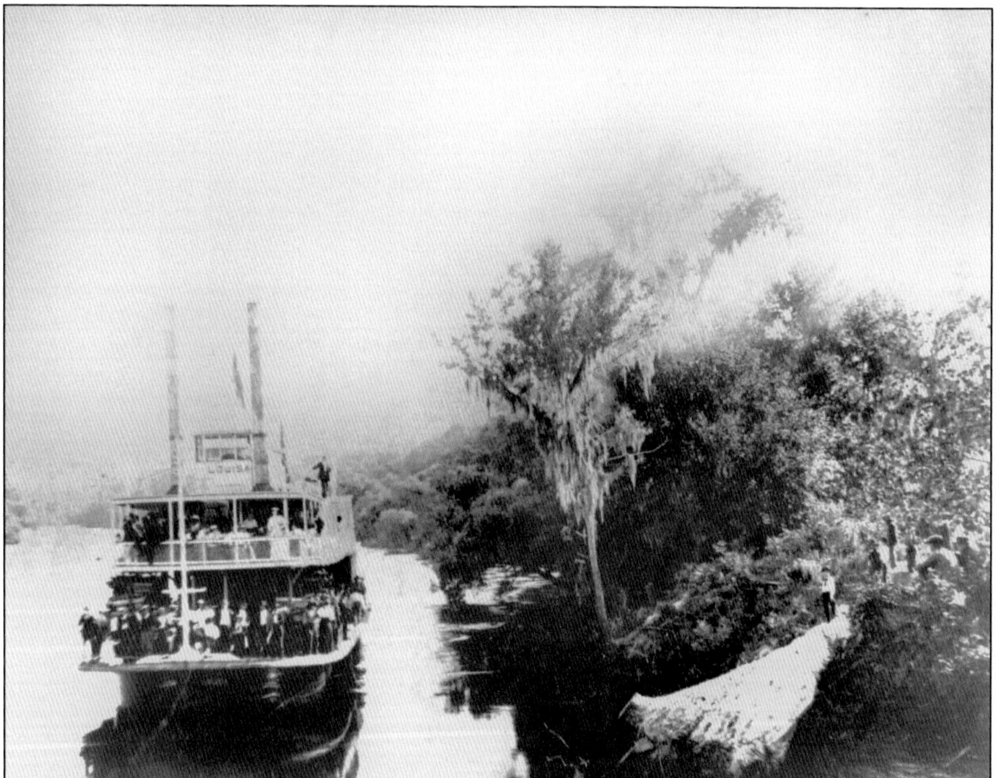

At one time, many steamboats plied the Suwannee River. One of those was *Louisa*, built in Georgia in 1890. In 1894, it was moved to the Suwannee River by Capt. E.L. Magruder, who also owned several other steamboats. *Louisa* is shown here around 1895, probably near Branford. After the hurricane of 1896, it was sold to interests in South Carolina and finally abandoned in 1904.

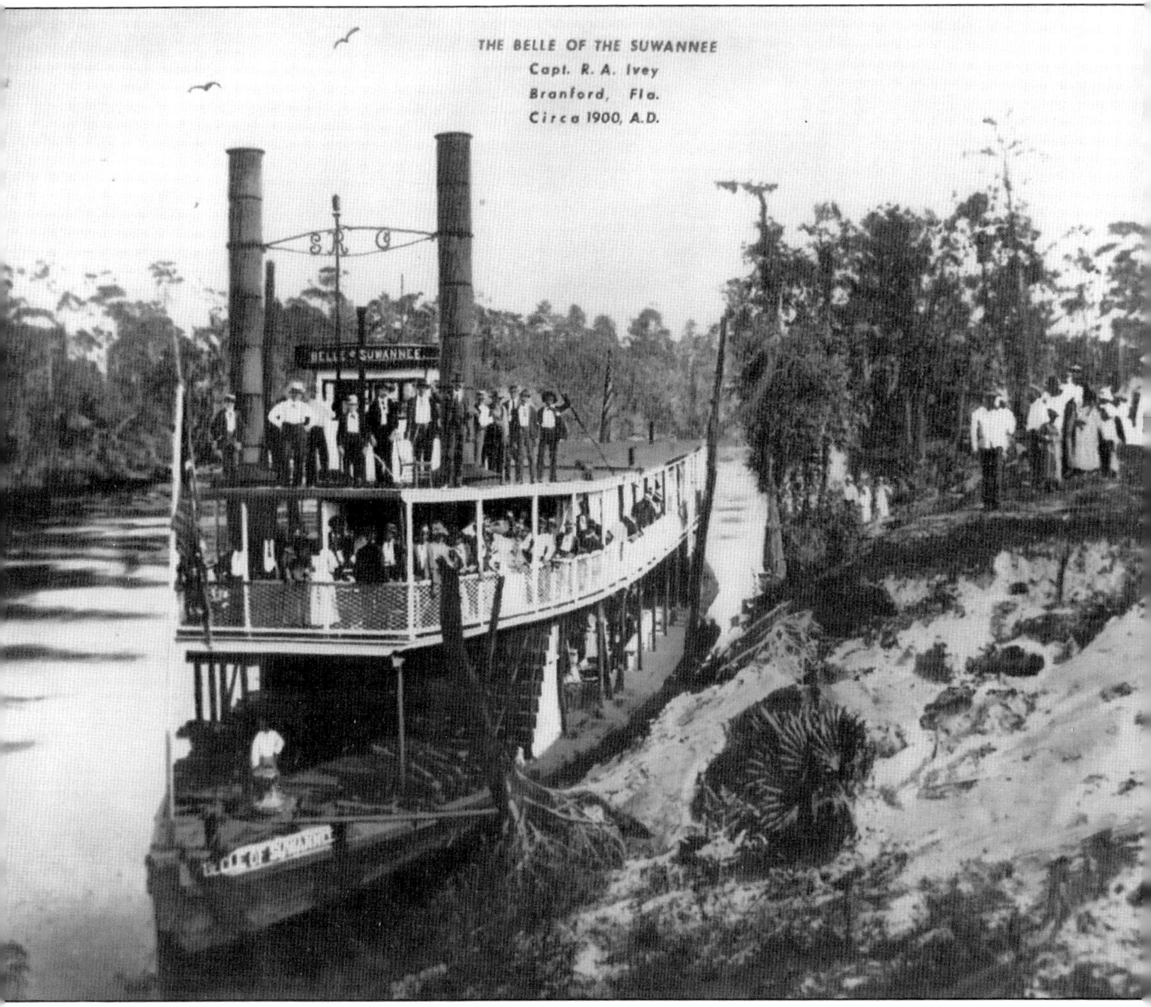

The most famous steamboat to cruise the Suwannee River during the 75-year era of steamboating was undoubtedly the *Belle of the Suwannee*, built in 1889 by local captain Robert Absalom Ivey and named for his daughter Bertha, the "belle" of his eyes. Ivey was a prominent landowner and businessman in the southern part of the county who built many steamboats at Branford, including *Belle of the Suwannee*, along with a well-known hotel there that served his many passengers. Famous for its bridal suite and menu of fresh river catfish, *Belle of the Suwannee* cruised the river for nearly a decade before the hurricane of 1896 wrecked the local economy. Sold to other interests, *Belle* sank off the mouth of the Suwannee River in 1900. It is shown here in happier times around 1895, most probably at Branford, loading and unloading passengers. (Florida State Photographic Collection.)

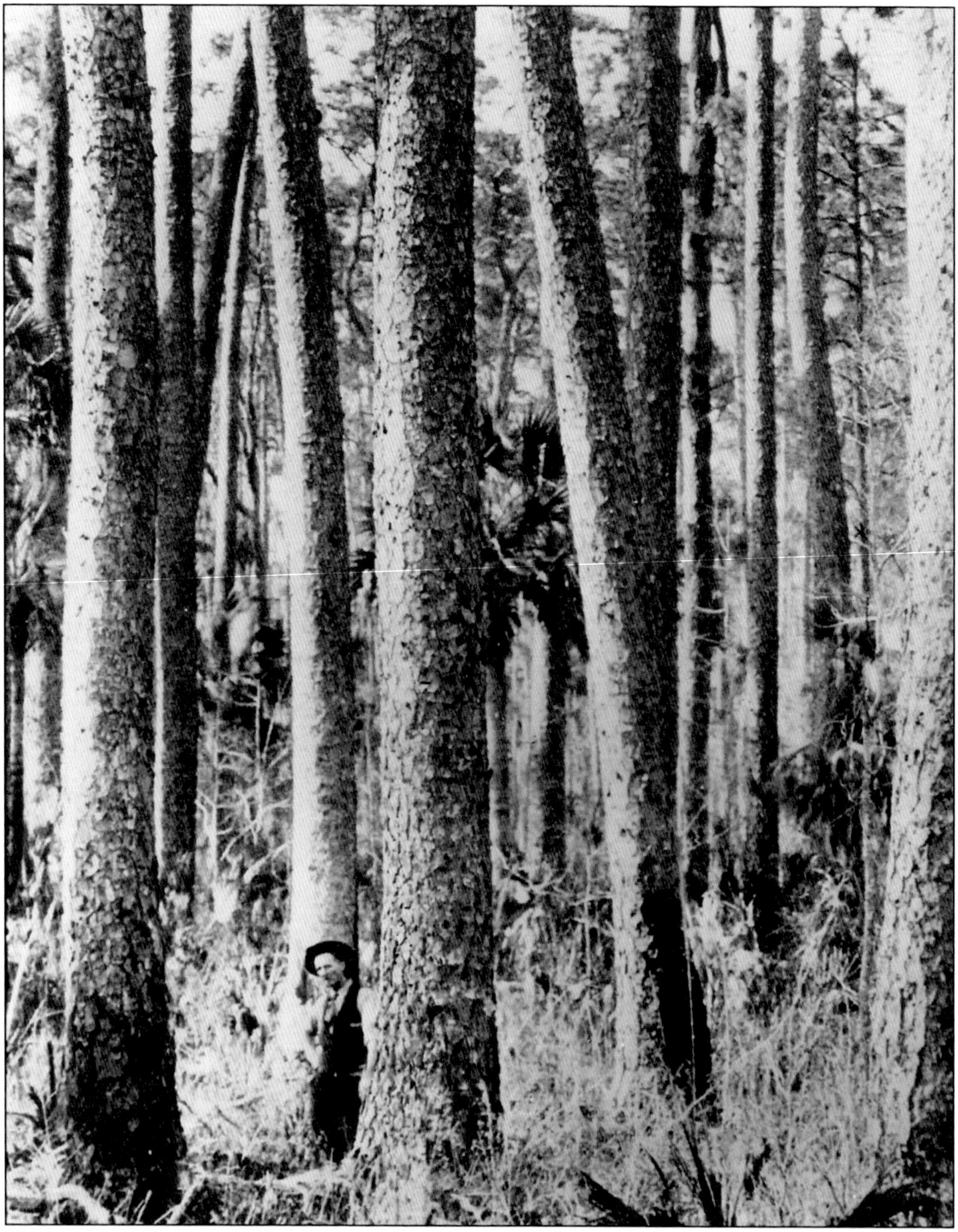

This picture, taken somewhere in Suwannee County at the turn of the century, shows some of the numerous stands of virgin longleaf pine that was a major factor behind the county's growth after the Civil War. The unidentified man standing at the base of the tree in the center of the picture is dwarfed by his natural surroundings. Spanish explorer Hernando de Soto and his men would have come across a similar view 350 years before as they traveled through this part of the United States. A multitude of timber companies spent years logging the vast virgin timber forests that covered the land for use in naval stores and commercial and residential construction. For those timber stands located near the Suwannee River, it was easiest to simply float the logs downriver to sawmills, strategically placed to collect and process them. (Florida State Photographic Collection.)

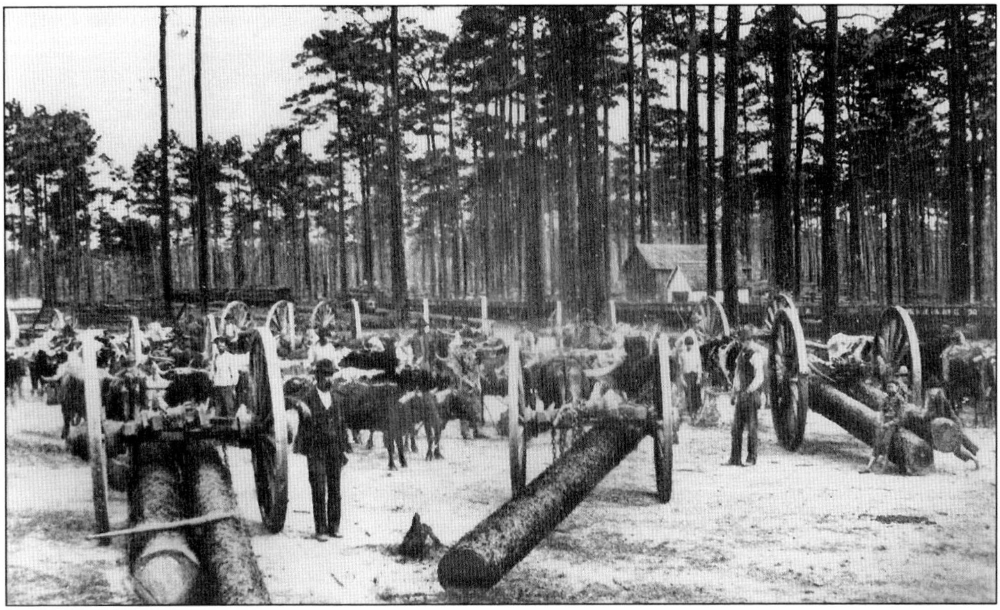

This timber would be cut by hand, transported on special horse- or mule-driven carts (seen above), and taken to the closest sawmill or railroad line for further processing (below). Numerous sawmills sprang up in Suwannee County to cut the thousands of board-feet that were shipped each day, and temporary lumber railroads dotted the land as an easier means of getting the products to the end users in more developed areas. This economic boom lasted from just after the Civil War through the early 1900s, when the majority of virgin timber had been "cut out." Second-generation growth allowed resurgence in the timber industry, but not at the same levels as the original. (Both, Florida State Photographic Collection.)

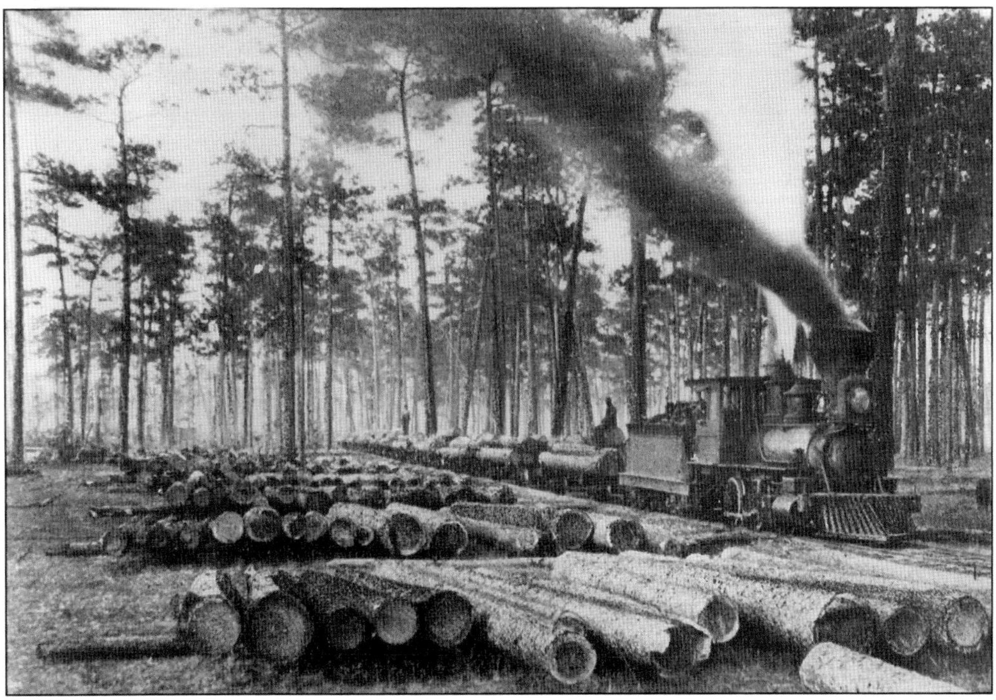

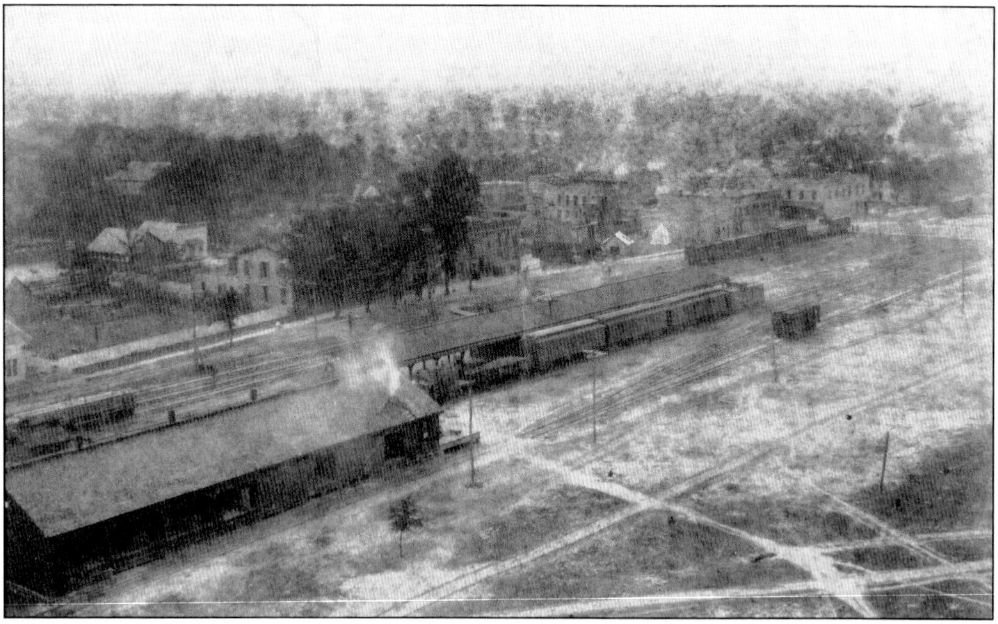

Thomas Dowling was one of the many men who made a fortune in Suwannee County. Around 1896, he built a magnificent two-story home on Duval Street, and the next year, using his own money, he built a waterworks across the street, which helped increase business. Dowling's home, water tower, and some attending structures stand today. These two pictures, taken between 1897 (when the water tower was built) and 1903 (when a new freight depot was constructed), were both shot from the water tower. The picture above shows the multitude of railroad lines passing through Live Oak at the turn of the century. The picture below shows some of the more prosperous homes along Duval Street and beyond.

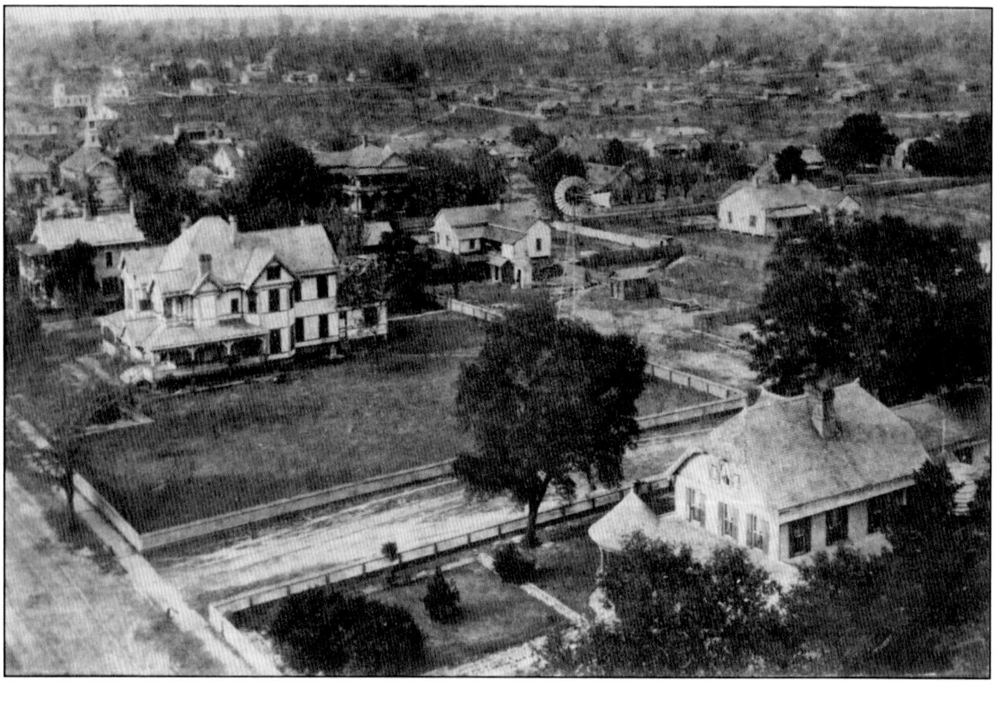

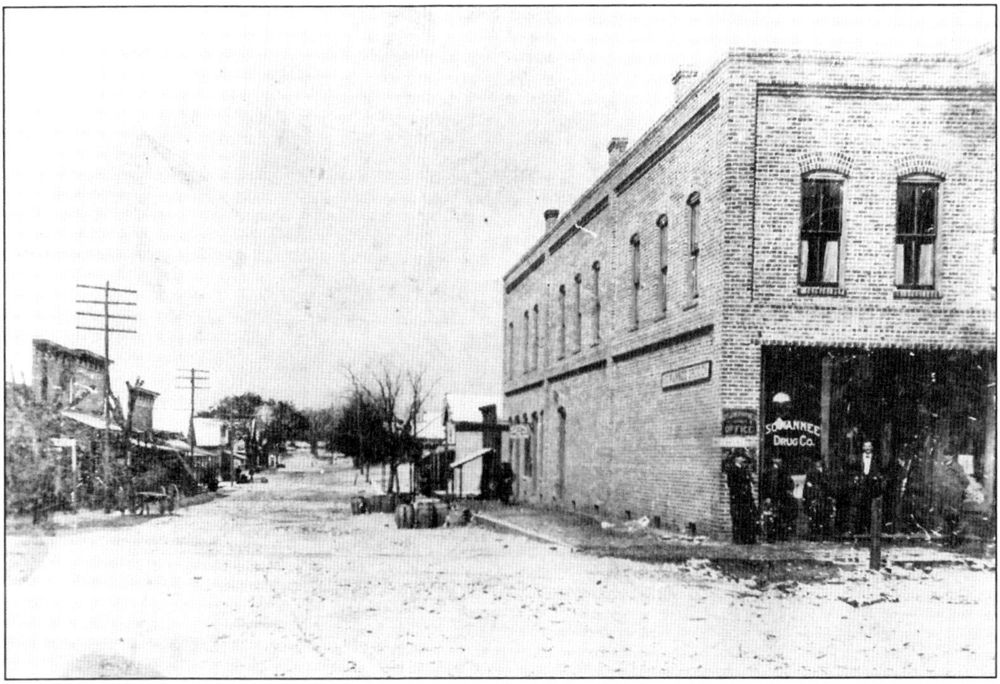

Despite the fact that Suwannee County is located in Florida, there have been several instances of snow during the cold winter months, most recently in 2010. This photograph from 1899 shows one such occurrence in downtown Live Oak. Shot looking west on Howard Street at its intersection with Ohio Avenue, the Suwannee Drug Company is on the right; it is now Xin Ming Chinese Restaurant. (Florida State Photographic Collection.)

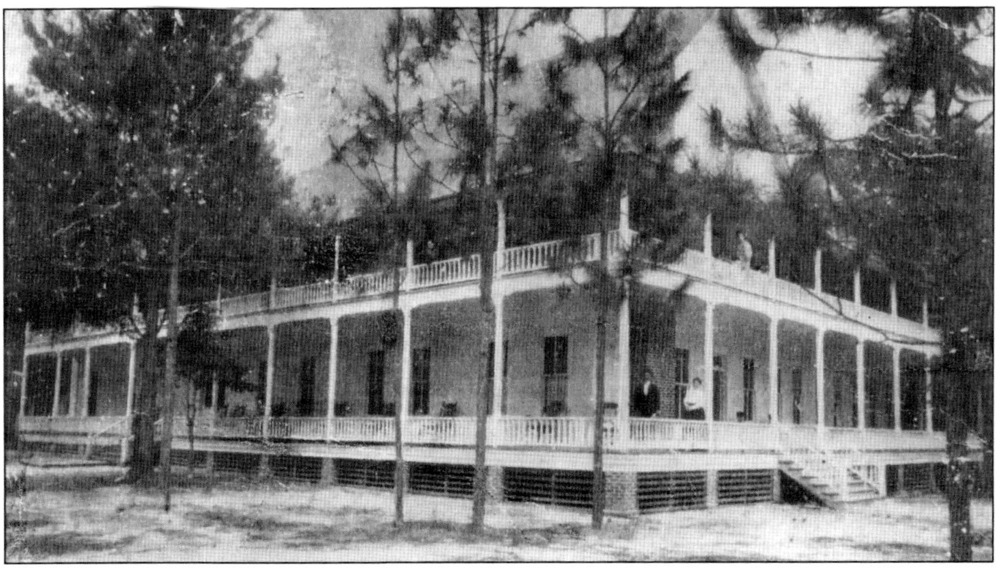

One of the famous local resorts at the turn of the century was the Park Hotel in what is now Dowling Park. It came complete with two swimming pools, a bowling alley, billiards, and hot and cold water and was a sportsman's paradise for fishing, hunting, and horseback riding. The nearby sulphur water was believed to have medicinal benefits. Unfortunately, fire destroyed the hotel in 1925. (ACV Archives.)

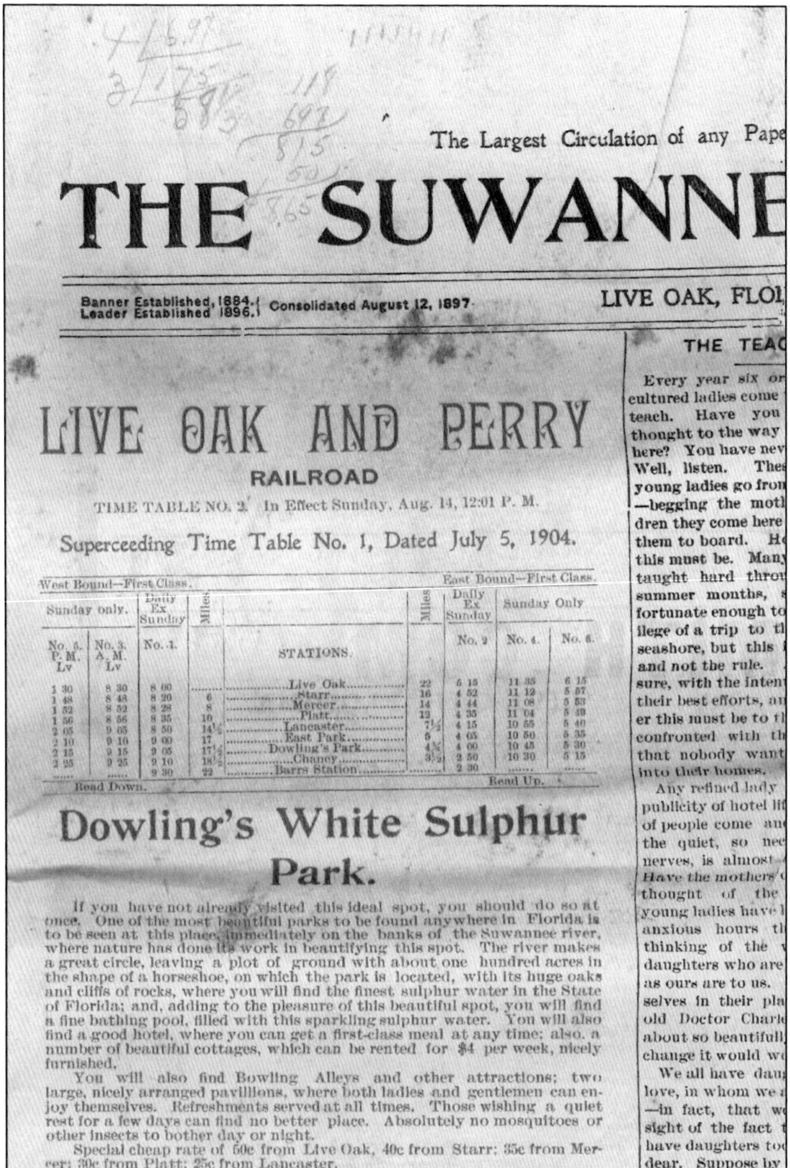

The Largest Circulation of any Pape

THE SUWANNE

Banner Established, 1884. Leader Established 1896. Consolidated August 12, 1897.

LIVE OAK, FLOI

LIVE OAK AND PERRY RAILROAD

TIME TABLE NO. 2 In Effect Sunday, Aug. 14, 12:01 P. M.

Superceeding Time Table No. 1, Dated July 5, 1904.

West Bound—First Class.						East Bound—First Class.		
Sunday only.		Daily Ex Sunday	Miles		Miles	Daily Ex Sunday	Sunday Only	
No. 5. P. M. Lv	No. 3. A. M. Lv	No. 1.		STATIONS.		No. 2	No. 4.	No. 6.
1 30	8 30	8 00	......	Live Oak	22	5 15	11 35	6 15
1 48	8 48	8 20	6	Starr	16	4 52	11 12	5 57
1 52	8 52	8 28	8	Mercer	14	4 44	11 08	5 53
1 56	8 56	8 35	10	Platt	12	4 35	11 04	5 49
2 05	9 05	8 50	14½	Lancaster	7½	4 15	10 55	5 40
2 10	9 10	9 00	17	East Park	5	4 05	10 50	5 35
2 15	9 15	9 05	17½	Dowling's Park	4¾	4 00	10 45	5 30
2 25	9 25	9 10	18½	Chaney	3½	2 50	10 30	5 15
......	......	9 30	22	Barrs Station	......	2 30	......	......
Read Down.						Read Up.		

Dowling's White Sulphur Park.

If you have not already visited this ideal spot, you should do so at once. One of the most beautiful parks to be found anywhere in Florida is to be seen at this place, immediately on the banks of the Suwannee river, where nature has done its work in beautifying this spot. The river makes a great circle, leaving a plot of ground with about one hundred acres in the shape of a horseshoe, on which the park is located, with its huge oaks and cliffs of rocks, where you will find the finest sulphur water in the State of Florida; and, adding to the pleasure of this beautiful spot, you will find a fine bathing pool, filled with this sparkling sulphur water. You will also find a good hotel, where you can get a first-class meal at any time; also, a number of beautiful cottages, which can be rented for $4 per week, nicely furnished.

You will also find Bowling Alleys and other attractions; two large, nicely arranged pavillions, where both ladies and gentlemen can enjoy themselves. Refreshments served at all times. Those wishing a quiet rest for a few days can find no better place. Absolutely no mosquitoes or other insects to bother day or night.

Special cheap rate of 50c from Live Oak, 40c from Starr; 35c from Mercer; 30c from Platt; 25c from Lancaster.

For any information regarding cottages, hotel accommodation, etc., apply to R. L. Dowling, or A. J. Skipper, Agt., Live Oak & Perry Railroad, Live Oak, Fla.

THE TEAC

Every year six or
cultured ladies come
teach. Have you
thought to the way
here? You have nev
Well, listen. Thes
young ladies go fron
—begging the motl
dren they come here
them to board. H
this must be. Many
taught hard throu
summer months, s
fortunate enough to
ilege of a trip to tl
seashore, but this
and not the rule.
sure, with the inten
their best efforts, an
er this must be to tl
confronted with th
that nobody want
into their homes.

Any refined lady
publicity of hotel lif
of people come an
the quiet, so nee
nerves, is almost
Have the mothers'
thought of the
young ladies have l
anxious hours tl
thinking of the
daughters who are
as ours are to us.
selves in their pla
old Doctor Charl
about so beautifull
change it would w

We all have dau
love, in whom we
—in fact, that w
sight of the fact
have daughters to
dear. Suppose by
tune's wheel one of
is thrown upon her
she decides to teach

To help spread news of the local resorts, the *Suwannee Democrat*, Suwannee County's major newspaper, regularly published advertisements touting the health benefits of the natural springs. The *Democrat* was the result of a consolidation of two earlier newspapers, the *Leader* and the *Banner of Liberty*, which themselves were reincarnations of even earlier newspapers stretching back to 1883. Newspapers were published in Suwannee County from at least 1869, but they were short-lived. In 1897, J.E. Pound purchased both the *Leader* and the *Banner* and formed the weekly *Suwannee Democrat*. Eventually, the paper was published twice a week, a tradition that continues today. Other newspapers have appeared in Suwannee County from time to time throughout its long history, but none have lasted as long as the *Democrat*. This portion of an original 1904 *Suwannee Democrat* shows railroad times as well as a description of the Park Hotel in Dowling Park. (SCCC.)

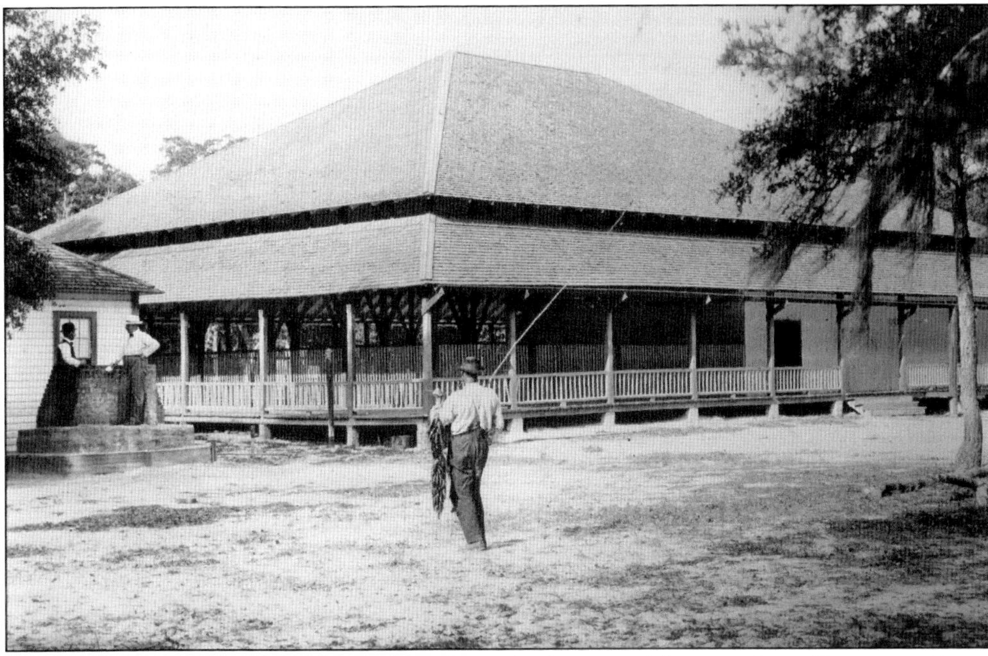

This photograph shows the Park Hotel Pavilion which was used for a number of functions. A man carrying a large string of fish is visible in the center of the picture. Local rumor is that the two men in the left background are local businessman Thomas Dowling (in dark derby) and Richard Sears (in light hat), of Sears, Roebuck, and Company, but there is no evidence to support this. (ACV Archives.)

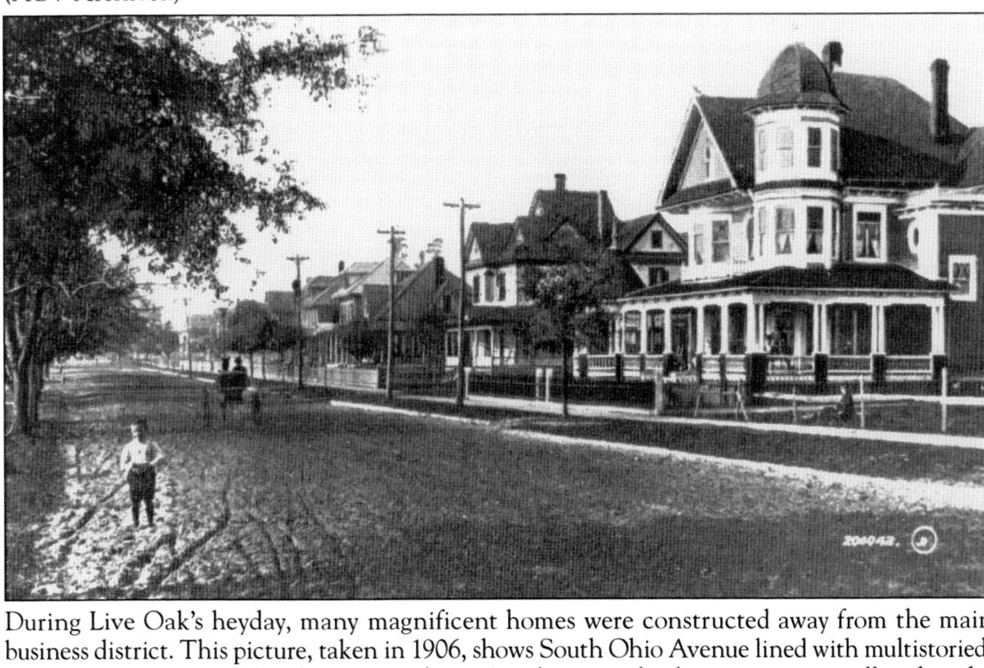

During Live Oak's heyday, many magnificent homes were constructed away from the main business district. This picture, taken in 1906, shows South Ohio Avenue lined with multistoried, showcase homes. Considered "way out of town" at the time, this location is now well within the city limits. All but one or two of these homes are long gone, replaced by commercial buildings and parking lots.

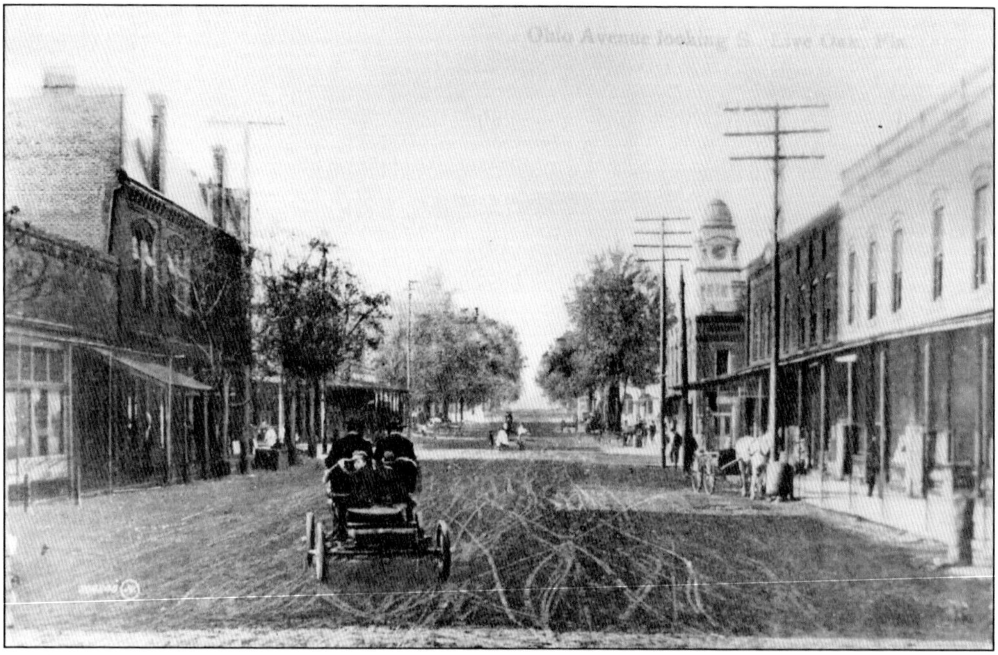

By the turn of the century, Live Oak was rapidly growing because of its location on several major railroads. This picture, shot in 1906 or 1907, shows Ohio Avenue looking south from the railroad tracks. The second-generation brick buildings in the foreground housed a variety of stores, and the courthouse, built in 1904, dominates the skyline in the right background.

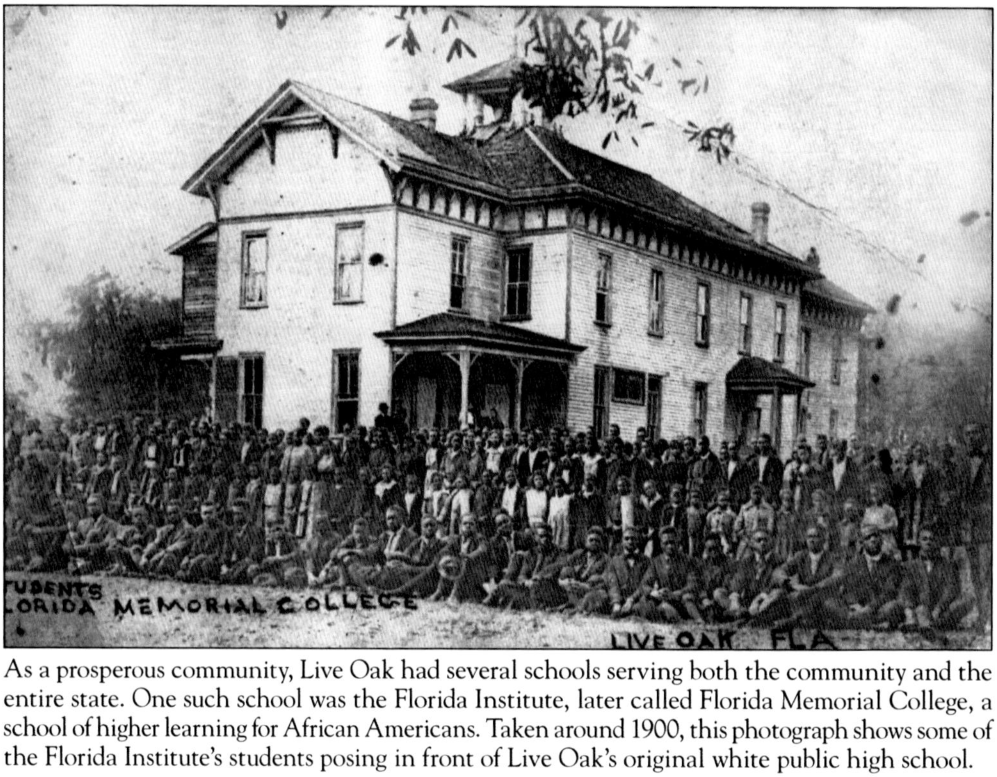

As a prosperous community, Live Oak had several schools serving both the community and the entire state. One such school was the Florida Institute, later called Florida Memorial College, a school of higher learning for African Americans. Taken around 1900, this photograph shows some of the Florida Institute's students posing in front of Live Oak's original white public high school.

The first purpose-built Suwannee County Courthouse was completed in 1874, replacing an earlier structure that had blown down in a storm. In 1904, it was moved across the street, and a new brick courthouse was constructed on the original location to meet the growing needs of the population. The 1904 courthouse continues to operate today in its original capacity.

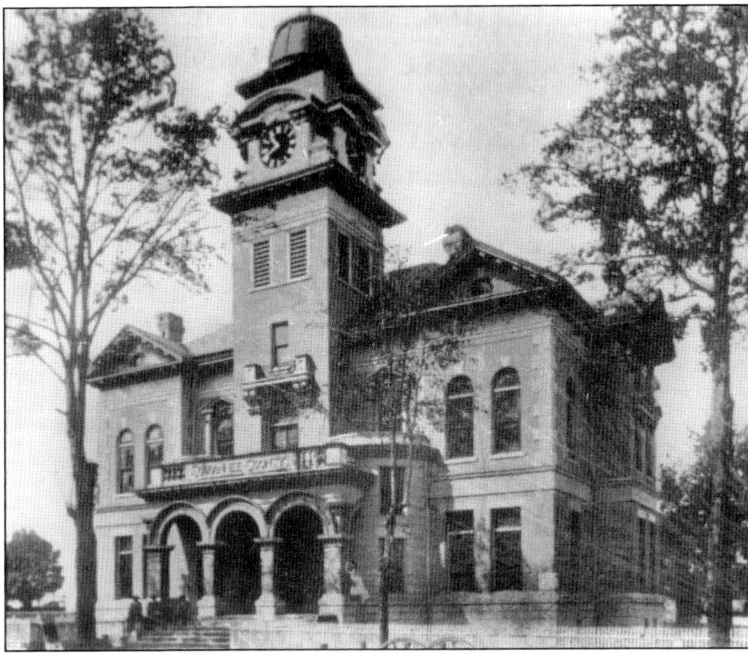

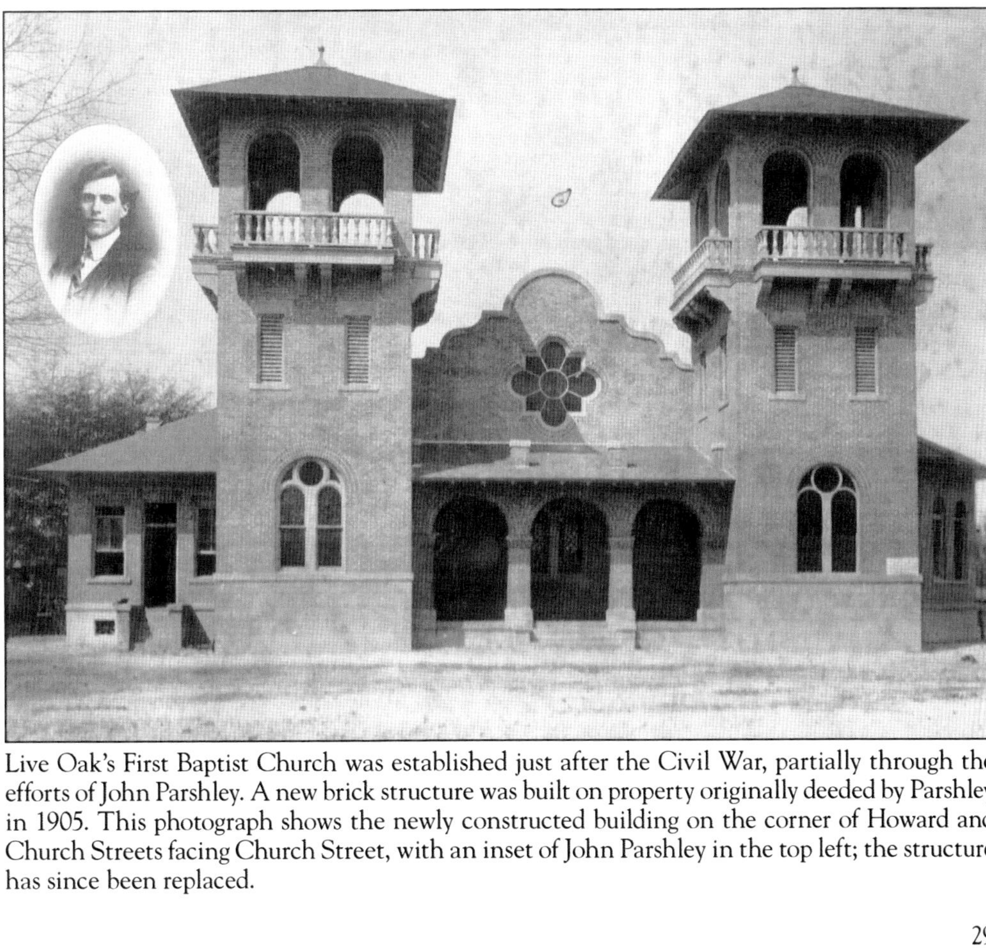

Live Oak's First Baptist Church was established just after the Civil War, partially through the efforts of John Parshley. A new brick structure was built on property originally deeded by Parshley in 1905. This photograph shows the newly constructed building on the corner of Howard and Church Streets facing Church Street, with an inset of John Parshley in the top left; the structure has since been replaced.

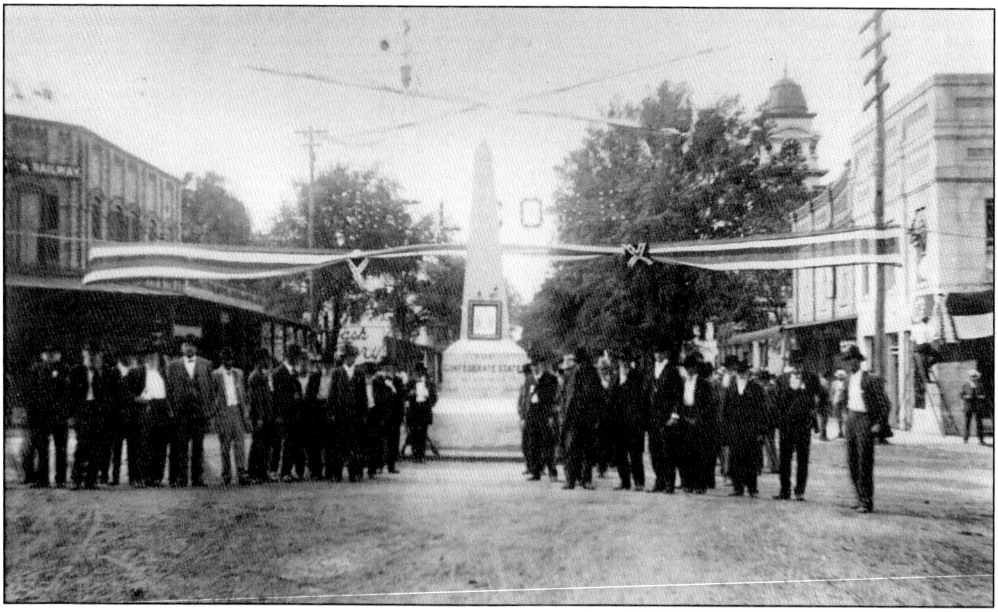

The veterans of the Civil War held state conventions in various locations to remember the comrades and cause that had died. In 1909, Florida's state convention of Confederate veterans was held in Live Oak, befitting one of the largest and most central cities in the state. A wood-and-plaster monument was erected for the occasion at the main intersection of Ohio Avenue and Howard Street, and thousands arrived to remember their youth. The pictures on this page show the center of Live Oak, with the monument in the middle of the intersection. The courthouse is visible in the right background of the first picture. (Both, Florida State Photographic Collection.)

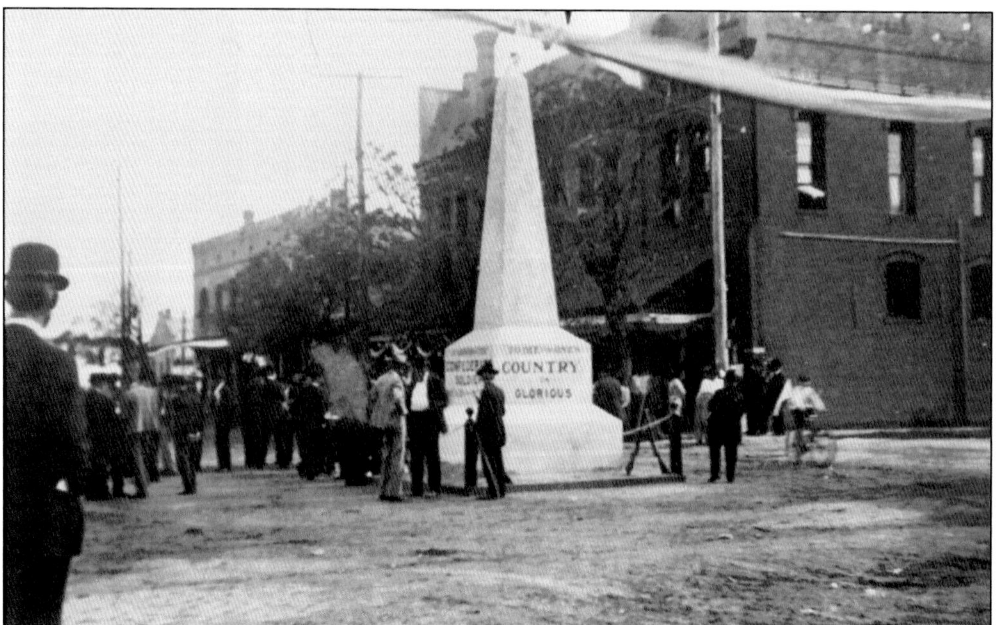

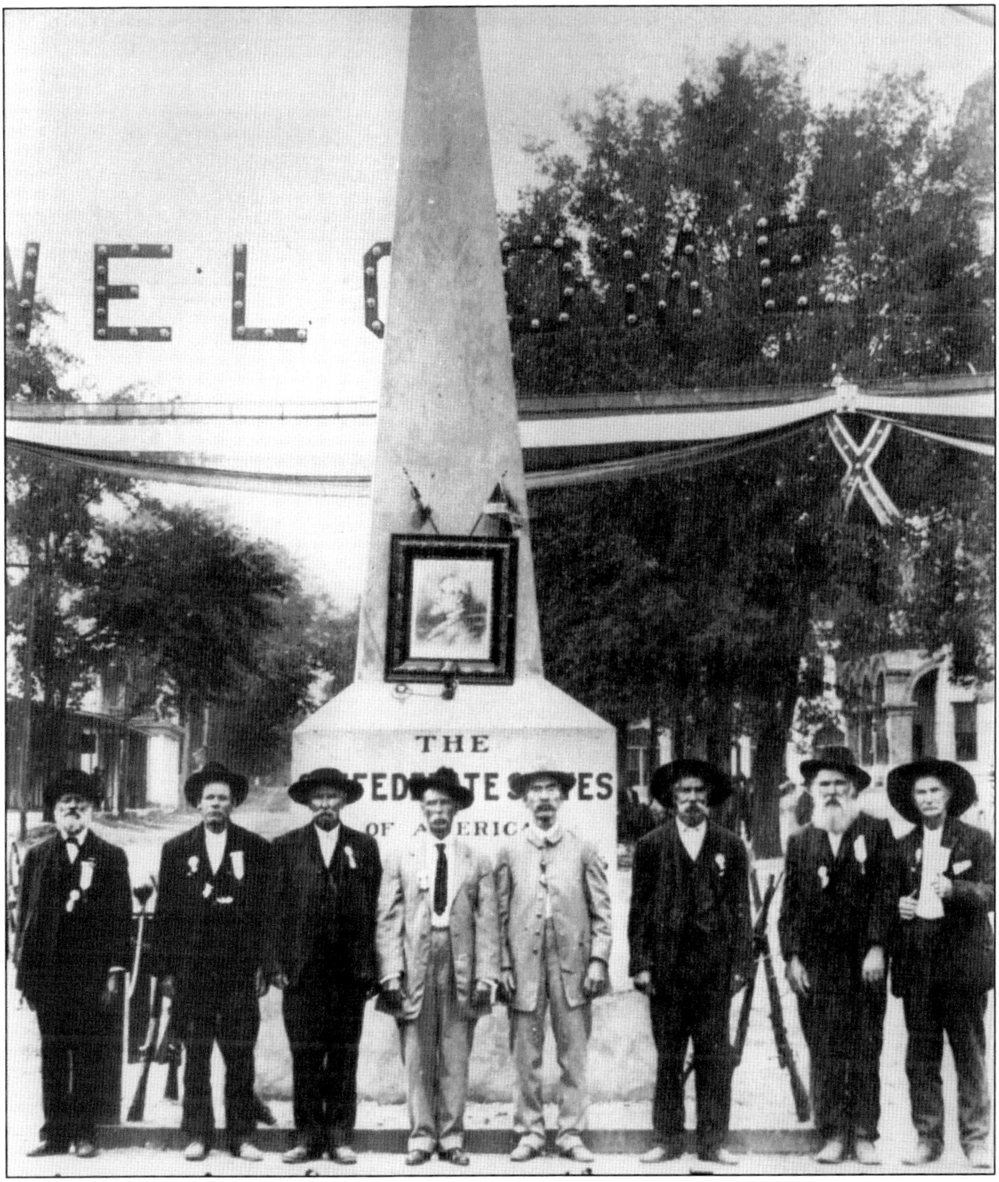

Many veterans from all over the South came to the 1909 Confederate Convention. This photograph shows men of the 1st Florida Reserve Regiment, Company D. The veterans are, from left to right, Joseph P. Webb, John D. Willis, Arnett Landing, S.W. Page, Sylvanus Mortimer Hankins, John T. Clark, Robert Pickles, and Andrew J. Loper, some of whom have descendants still living in Suwannee County. The wood-and-plaster monument behind them has a picture of revered Gen. Robert E. Lee, with words of encouragement and remembrance on the four sides of the base. In the right background, barely discernable through the trees, is the Suwannee County Courthouse and nearby post office. In the left background is the Parshley Building and Suwannee Hotel; all four of these buildings had been constructed in the previous five years and showed the prosperity of Live Oak at the time.

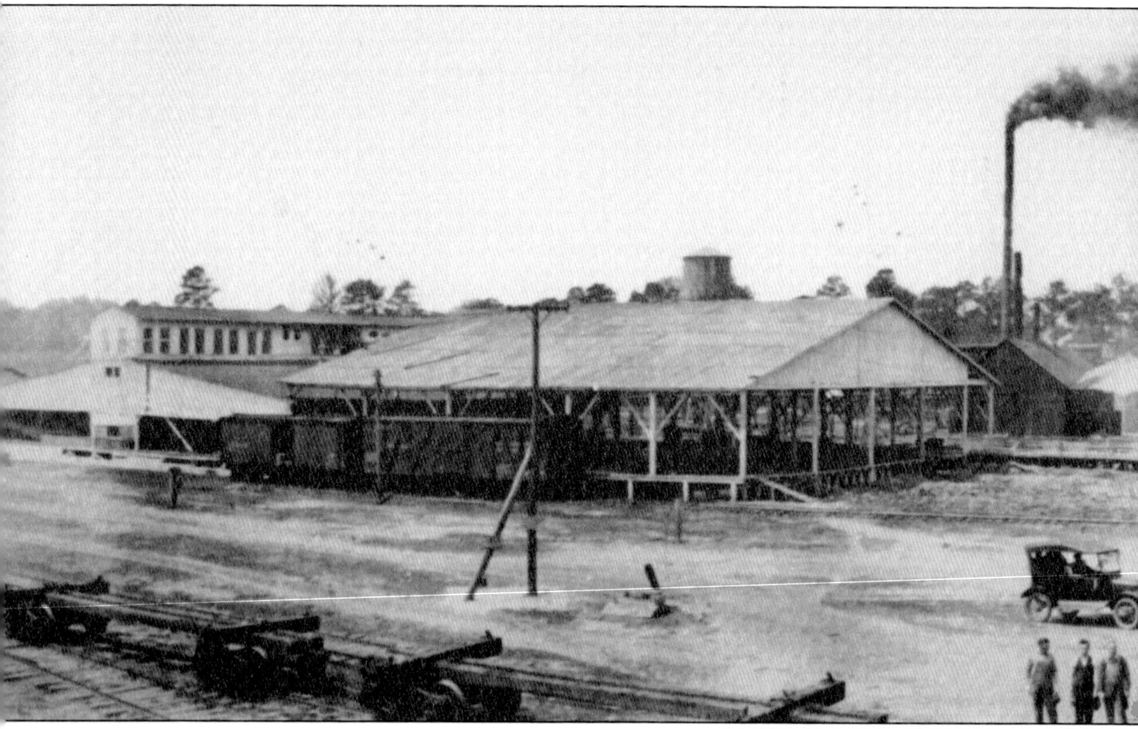

Logging in the late 1800s and early 1900s was a major industry in Suwannee County. Thomas and Robert Dowling had originally established a sawmill in Live Oak, but by the beginning of the 20th century, it had been "cut out," creating an ever-increasing distance between the remaining stands of timber and the mill. To ease this problem, the Dowlings eventually constructed this

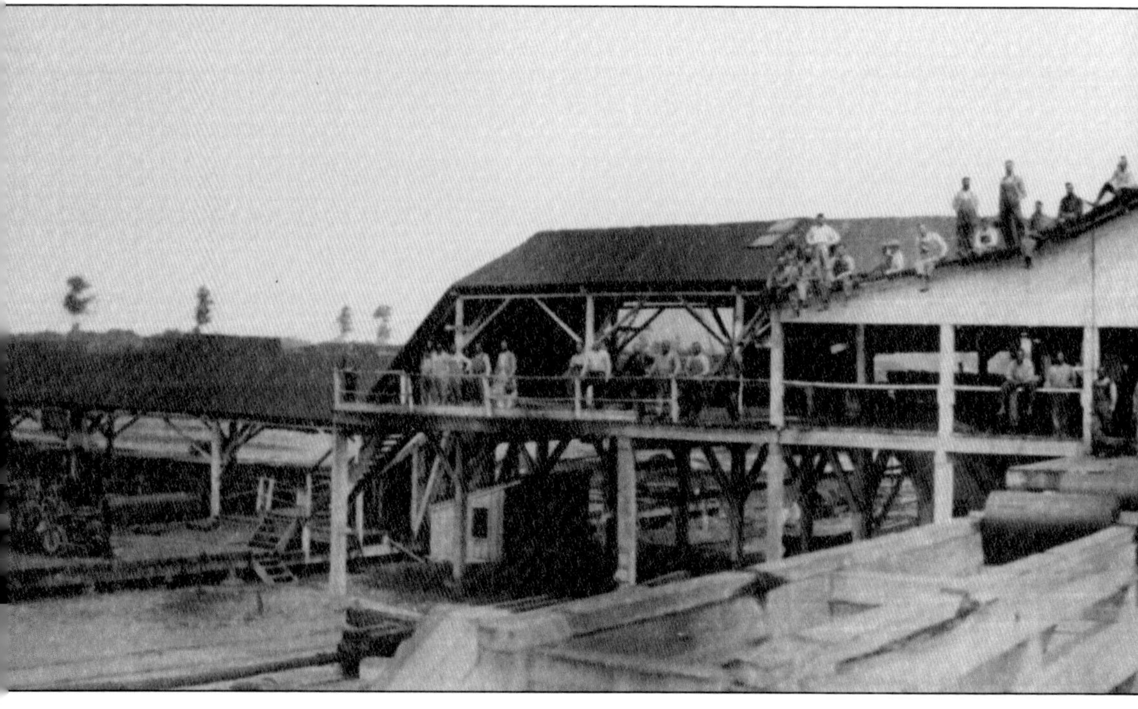

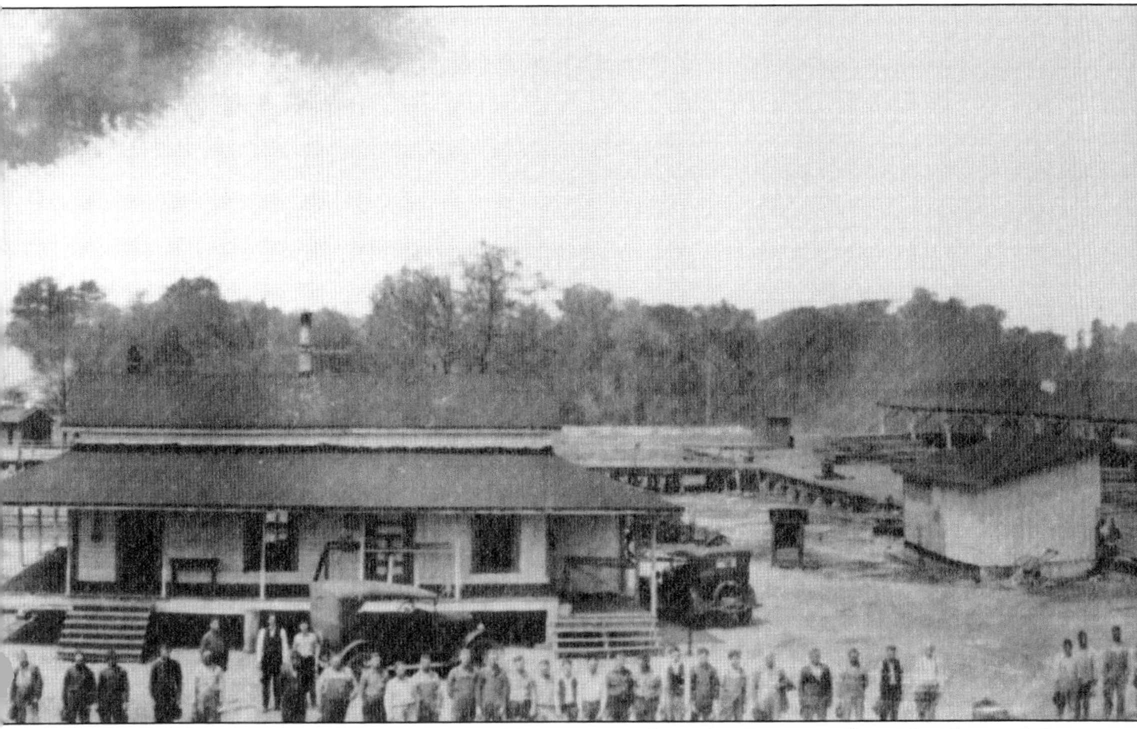

sawmill in Hudson-upon-the-Suwannee (shown around 1913). The sawmill and holdings of the Dowling Lumber Company were sold to Richard W. Sears, of Sears, Roebuck, and Company, in 1910 and incorporated as the Standard Lumber Company. The sawmill finally closed in 1929 and burned down the next year. (Both, ACV Archives.)

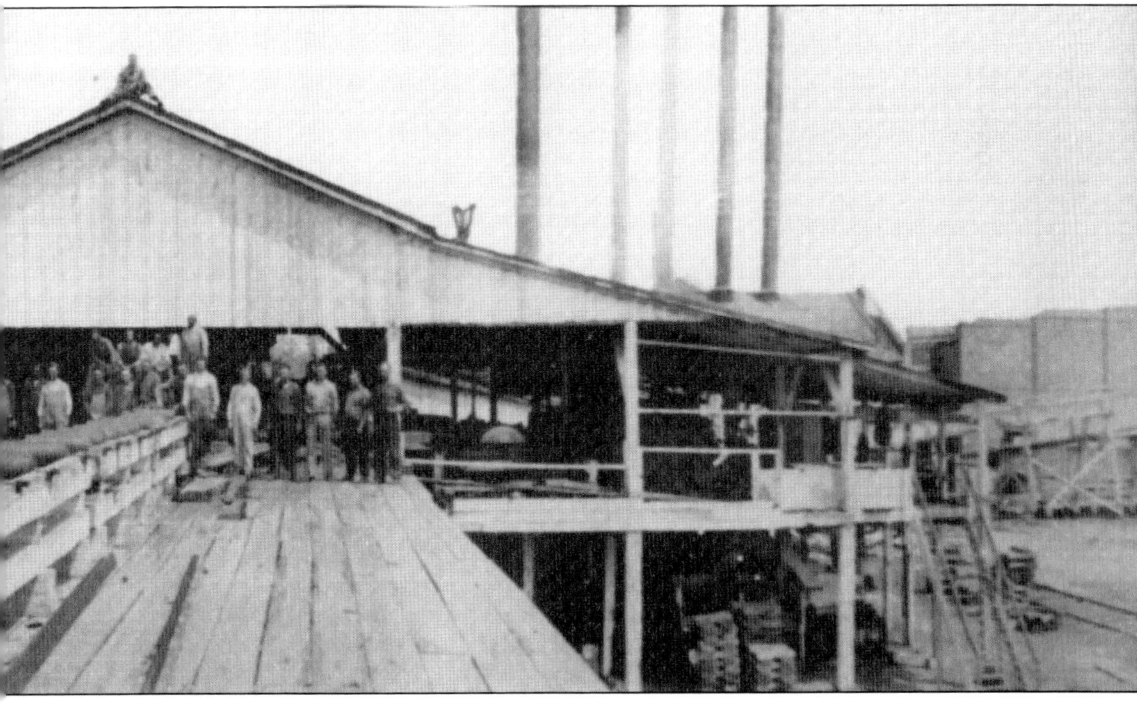

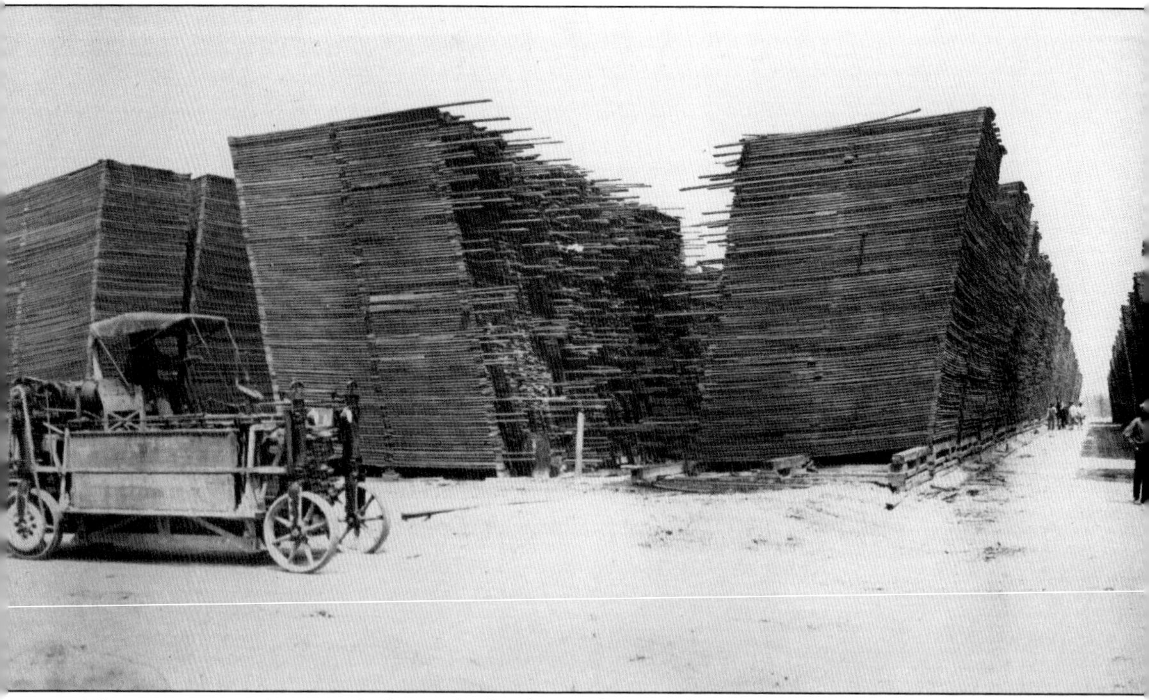

This panoramic photograph shows the lumberyard at Dowling Park around 1915, representative of several major lumberyards that served throughout the county. The stacks of cut timber dwarf the men in the photograph. The strange vehicle on the left-hand side of the photograph is a Ross Lumber Carrier, first built in 1913 by Harry B. Ross. It was powered by electricity and had only front-wheel steering but could lift 12,000 pounds and was, therefore, indispensable to sawmills. (ACV Archives.)

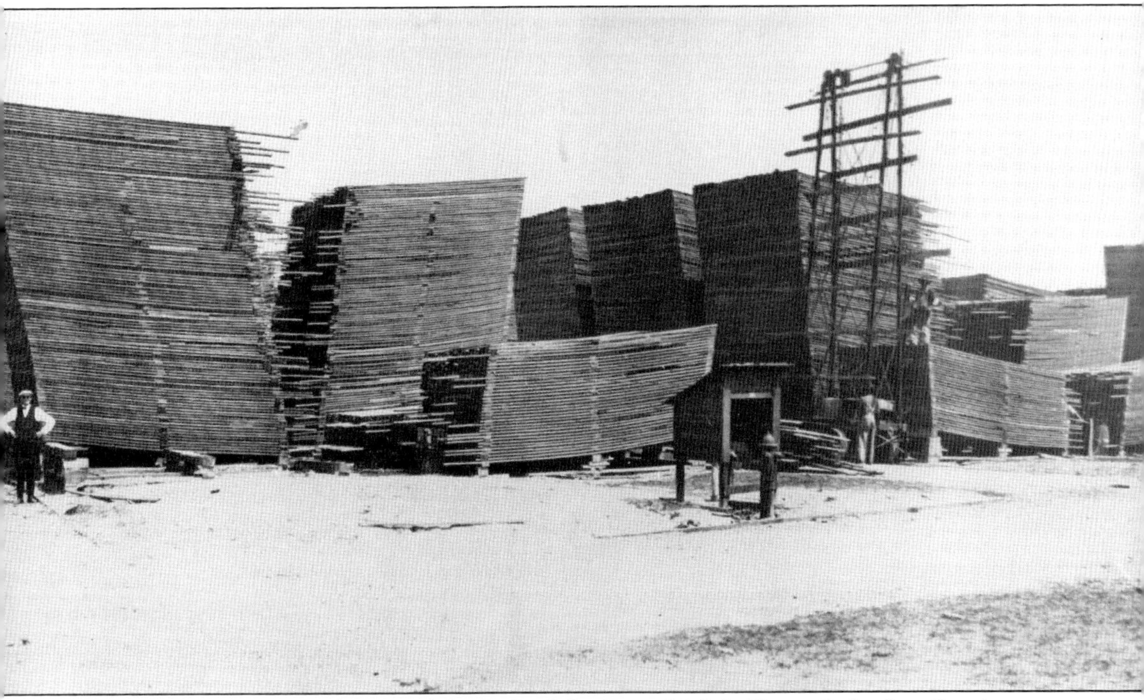

The lumberyard is now the site of the Park of the Pines Mobile Home Park; the alleys between the huge stacks of lumber are now roads in the Park. (ACV Archives.)

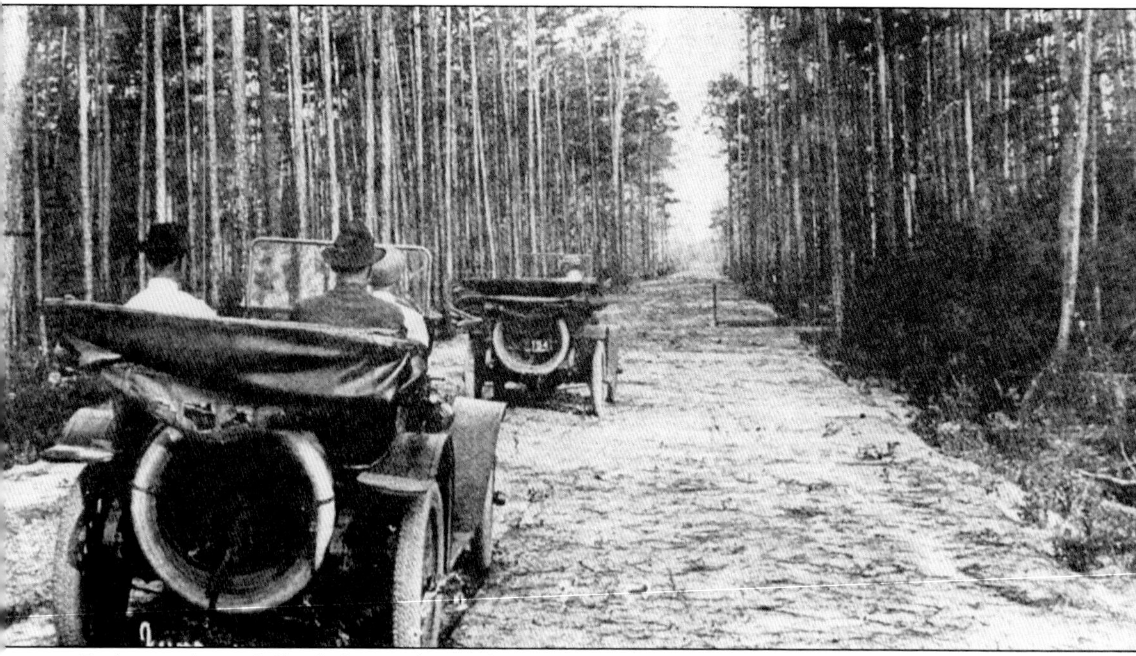

Early travel was difficult for residents of Suwannee County. Numerous trails had been made in the virgin forests by frequent travel of men, horses, and wagons, but good bricked or paved roads were still a few years in the future. This photograph from 1916 shows a typical road leading to the county seat of Live Oak; the best roads within Suwannee County would have been similar to this one. Automobile owners would routinely carry along axes so that they could dig out the numerous stumps along the way; owners who merely swerved around the tree stumps were seen as uncouth. Even in this period, it was not uncommon to find superstitious country folk who saw automobiles as tools of the devil, and they would attempt to shoot the owners when given the chance, especially after a few homemade alcoholic beverages. (Florida State Photographic Collection.)

Two

Live Oak

Built along the Pensacola & Georgia Railroad in 1859, Live Oak was named for a popular tree under which railroad workers rested and ate lunch. When a railroad depot was built near the tree, it was only natural for the small community that sprung up around it to be called Live Oak. During the Civil War, the Confederacy decided to create a north-south railroad link into Georgia through Live Oak, hoping to ease the supply problem of needed foods and supplies into other parts of the Confederacy. The railroad junction was completed in early 1865, too late to help the Confederacy, but it opened up the interior of Florida to settlement after the Civil War. This increase in prosperity helped Live Oak to become the county seat in 1868. An election held the following year confirmed Live Oak as the county seat, and it has remained such ever since.

Live Oak was incorporated as a town on April 21, 1878, allowing more local control of the community. In 1903, Live Oak became a city and was also the largest community in Suwannee County. In fact, by the close of the 1905 state census, Live Oak was the largest inland city and fifth largest city in all of Florida. However, Live Oak soon lost its status because of explosive South Florida growth. The devastation of the cotton crop by the boll weevil near the end of World War I nearly finished the city as an economic powerhouse, and business stagnated with the coming of the Great Depression. Politically, the town remained in the forefront for another four decades, until redistricting took into account the massive growth of southern Florida. Today, Live Oak remains the largest community and only full-fledged city in Suwannee County.

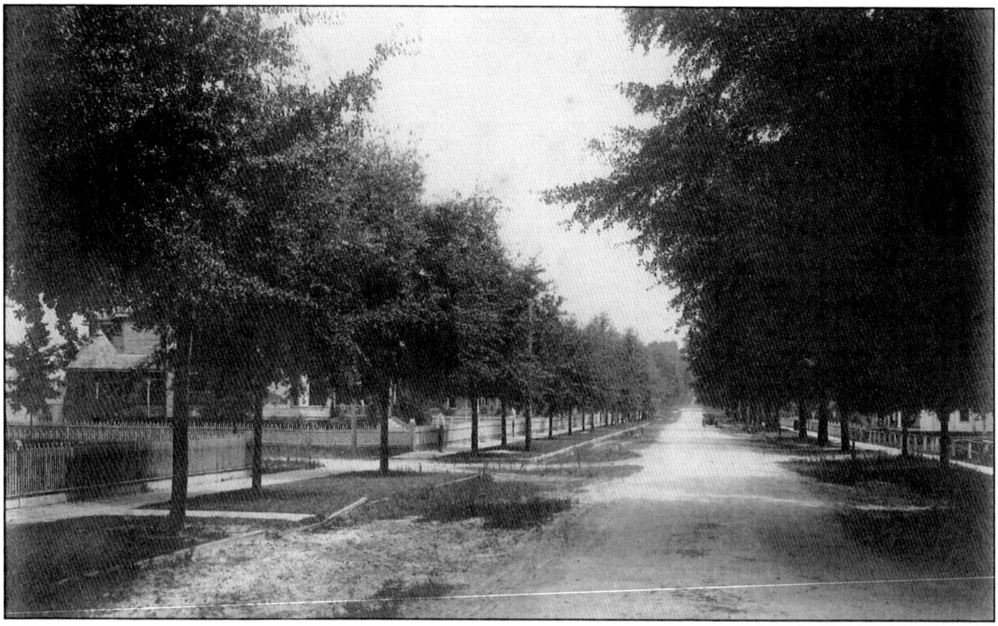

Despite the fact that Live Oak was soon eclipsed as the fifth largest city in Florida by growing South Florida cities, it was still a bustling and important community with many civic improvements. One of the widespread improvements was the addition and repair of streets and sidewalks along the major thoroughfares, as these two pictures show. The picture above, taken prior to 1913, shows some of the influential homes on South Ohio Avenue, looking north, with millionaire "Captain" Hillman's house to the extreme left. Prominent in the picture are the dirt roads and haphazard look of the right-of-ways, as well as a large numbers of live oak trees that lined the street. In the picture below, taken in 1913 from almost the exact location, things have improved dramatically. Sadly, today all of these live oak trees and nearly all of the homes are gone. (Both, author.)

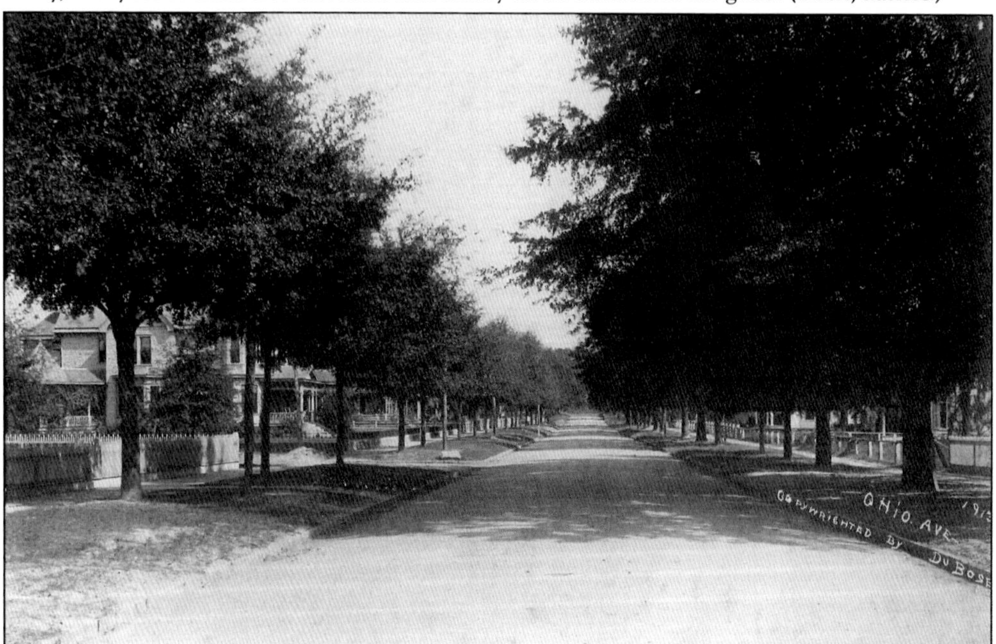

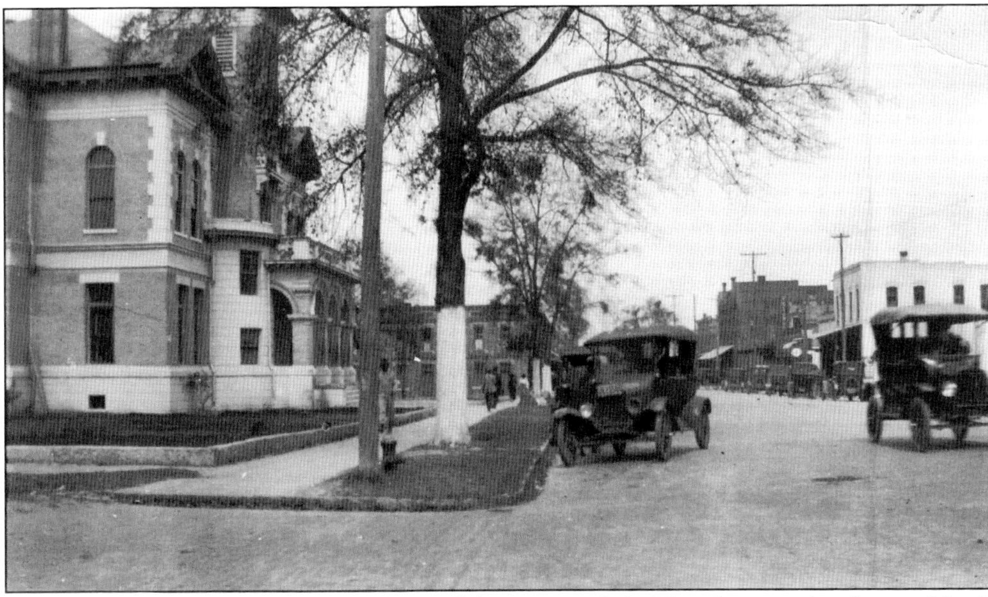

Ohio Avenue has long been a major thoroughfare in Live Oak. This photograph, taken on March 20, 1919, shows a busy Ohio Avenue, looking north. The courthouse is shown on the left with numerous businesses behind and across the street from it. By this point, automobiles have all but replaced horses as the method of travel for most of Suwannee County's residents.

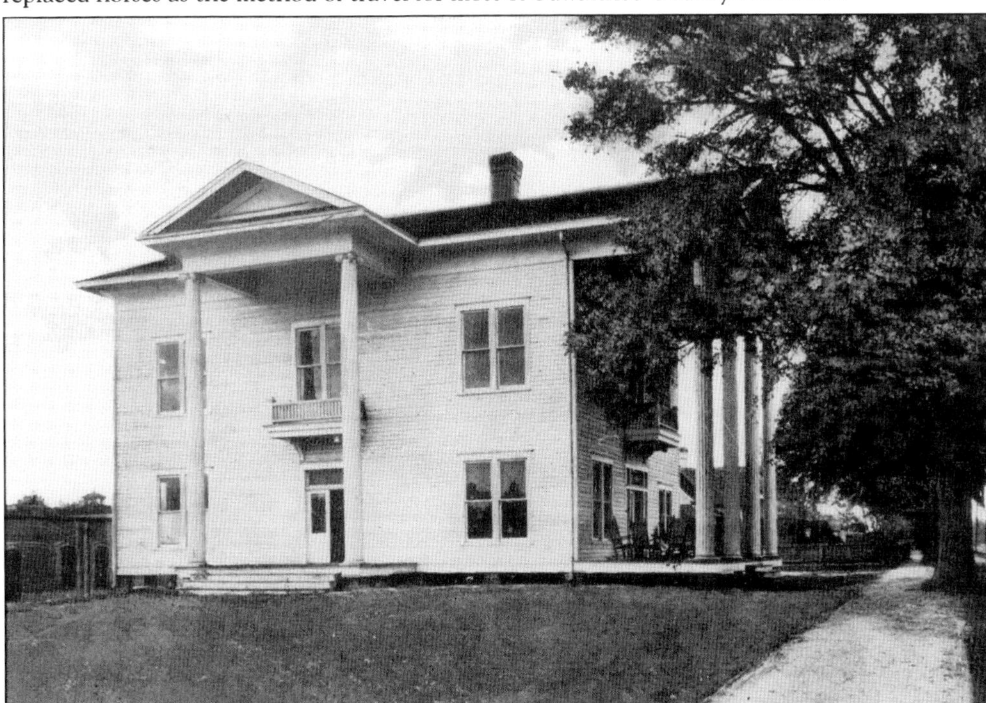

Live Oak has been blessed with numerous civic organizations throughout the years. One of the many long-running organizations is the Elks Lodge, which was originally established in the first part of the 20th century. Among their accomplishments was this large home on the corner of Suwannee Avenue and Conner Street, built to serve the needs of the community. (SCCC.)

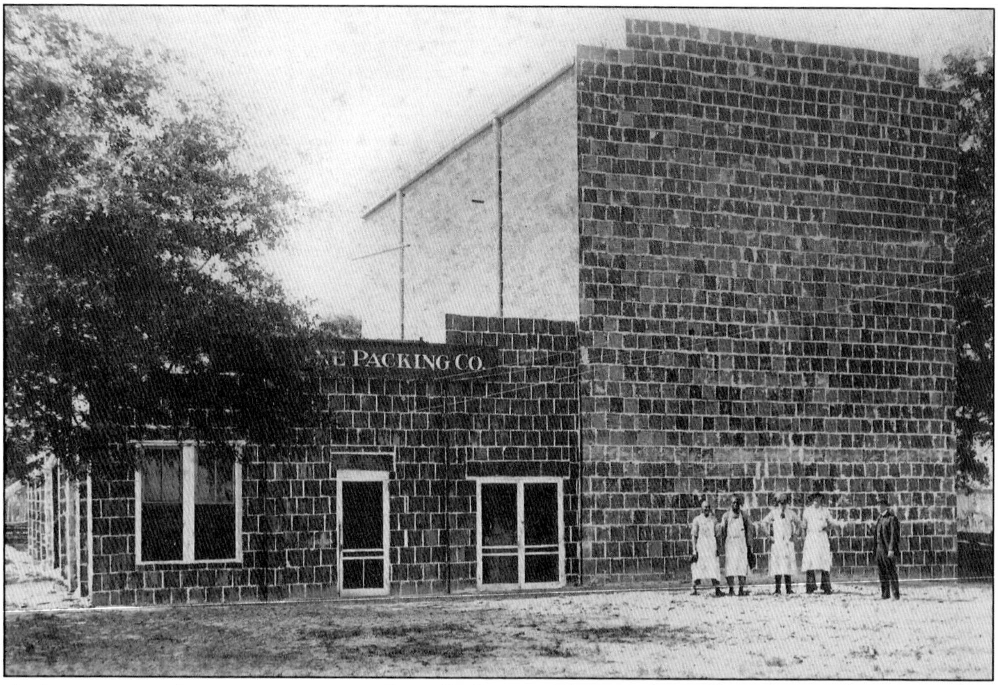

As is necessary for any community, Live Oak sported a number of butcher and meatpacking businesses. Perhaps the longest lasting of these businesses was the Suwannee Packing Company, commonly called Suwannee Pack. Established in the early 20th century to provide meat for the residents, Suwannee Pack finally closed its doors at the turn of the next century. (Florida State Photographic Collection.)

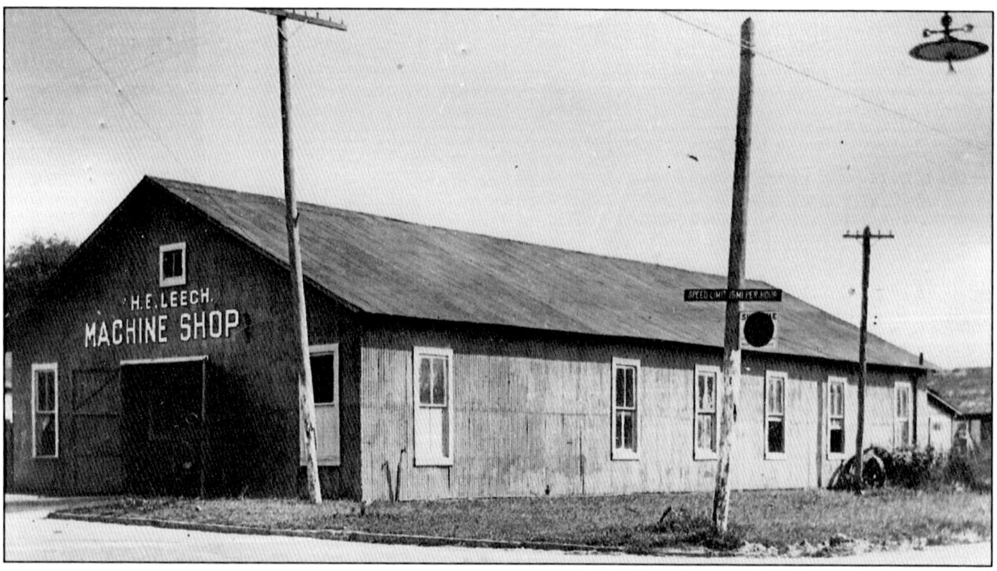

Another important business at the beginning of the 20th century was a machine shop to provide repairs to the fragile, accident-prone "horseless carriages" of the day. Among these machine works was the business of H.E. Leech, who established his shop on the corner of Howard and Houston Streets. Shown in 1920, this location is now a parking lot for the First Baptist Church. (Florida State Photographic Collection.)

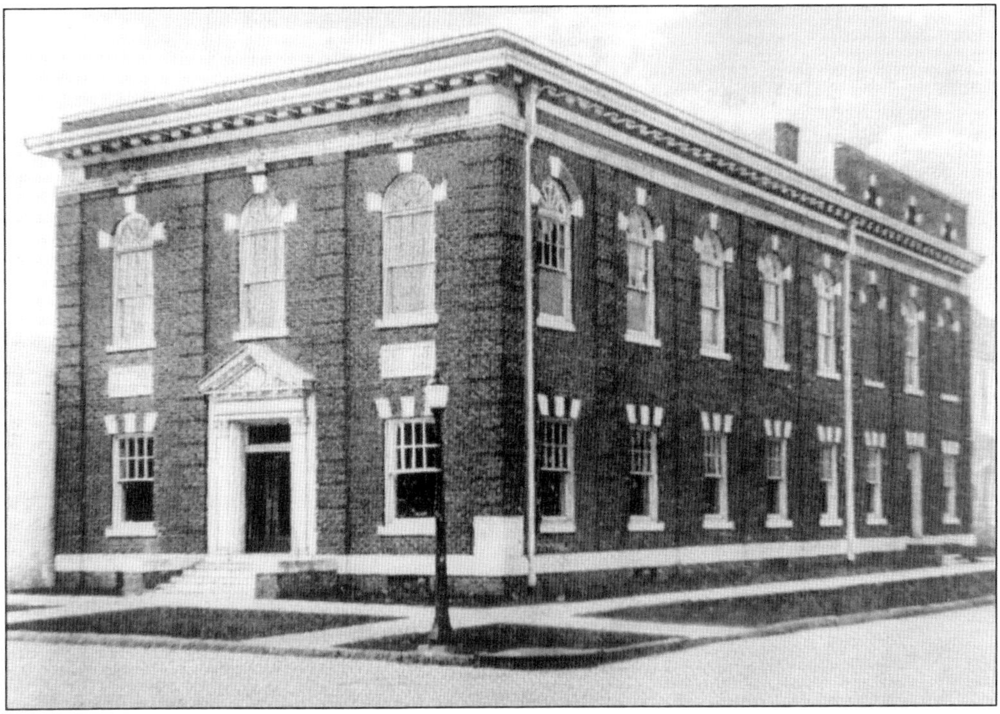

One of the oldest organizations in the county is the Free Masons, having been established even before Suwannee County. The Live Oak lodge was eventually located on the corner of Ohio Avenue and Duval Street, where its first building also served as armory for the local Suwannee Rifles militia, a church, and town hall. This brick building was constructed in 1922 and served for many years before being lost. (Florida State Photographic Collection.)

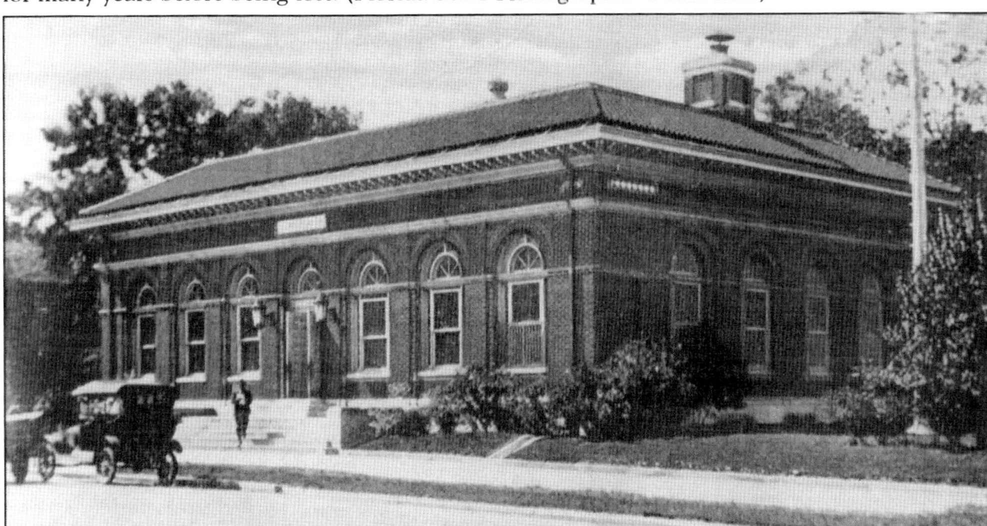

Live Oak's first post office was established in 1866, and a new building was constructed next to the courthouse in 1906. It was soon eclipsed, as a newer post office was built on the corner of Ohio Avenue and Parshley Street in 1915. Now nearly 100 years old, the Live Oak Post Office continues to serve the community and looks much as it did in this 1922 postcard. (Florida State Photographic Collection.)

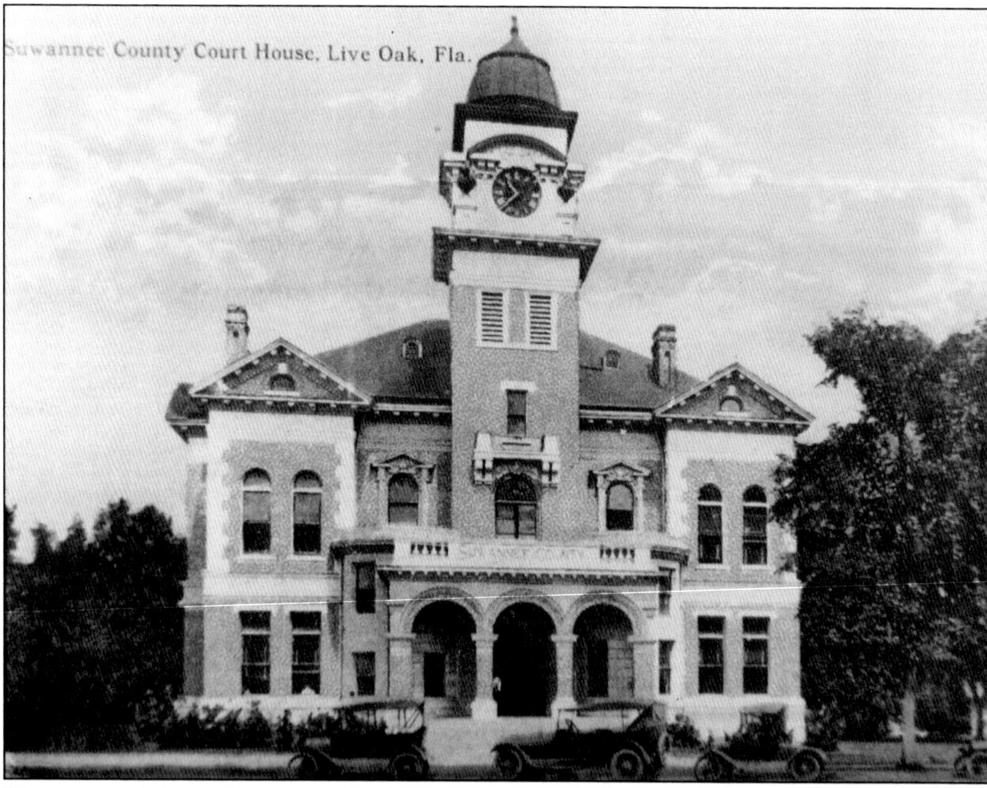

This postcard from 1922 shows the Suwannee County Courthouse on South Ohio Avenue. The change from horse-drawn carriages to horseless carriages is now complete, with a variety of automobiles parked in front of the county's government hub. Note the number of live oak trees surrounding the courthouse, most of which had been cut down by the 1960s. (SCCC.)

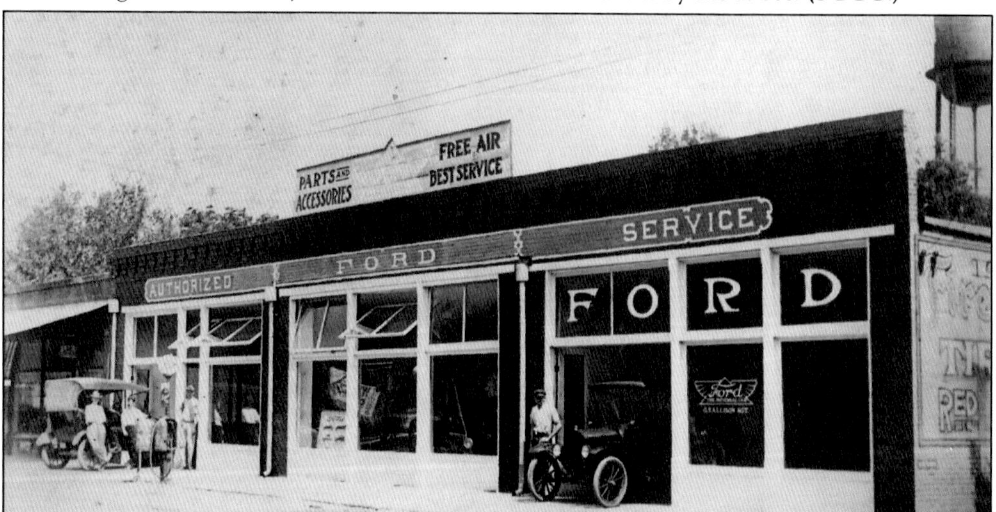

As horses and buggies were replaced by automobiles after the turn of the century, clever businessmen quickly adapted to the changes. A Ford dealership was operated by George F. Allison on East Howard Street, serving the transportation needs of the community for many years. Dowling's original water tower is visible in the background at far right. (Florida State Photographic Collection.)

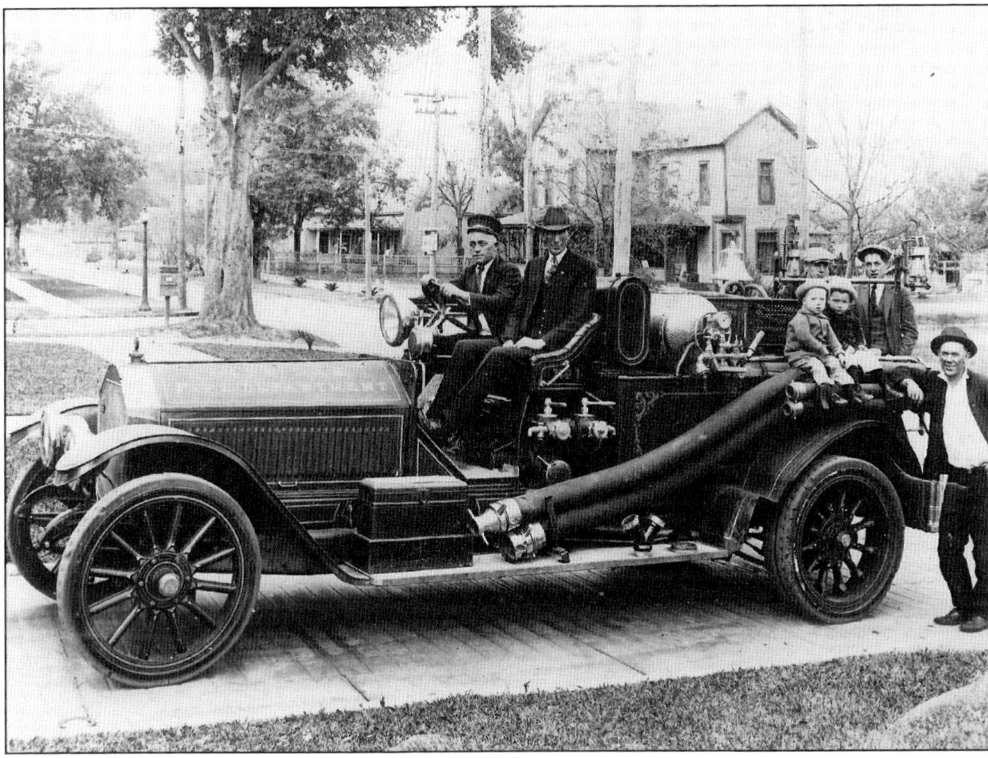

In 1918, Live Oak purchased its first motorized fire engine, affectionately called "Betsy." This picture shows Betsy in her early years, probably around 1925. The thin man in the left passenger seat is Luke Haddon, a longtime fire chief who served from 1915 until his death in 1960, ironically during Fire Prevention Week. "Betsy" still exists and is lovingly maintained by the Live Oak Fire Department.

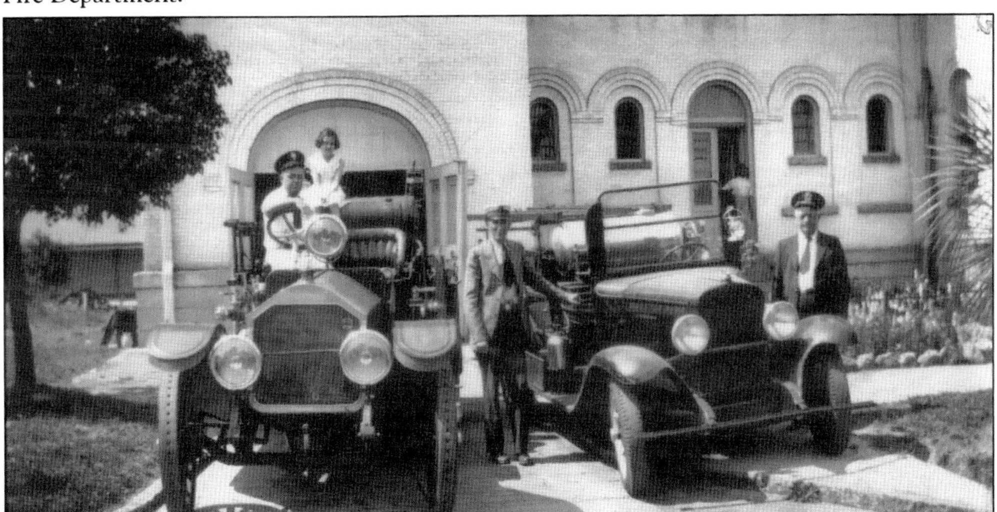

This photograph from 1935 shows two of the fire department's trucks, with "Betsy" on the left. From left to right, Joab Creekmore and daughter Delores sit on Betsy, while longtime fire chief Luke Haddon stands between the trucks and chief of police Bert Creekmore stands to the right. The 1908 city hall is in the background.

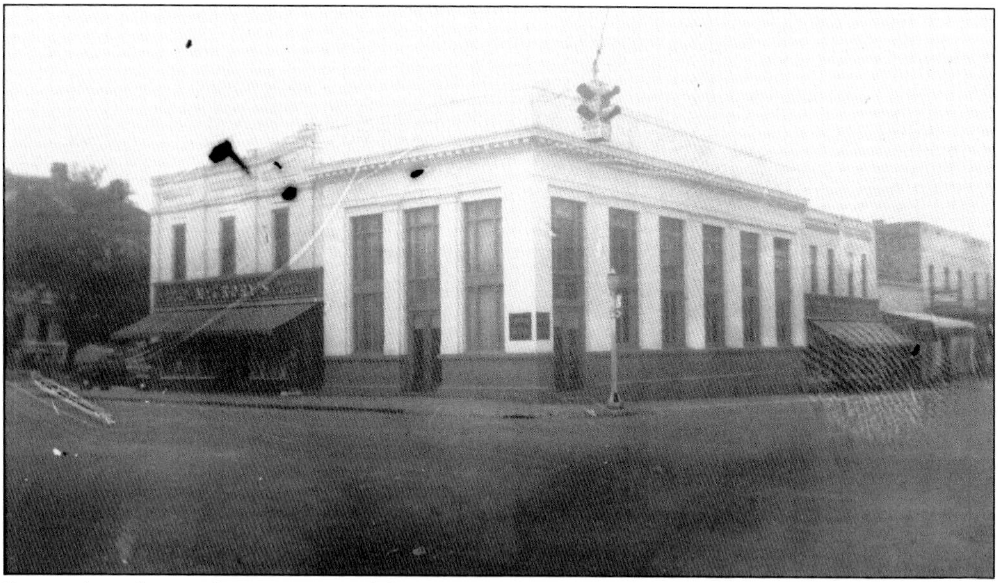

Situated on the southwest corner of the main intersection of Howard Street and Ohio Avenue, this brick structure served as the Commercial Bank building for many decades. After Hurricane Dora in 1964, the Commercial Bank moved farther down Ohio Avenue. The building, shown in 1942, is currently the office of Rhett Bullard, attorney at law.

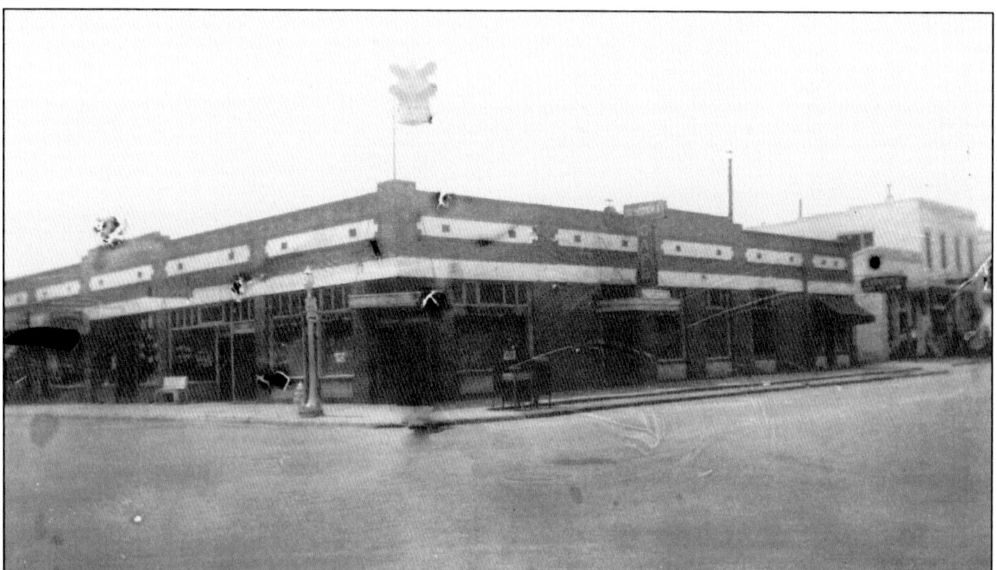

The Seminole Café was a watering hole for white residents for many years. Sited on the southeast corner of the main intersection of Howard Street and Ohio Avenue, it eventually closed its doors. After serving for three decades as the Suwannee Travel Agency, the building is now the location of the B.W. Helvenston Insurance Agency, established in 1892. This photograph shows the café in 1942.

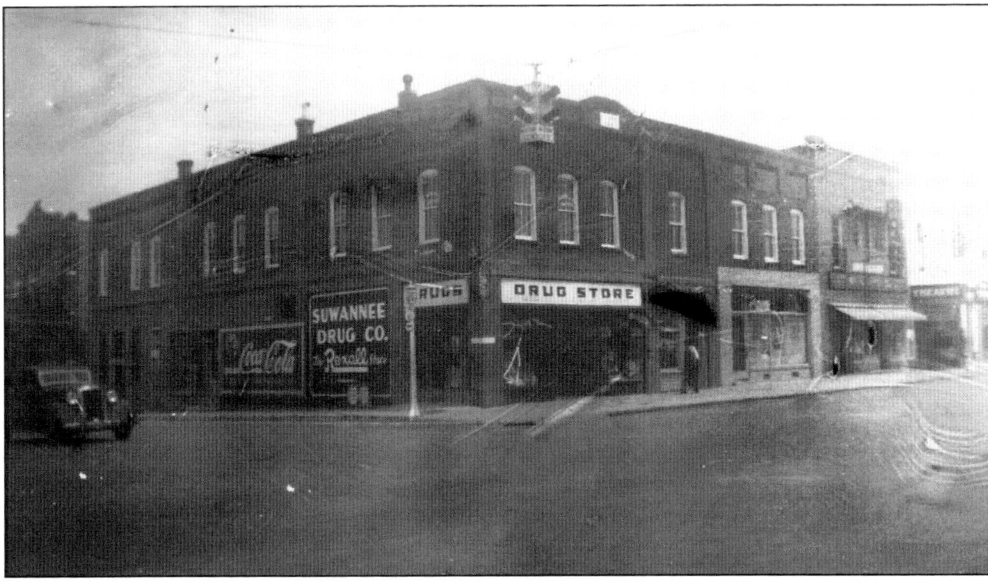

Located on the northwest corner of the main intersection of Howard Street and Ohio Avenue, the Suwannee Drug Company served the residents of Live Oak for many years. Shown here in 1942, it is now the location of the Xin Ming Chinese Restaurant. Barely noticeable on the far right is one of Live Oak's theaters.

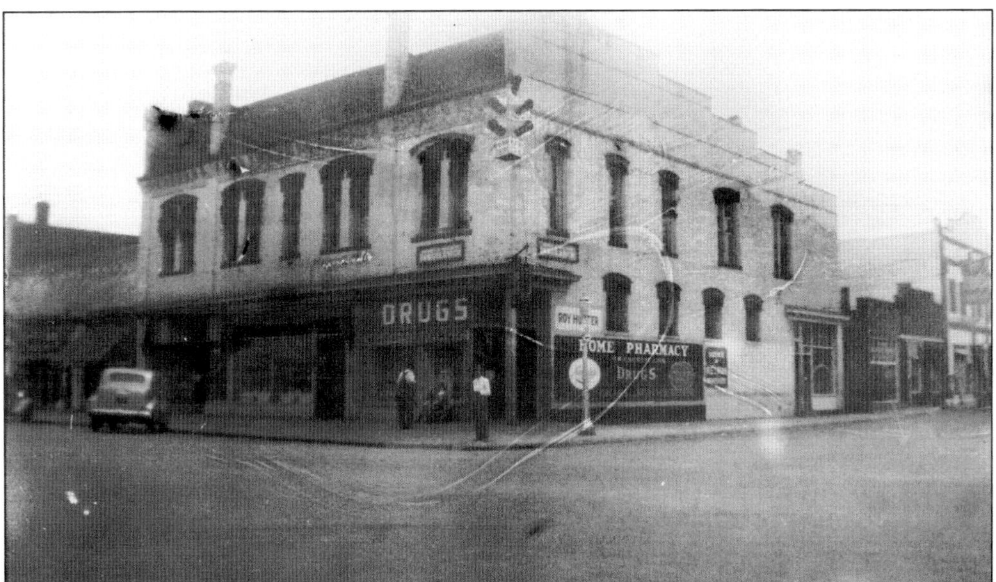

Dr. Roy Hunter, a longtime Live Oak resident, ran the Home Pharmacy on the northeast corner of the main intersection of Howard Street and Ohio Avenue. The building, shown here in 1942, is now the location of Insurance World. Another of Live Oak's theaters, the Alimar, is on the far right.

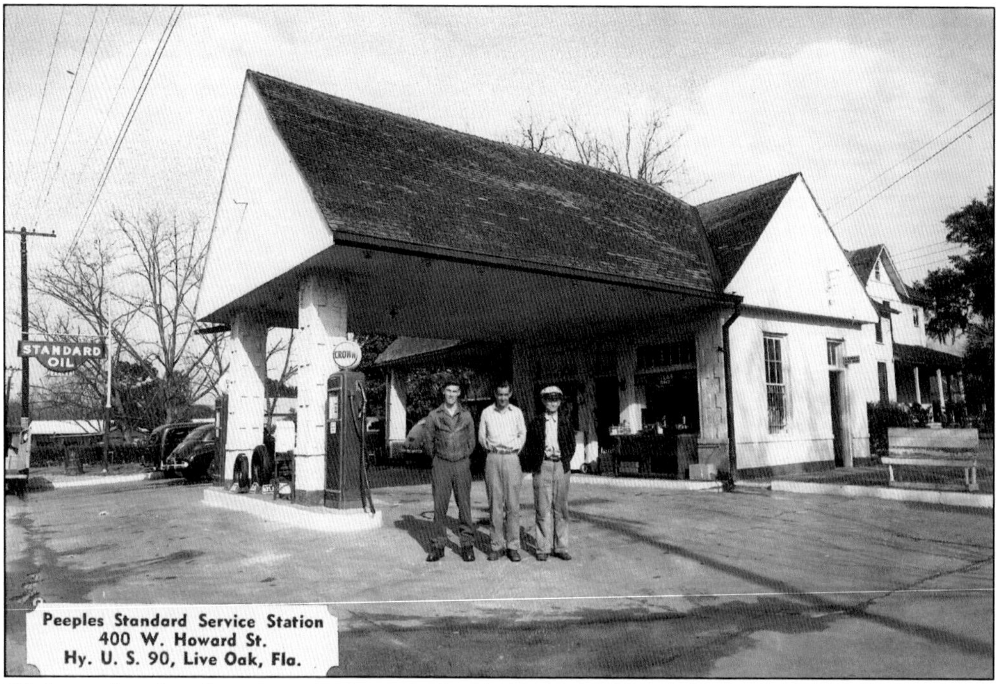

Within a few decades, most residents had at least one automobile they could call their own. Garages sprang up around the city to provide fuel and friendly service. One of those many garages was the Peeples Standard Oil Service Station, located at 400 West Howard Street, shown here in the 1940s. (Florida State Photographic Collection.)

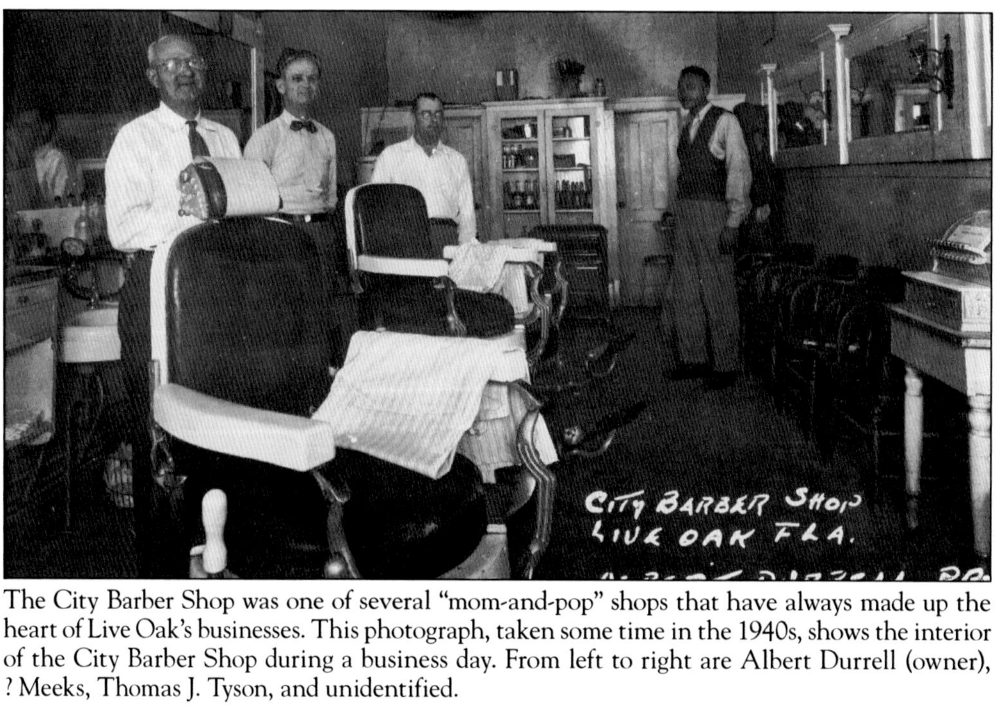

The City Barber Shop was one of several "mom-and-pop" shops that have always made up the heart of Live Oak's businesses. This photograph, taken some time in the 1940s, shows the interior of the City Barber Shop during a business day. From left to right are Albert Durrell (owner), ? Meeks, Thomas J. Tyson, and unidentified.

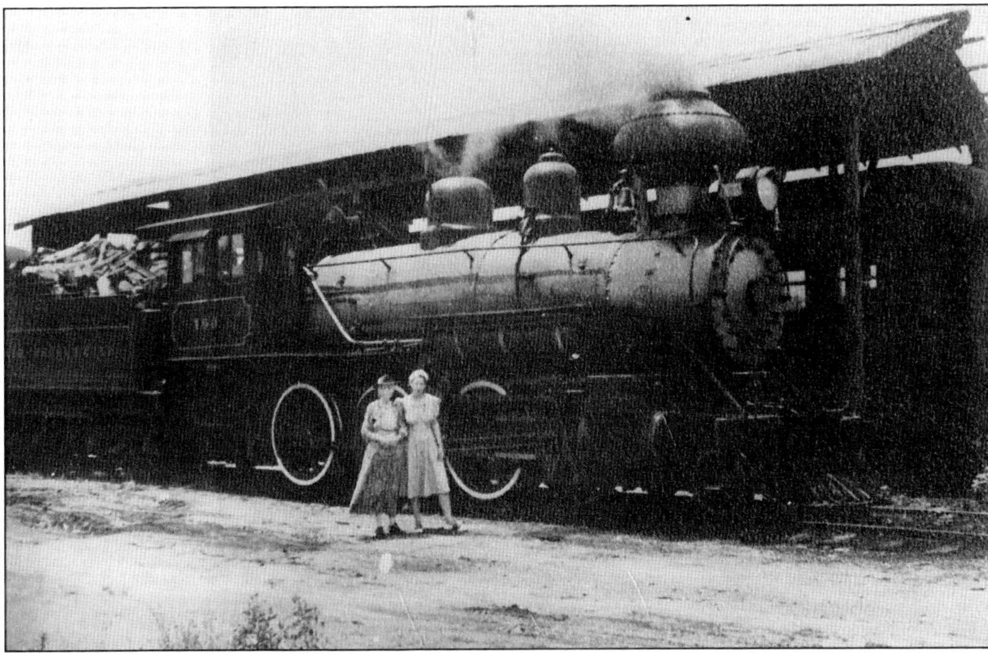

The most famous railroad in Suwannee County would probably be the Live Oak, Perry & Gulf (LOP&G) Railroad, chartered in 1906 from the holdings of older railroads. This short line was alternatively called the "Loping Gopher" and "Livin' on Peas and Grits" because of the bumpy and rural nature of the line. This railroad hauled passengers and freight for many years, and part of it continues to operate today as the Georgia & Florida Railway. The photograph above shows LOP&G engine No. 100 some time around World War II, while the photograph below shows engine No. 102 around the same period. In both pictures, the "cabbage stack" funnel that kept sparks from flying is visible.

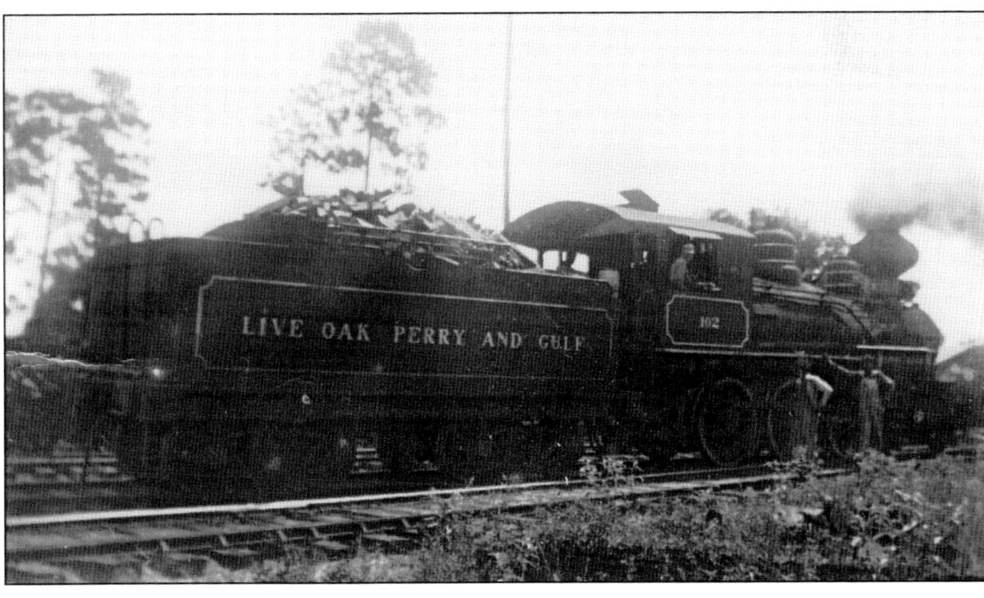

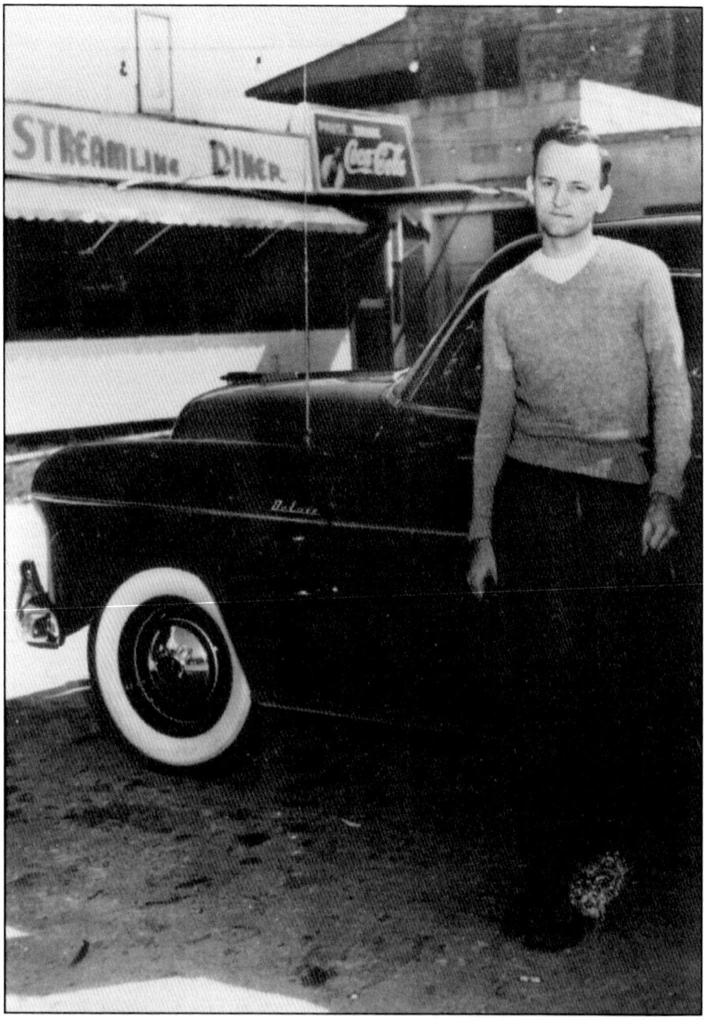

Among the mom-and-pop shops in downtown Live Oak was the Streamline Diner. Situated just west of the intersection of Howard Street and Pine Avenue, it served meals to white patrons during the long period of segregation. This photograph, taken in the 1940s, shows one of its patrons standing by his car.

This photograph, taken in the mid-1900s, shows East Howard Street, looking toward the main intersection of Ohio Avenue and Howard Street. Among the businesses in the picture are the Alimar Theatre (later burned down), Grantham Chevrolet and Oldsmobile Dealership (later torn down), and the Sinclair Dodge Dealership, which is currently the home of the *Suwannee Democrat*, the local newspaper.

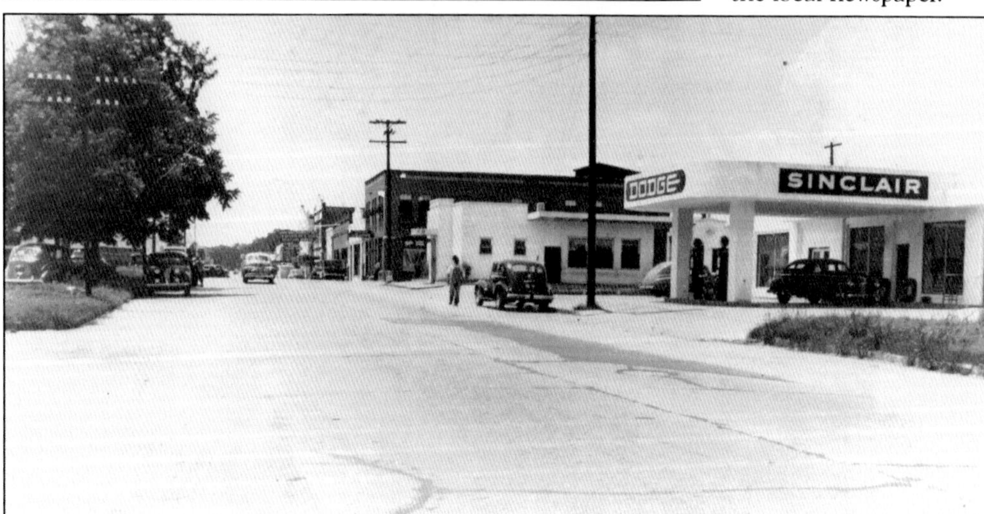

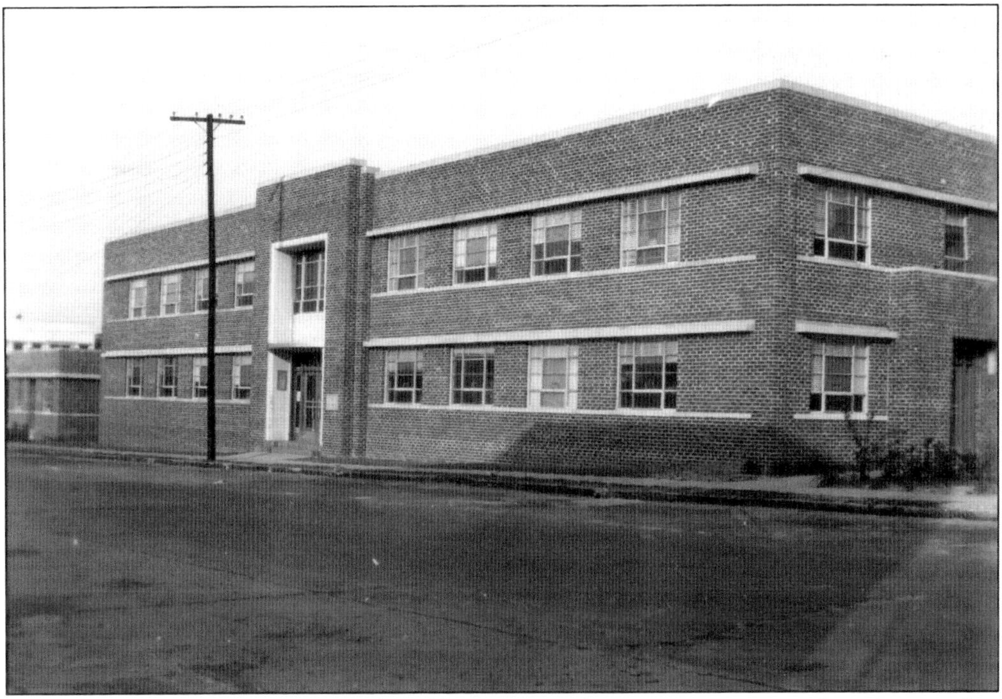

The Suwannee County Agricultural Building on Pine Avenue was constructed on the site of an old county jail. After many years of service as an agricultural building and health department, the building was renovated at the end of the 20th century for use by the county's tax collector and property appraiser, who continue to inhabit it today. It is shown in 1951.

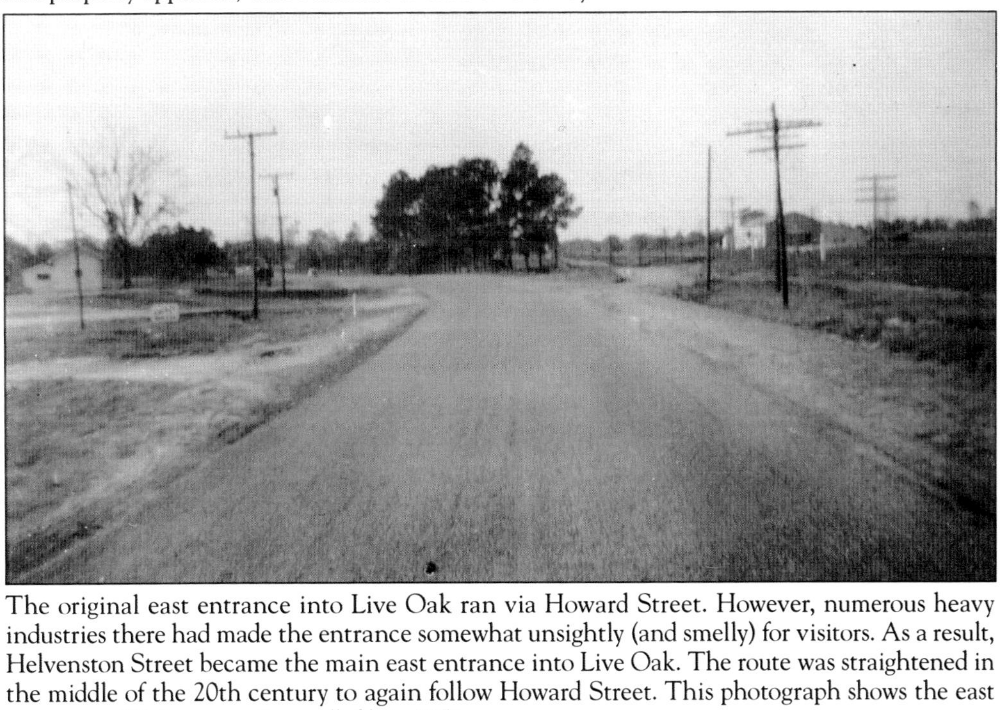

The original east entrance into Live Oak ran via Howard Street. However, numerous heavy industries there had made the entrance somewhat unsightly (and smelly) for visitors. As a result, Helvenston Street became the main east entrance into Live Oak. The route was straightened in the middle of the 20th century to again follow Howard Street. This photograph shows the east entrance of Helvenston Street (left) in 1954.

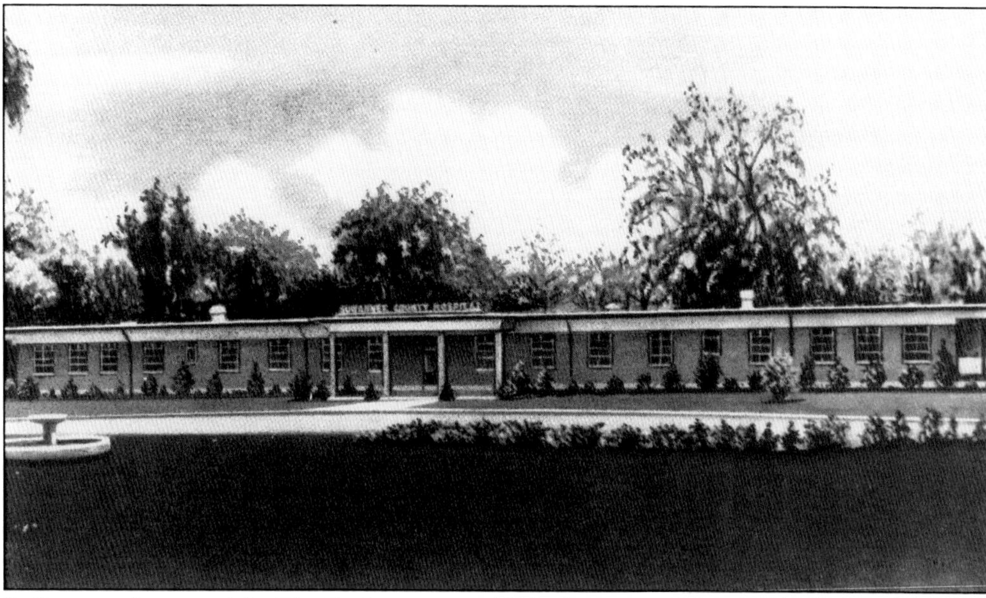

Built upon the site of the Florida Institute in 1948, the county's first public hospital was also the first constructed under the Hill-Burton Act of 1948, which gave federal assistance for public welfare projects. Serving the community for many years, it was eventually torn down to make way for housing. The author was one of many babies born there.

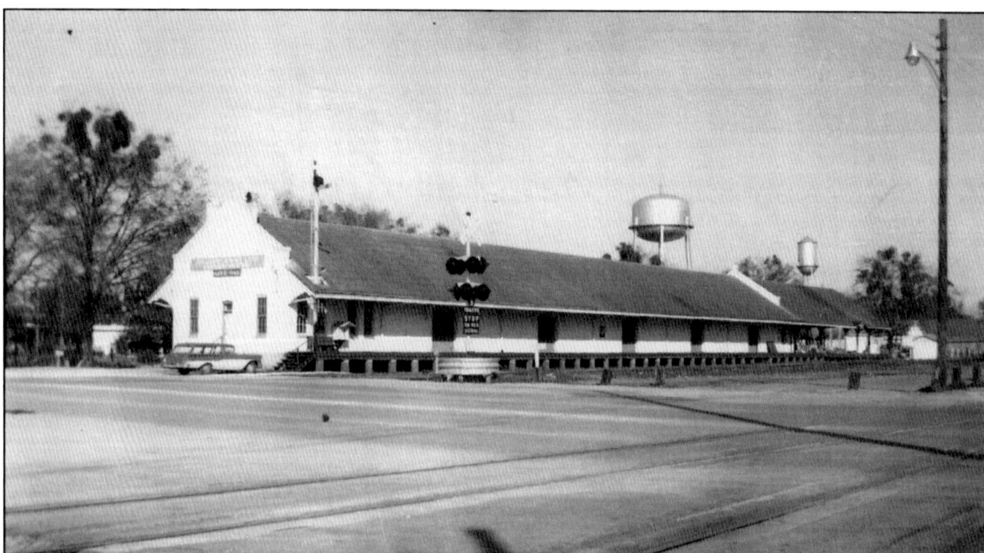

The Atlantic Coastline Freight Station was completed in 1903 near the corner of Ohio Avenue and Duval Street, replacing an earlier structure just south of it that had outlived its usefulness. The freight station served the community for many decades but was eventually closed. The abandoned station became a focus of historic restoration in early 1980s, eventually reopening as the Suwannee County Historical Museum.

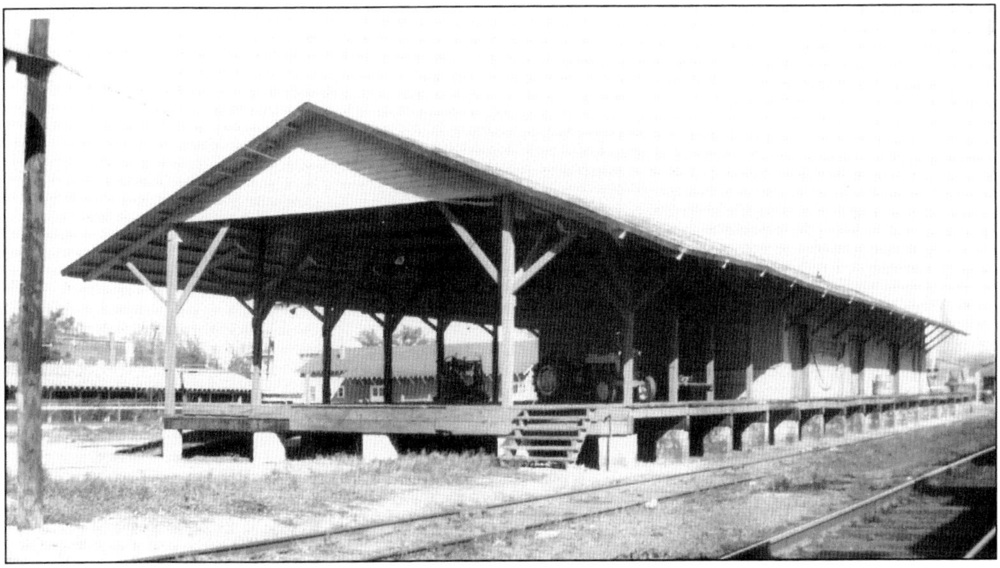

Live Oak was a major railroad hub from almost the beginning of its existence, and even into the second half of the 20th century, several railroads maintained depots there. This photograph shows the Seaboard Air Line (SAL) freight station just north of downtown Live Oak in 1960. In the first photograph, looking roughly northeast, the Masonic lodge is in the left background, and city hall can barely be seen through the posts of the overhang. In the lower photograph, looking roughly northwest, the building of Huffman and Gilmore Feed, Seed, Farm, and Garden Supply can be seen behind the freight station. The SAL freight station was eventually torn down to make way for parking space.

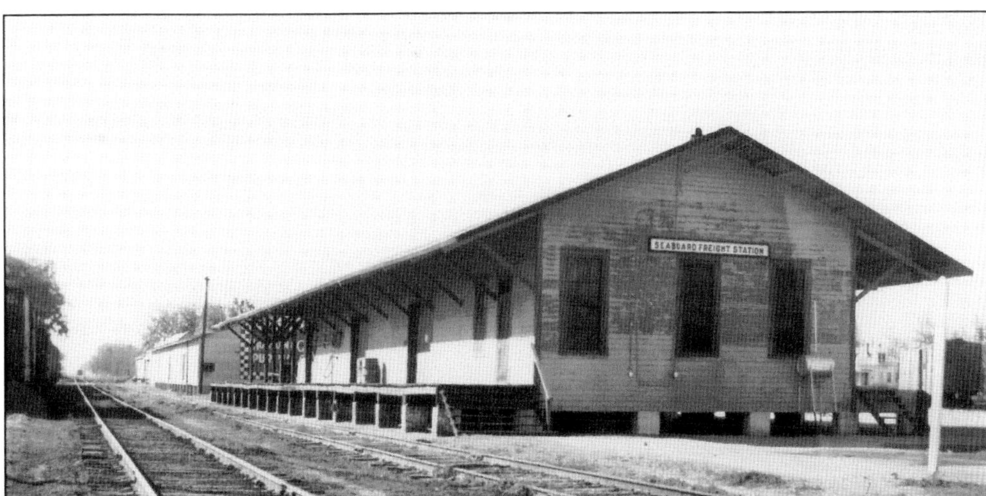

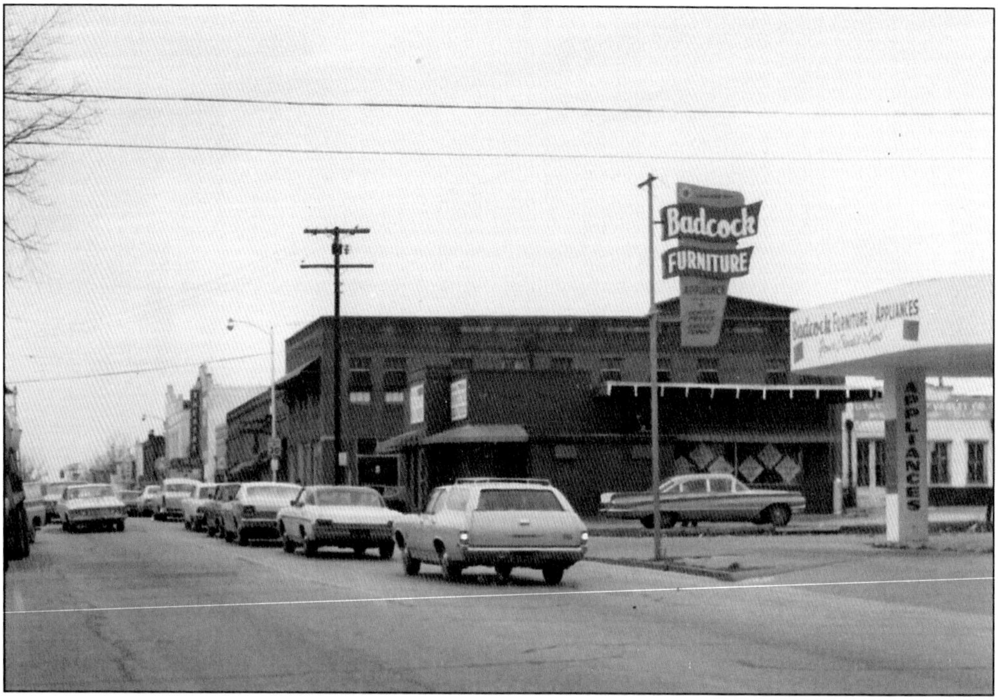

By the 1960s, many of the original buildings in Live Oak had been replaced by newer structures. This photograph, taken during the 1960s, shows East Howard Street, looking west. The building to the extreme right, Badcock Furniture and Appliance, is now the home of the *Suwannee Democrat*. All but two or three of the buildings shown in the picture still stand today. (Florida State Photographic Collection.)

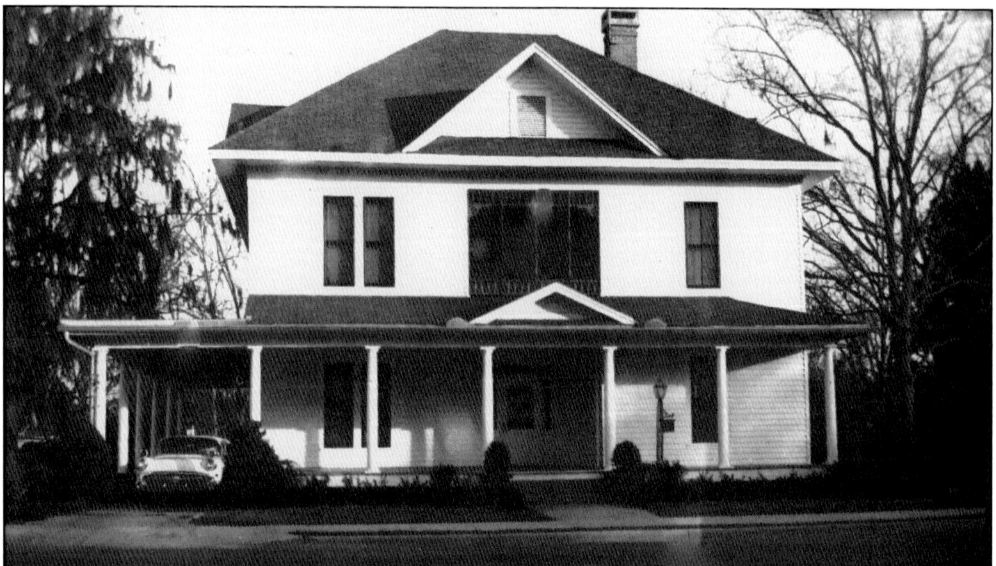

As Live Oak expanded, so too did the number of businesses. Many times, these businesses took up shop in older homes along main thoroughfares. One such business was the Suwannee Funeral Home, originally located on South Ohio Avenue in what had been the location of some of the most influential families in the city 50 years before.

Three

Other Communities

A variety of communities have existed throughout Suwannee County's history. Some continue to thrive, but others have not been so fortunate; many communities dried up when their residents moved to more productive areas, using automobiles and newly built roads.

The town of Branford was originally called Rowland's Bluff. The town became a major steamboat and railroad port during the last years of the 19th century, until a major hurricane wiped out much of the industry in 1896. Branford slowly rebuilt and today is a bustling town in Suwannee County that retains its local government.

Originally known as Hudson-upon-the-Suwannee, Dowling Park was founded in the late 1800s. After the Dowling family moved its lumber and railroad operations to the area around the turn of the century, the community's population exploded, and it was renamed Dowling Park. In 1913, an orphanage and home was created on land donated by Thomas Dowling; it became the Advent Christian Village, Florida's first retirement center and originally meant for "old and worn-out preachers."

McAlpin was founded in 1882 and named for Daniel McAlpin, an early publisher of what would become the *Suwannee Democrat*. Its main products during the end of the 19th century were naval stores and cotton, but as markets shifted to larger cities, McAlpin became more rural.

O'Brien was originally called Dab's Hole after a prominent sinkhole in the area. As with many other communities in Suwannee County, it began to fade when lumber, turpentine, and cotton were no longer produced in large quantities and markets shifted to larger towns, such as Live Oak. Today, it retains a post office and assorted businesses.

Wellborn was originally called Little River and can be considered to have been founded in 1830 by George McClellan, an early settler. In 1860, Louis Wellborn Dubose, an engineer from Tallahassee, was given 162 acres in appreciation for work performed on the east-west railroad. The land was surveyed in 1860 and called Wellborn; today, the community continues to attract thousands to its Blueberry Festival every year.

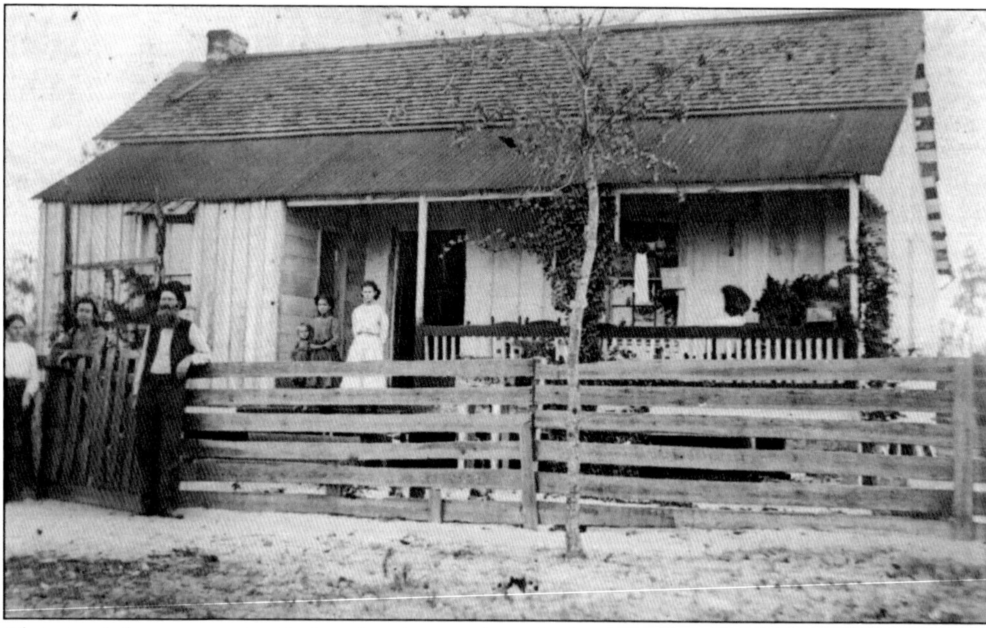

This simple home was classified as the oldest in Branford at one point in the late 20th century and was the home of Minnie Dees Brown Rankin Brown Peak Brown. Her interestingly long name comes from the fact that she was married several times, including to Levi Rankin, the bearded man in both of the photographs. The children on the porch in the earlier photograph (above) are Bertie, Nellie, and O.D., all Minnie's children. Nellie lived in the home after the death of her mother, Minnie, and worked at the drugstore in Branford, where she was well known by the community. (Both, Susannette Howell Baxter.)

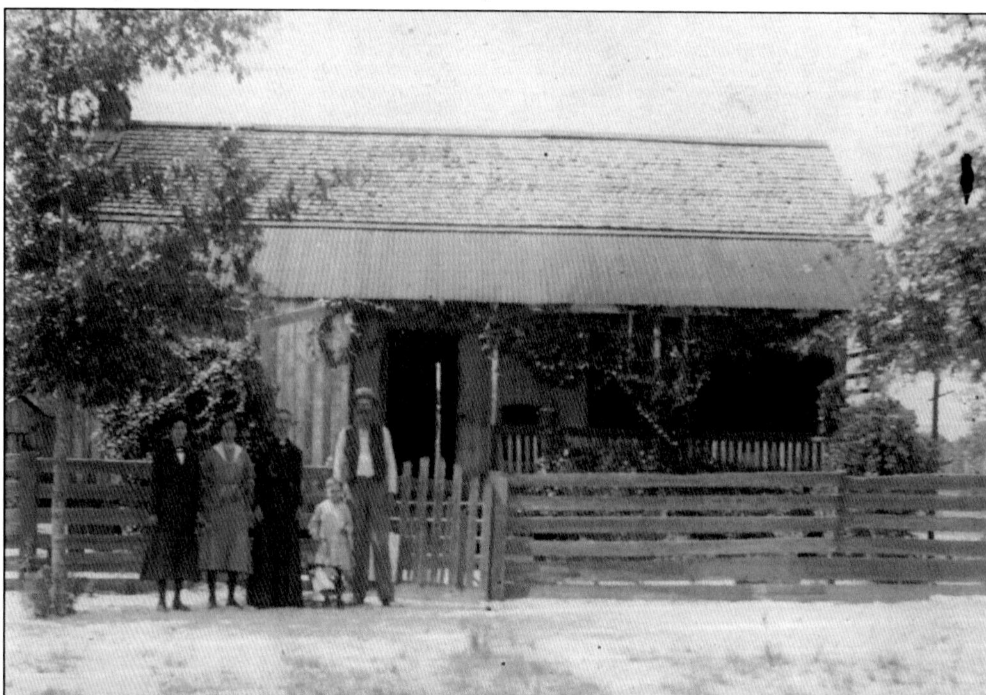

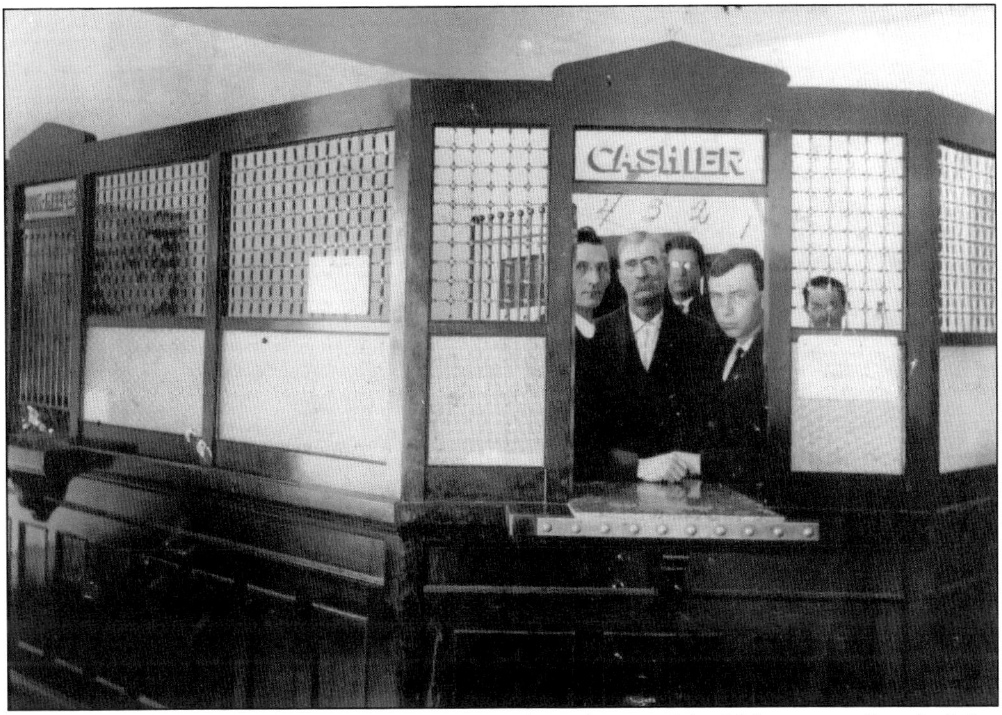

Live Oak was not the only community growing in the early part of the 20th century; Branford also saw the rise of businesses, including the aptly named Branford State Bank. This photograph, taken on opening day in 1911, shows, from left to right, Henry Heath, Sam Martin, Walter Clements, and Fred D. Phillips. The oak counter is now on display at the Suwannee County Historical Museum. (Suwannee County Historical Commission.)

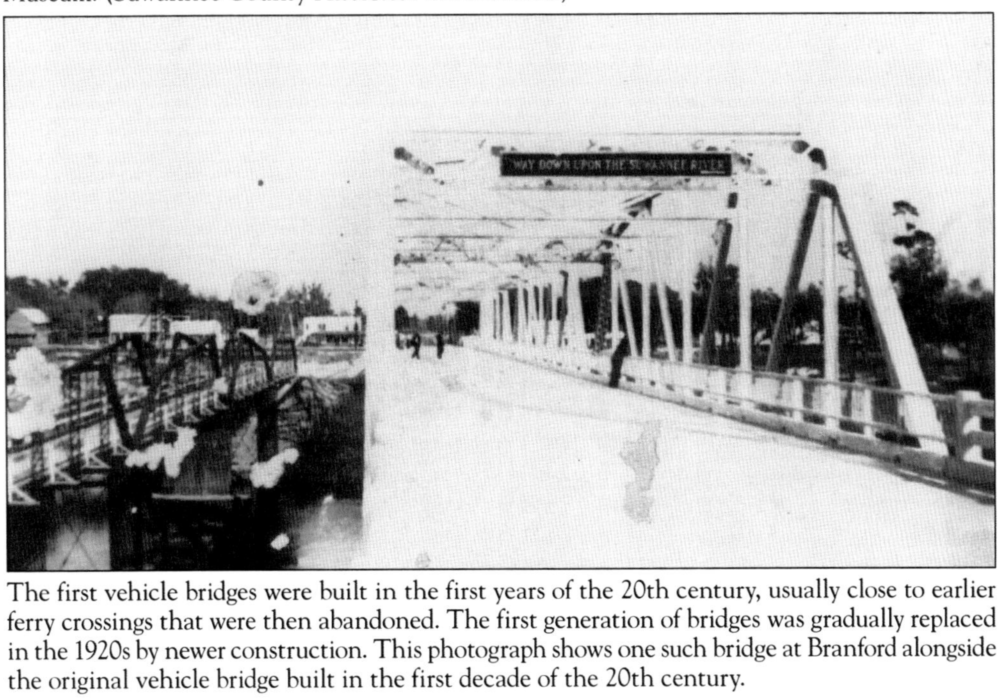

The first vehicle bridges were built in the first years of the 20th century, usually close to earlier ferry crossings that were then abandoned. The first generation of bridges was gradually replaced in the 1920s by newer construction. This photograph shows one such bridge at Branford alongside the original vehicle bridge built in the first decade of the 20th century.

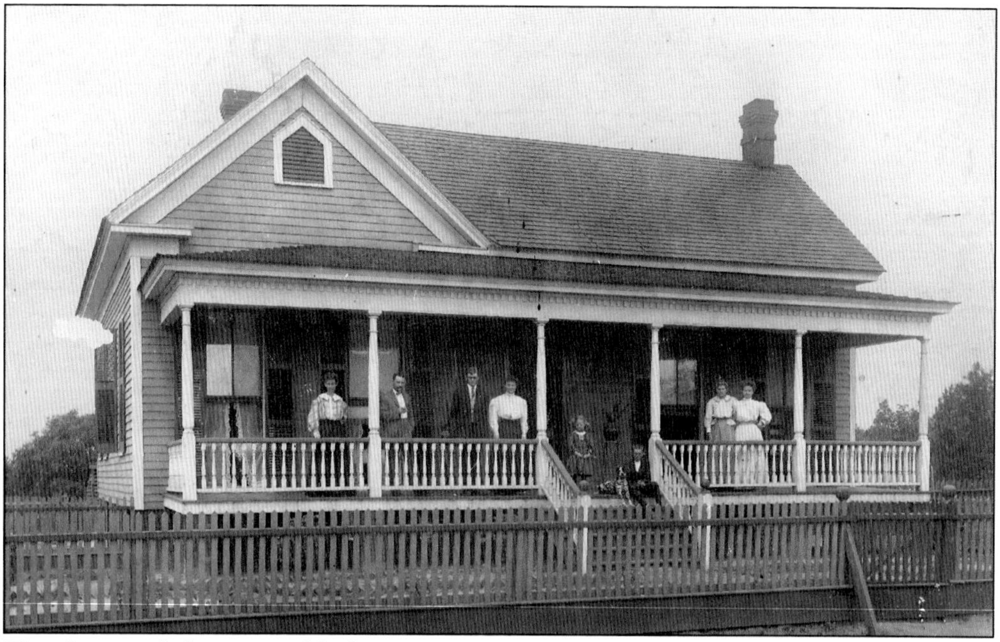

This photograph shows one of the homes in Dowling Park around 1900, with various unidentified adults and children in front. It is likely that the home was used as a boardinghouse for workers at the local sawmill during this period. The house still stands on County Road 250, just outside the main entrance to the Advent Christian Village. (ACV Archives.)

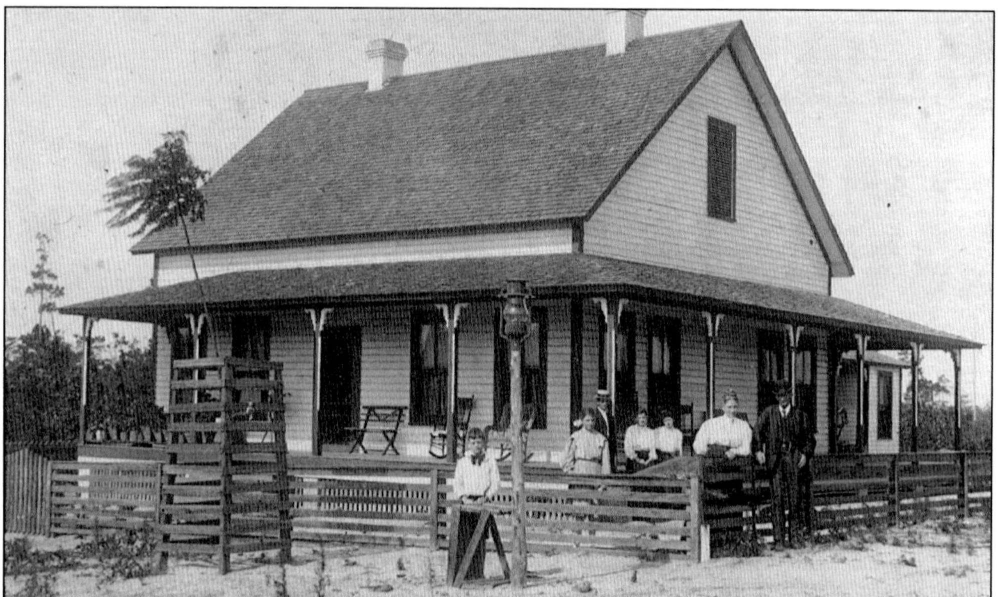

This photograph shows the home of Wiley Jordan, first postmaster of Dowling Park, around 1906. Within two years of becoming postmaster, he took a traveling salesman job and turned his duties over to his 22-year-old daughter Ruby. She would later marry Henry Strickland and become mayor of Live Oak in 1924, the first female mayor south of the Mason-Dixon Line. In this photograph are, from left to right, Jordan children Edward (by lamppost), Pauline, Clifford, Bertha, and Ruby, with Grandma and Grandpa Jordan to the right. (ACV Archives.)

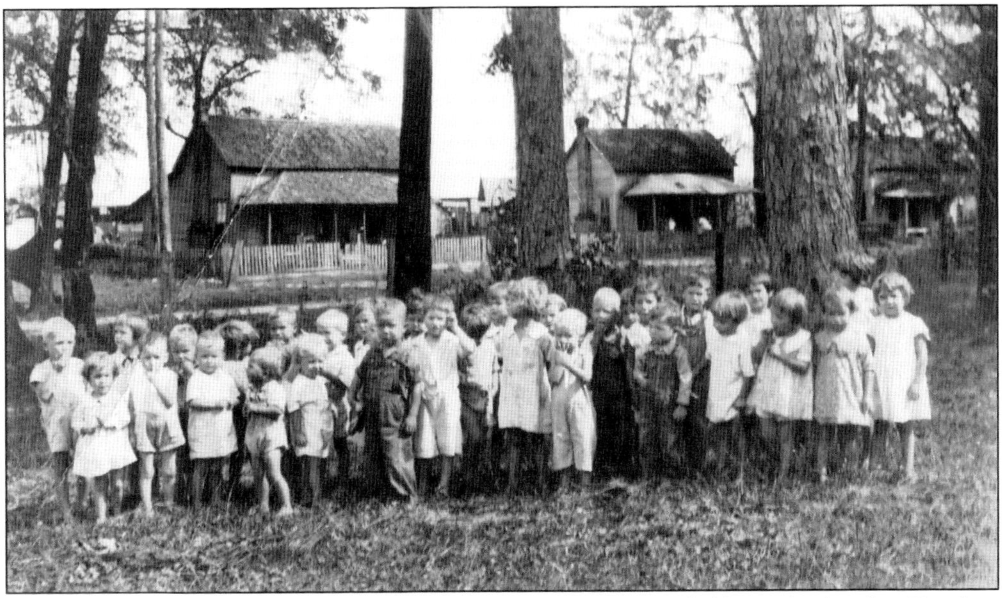

This photograph, taken around 1908, shows some of the young children who lived in Dowling Park. Most probably, they are children of some of the millworkers who lived in the cottages shown in the background. Upon reaching school age, they would have attended the school in Dowling Park; African American children would have had to walk approximately two miles to school in nearby Lancaster. (ACV Archives.)

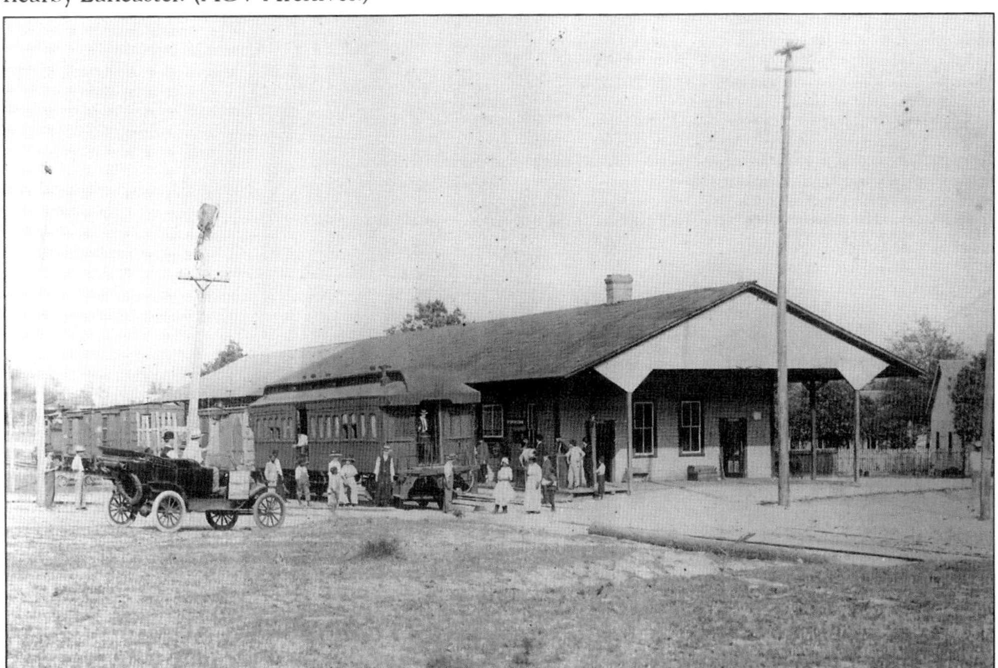

By the second decade of the 20th century, Suwannee County was crisscrossed by a number of railroads, each with depots at most of the communities through which they traveled. This photograph shows one such depot, probably at Dowling Park, around 1910. A detailed examination of this photograph shows that the depot's entrances are labeled "white" and "colored."

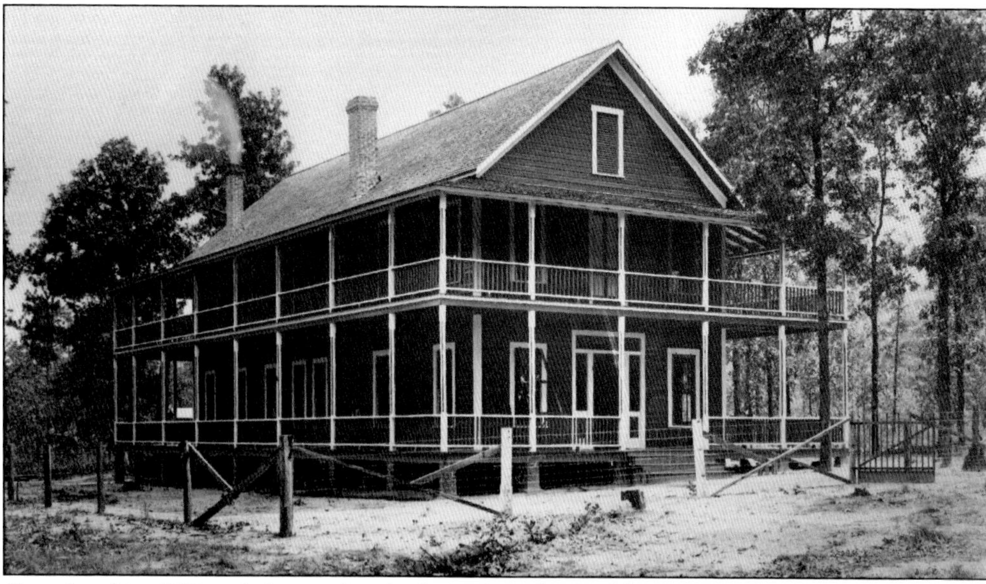

Completed in 1913 and shown shortly thereafter, this building in Dowling Park served as the children's dormitory for the Advent Christian Village, with space for a matron, children, and retirees or visitors. The home burned on December 23, 1925, Christmas gifts and all. The surrounding community pitched in to give the children a wonderful Christmas, and a new brick building was soon constructed on the same site. (ACV Archives.)

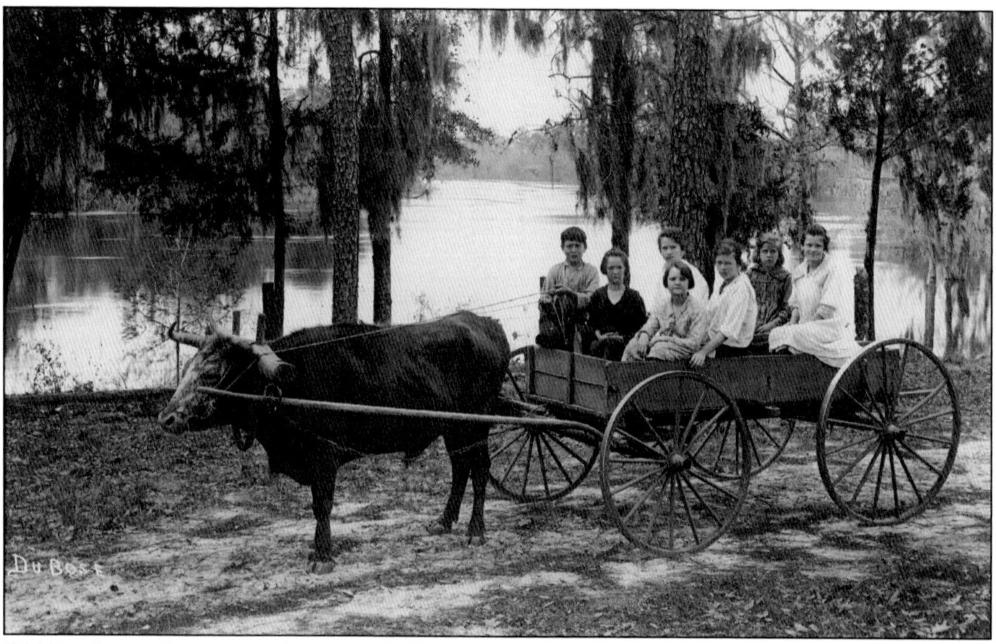

Old Buck was the name of an ox used by the Advent Christian Village in its early years for everything from planting crops and hauling coffins to carrying luggage from the Live Oak, Perry & Gulf Railroad to the local hotel. In this photograph, taken in 1916, Old Buck takes some of the village's orphans on a ride alongside the banks of the Suwannee River. From left to right are (first row) Ted Setzer, Eula Setzer, and Leona Hope; (second row) Thelma Andrews and Rena Andrews; (third row) Colene Setzer and Viola Andrews. (ACV Archives.)

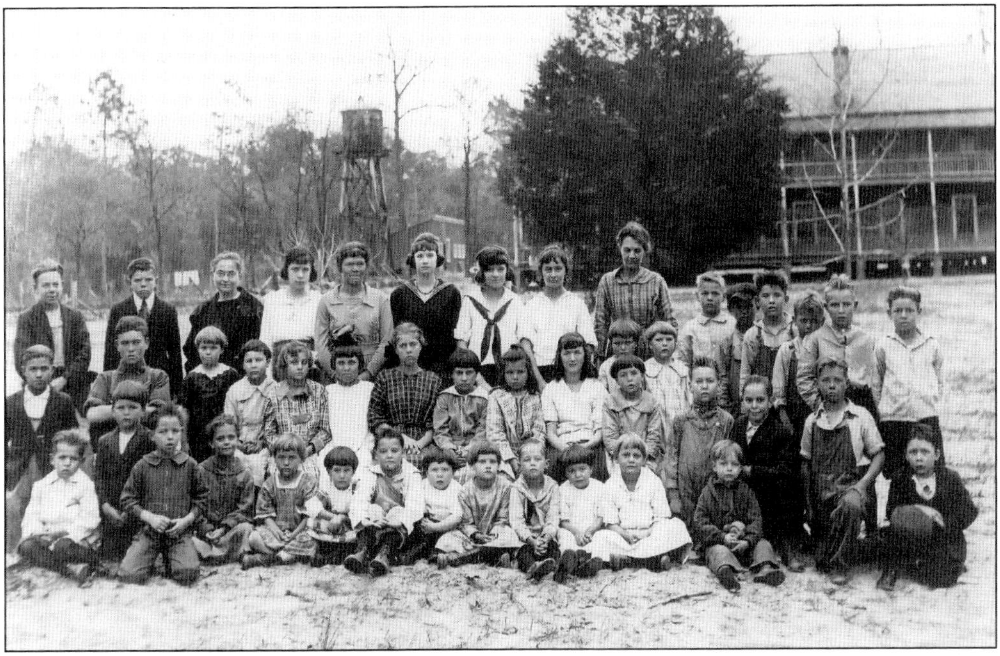

This photograph, taken in 1919 or 1920, shows the orphans of the Advent Christian Village in Dowling Park, some of whom are the same children shown in the 1916 photograph on the preceding page. The two-story orphans' home (which burned in 1925) and the water tower are visible in the background. (ACV Archives.)

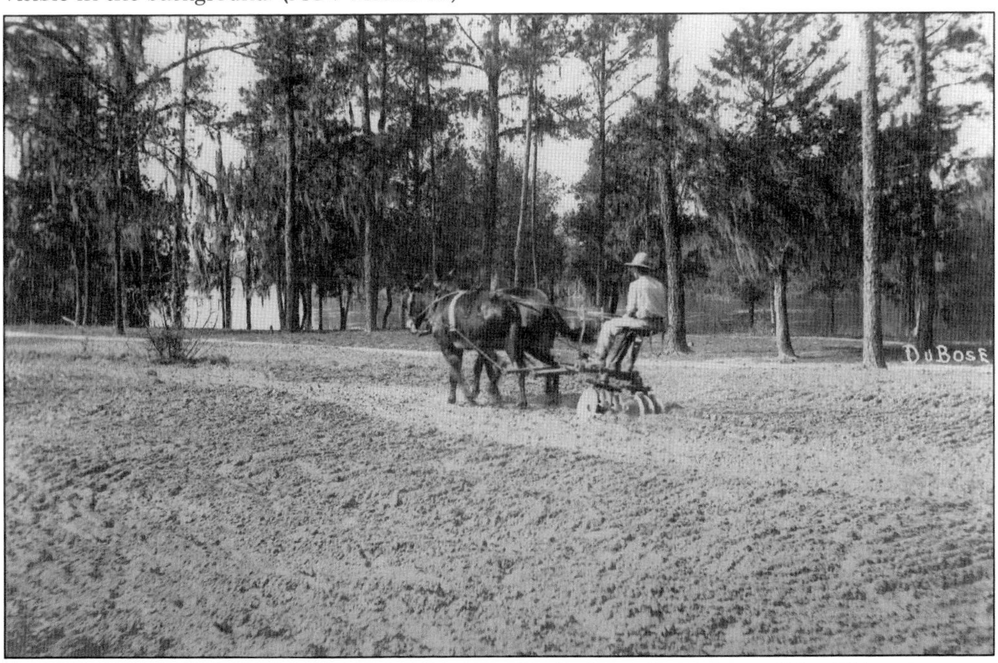

This photograph, taken around 1920 in Dowling Park, shows local farmer John Elder plowing a field alongside the Suwannee River using two mules; tractors were still few and far between in the rural parts of the county. This is one of several photographs taken by local photographer H.B. DuBose that can be found on the pages of this book. (ACV Archives.)

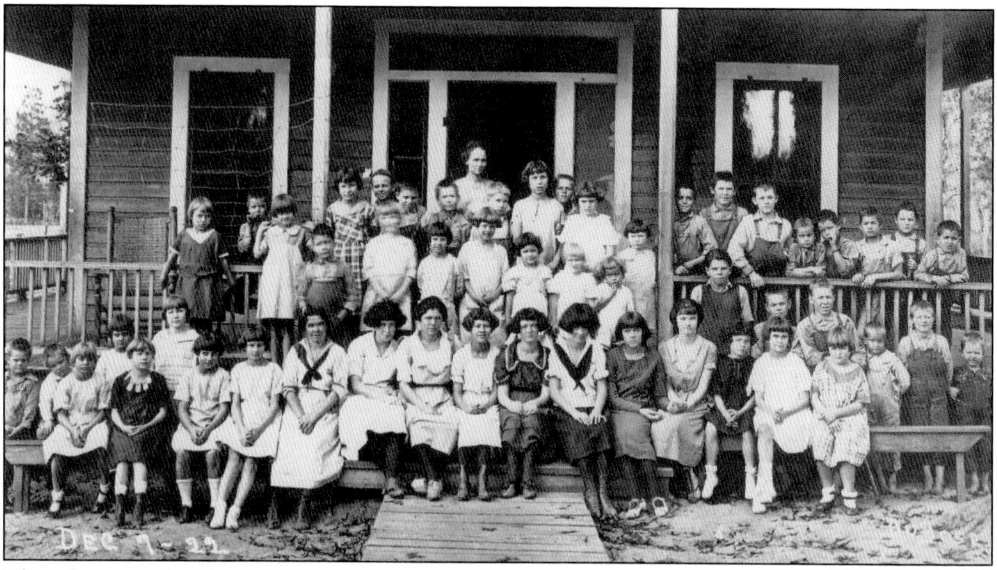

This photograph, taken on December 7, 1922, in front of the orphans' home, shows the orphans and matron of the Advent Christian Village in Dowling Park. Some of the children shown in the photograph include, in no particular order, Stella Parsons, Lorene Tedder, Ula Setzer, Viola Andrews, Colene Setzer, Thelma Andrews, Marvin Lee, Richard Lee, Frank Livingston, Roy Livingston, Edna Livingston, and Mary Mae Livingston. Mrs. Lee, the matron, is in their midst. (ACV Archives.)

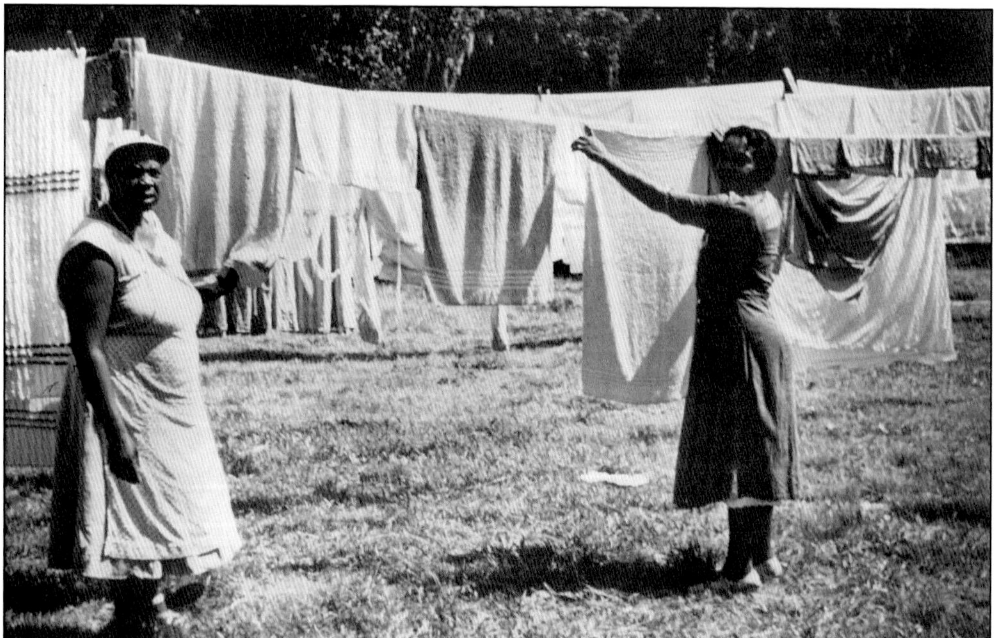

Among other necessities at the Advent Christian Village was laundry duty for the numerous children and staff. This 1950s photograph shows Sophie McCray and Alice Ford, staff members of the village and close friends of the director's family, hanging out laundry. The laundry building was across from the director's house and diagonally across from the present ceramics building. (ACV Archives.)

Matthew and Myrtle Carter, of Waycross, Georgia, are credited with saving the Advent Christian Village. As director between 1955 and 1963, Carter was responsible for eliminating a huge debt at the home and making it a debt-free institution by the time he retired in 1963. This photograph, apparently taken in the 1950s, shows the Carters in their Sunday dress. (ACV Archives.)

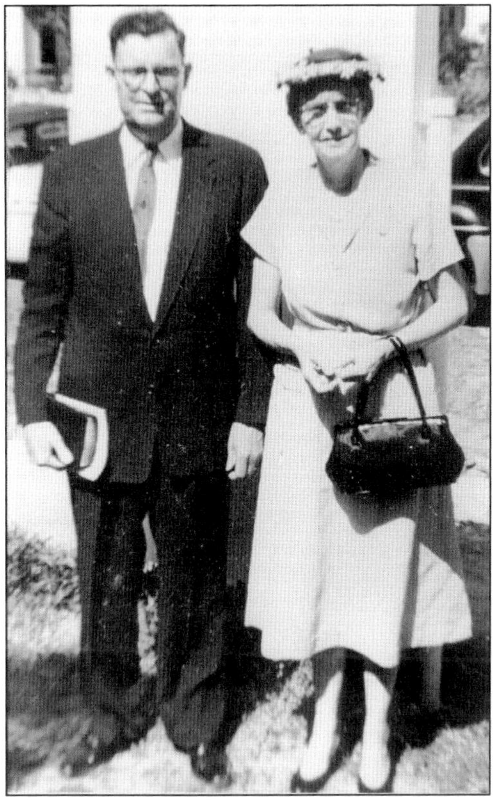

As with most public school systems, the county's early youth were mainly educated in small, rural, one- or two-room schools that were little more than glorified homes. A single teacher would educate all grade levels with the limited supply of books and materials on hand. This photograph shows the Ladyland School, situated in the southwestern portion of the county, around 1900. (Susanette Howell Baxter.)

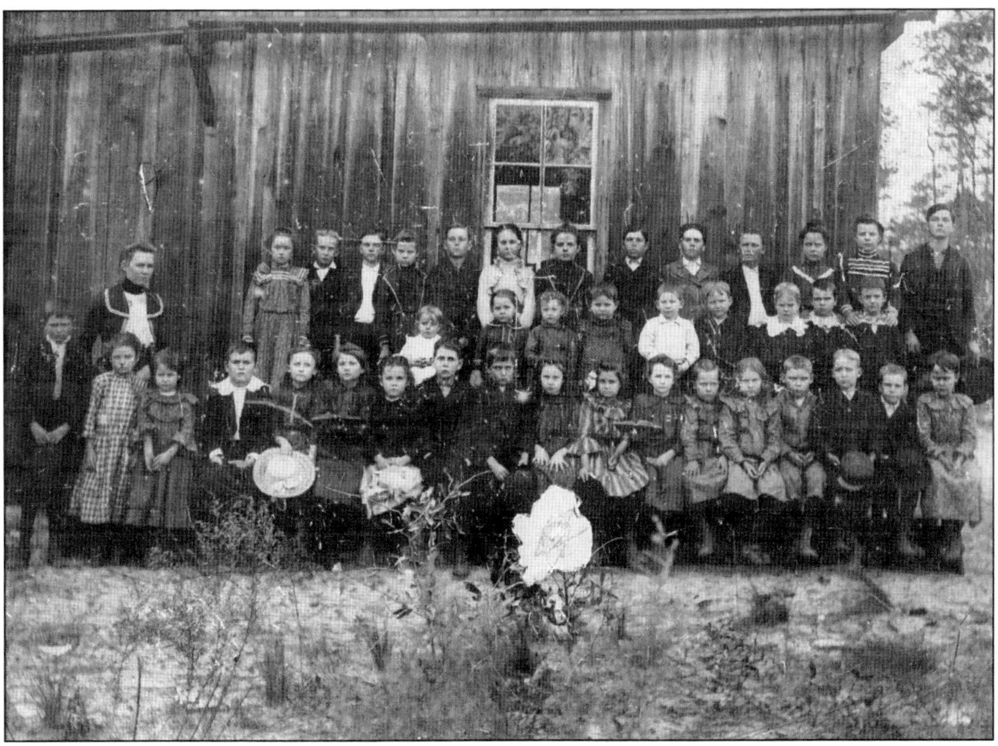

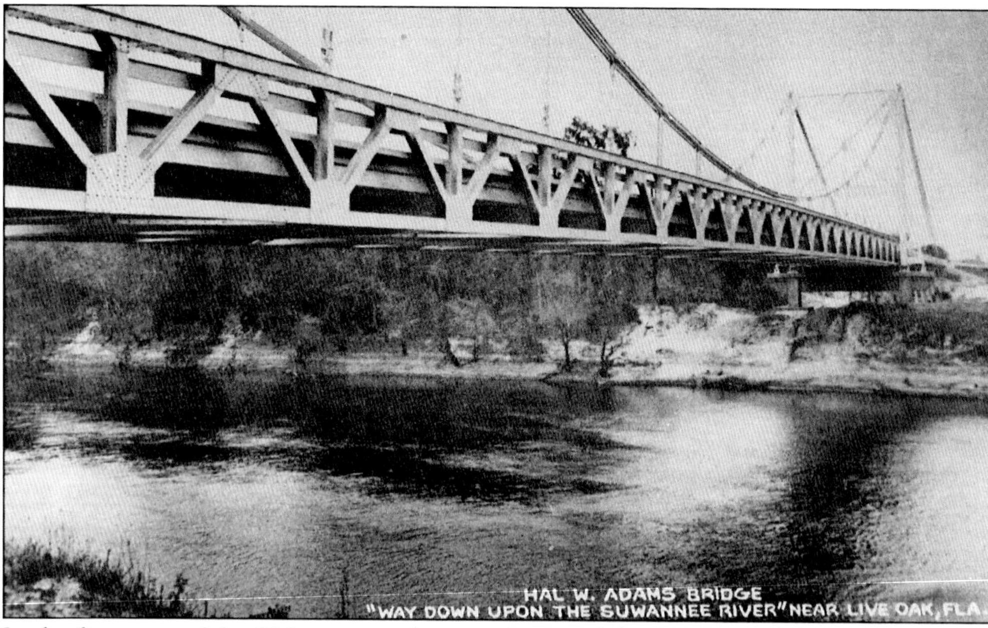

In the first years of the 20th century, the rise of automobiles necessitated the construction of vehicle bridges across the Suwannee River. This is the Judge Hal W. Adams Bridge, connecting Suwannee and Lafayette Counties, built in 1947 to replace an earlier bridge. It was the first suspension span bridge in Florida. (Florida State Photographic Collection.)

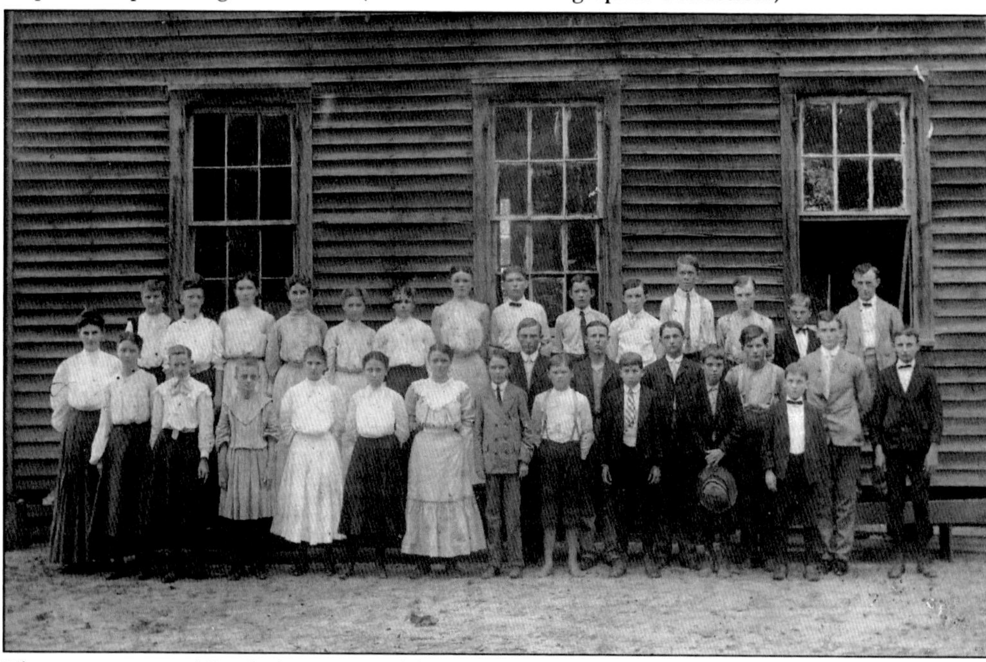

The community of Rixford was named for George R. Rixford, a naval stores manufacturer and owner of sawmills, gristmills, rice mills, and cotton gins in the small hamlet north of Live Oak. Established shortly after the end of the Civil War, Rixford was one of the many communities that could boast of a school. This photograph, taken around 1910, shows students in front of the school. (*Suwannee Democrat.*)

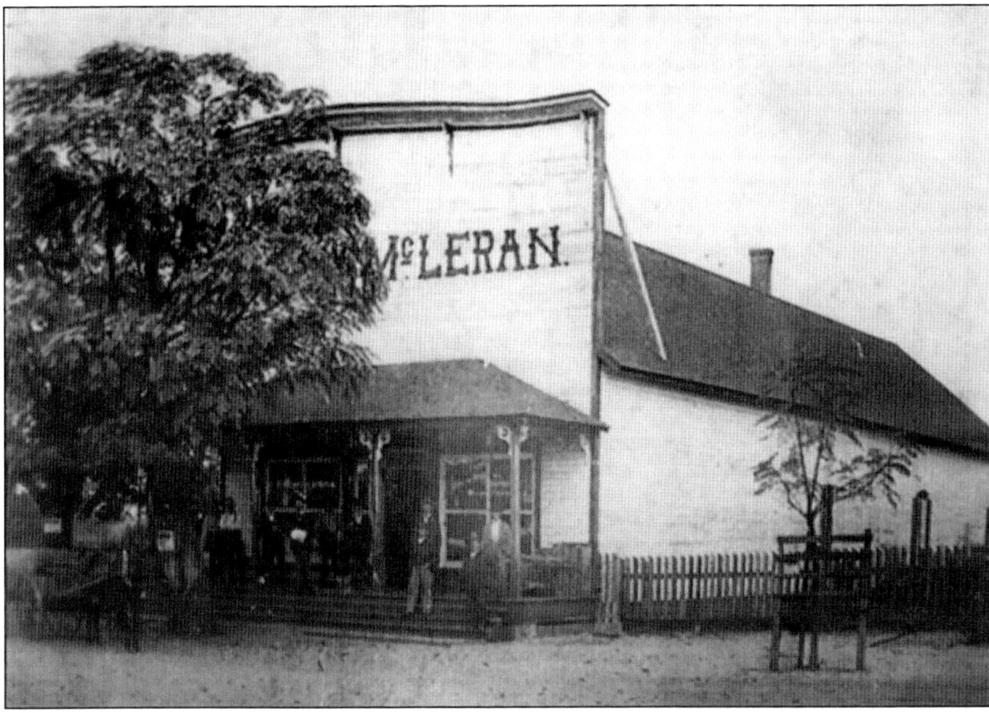

A.W. McLeran was an early settler of Wellborn who opened a general mercantile store there in October 1884. The store continued in operation through his son Thurston until 1972, when it finally closed. The building has since been refurbished and remains one of the oldest buildings in Wellborn. The photograph above shows it as a one-story building early in its career; it eventually was renovated to become two stories. The photograph below shows the John A. McMullen home in Wellborn in 1941. (Above, Kenneth Thrower; below, Suwannee River Regional Library.)

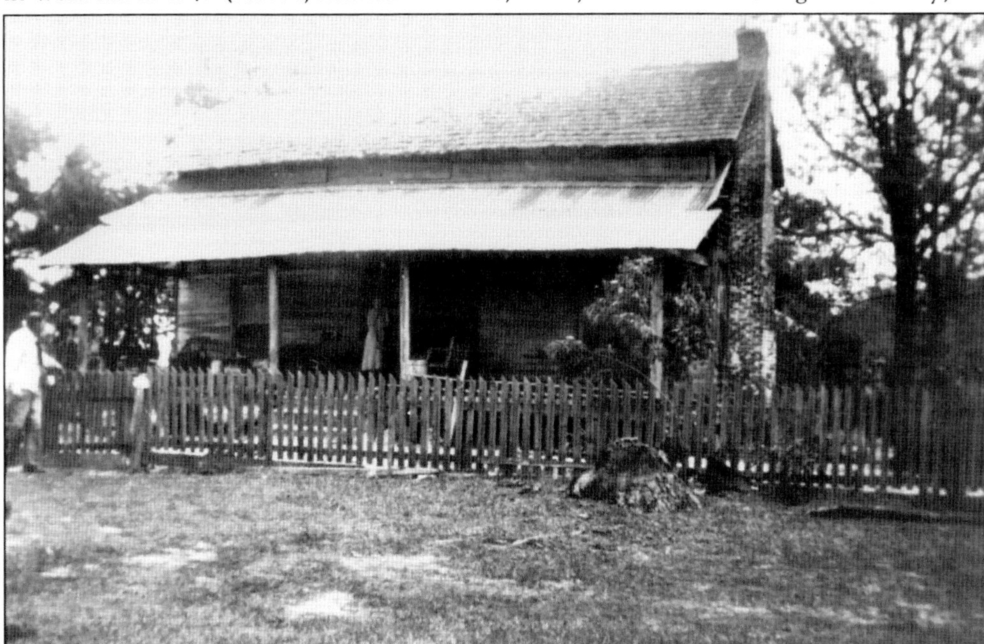

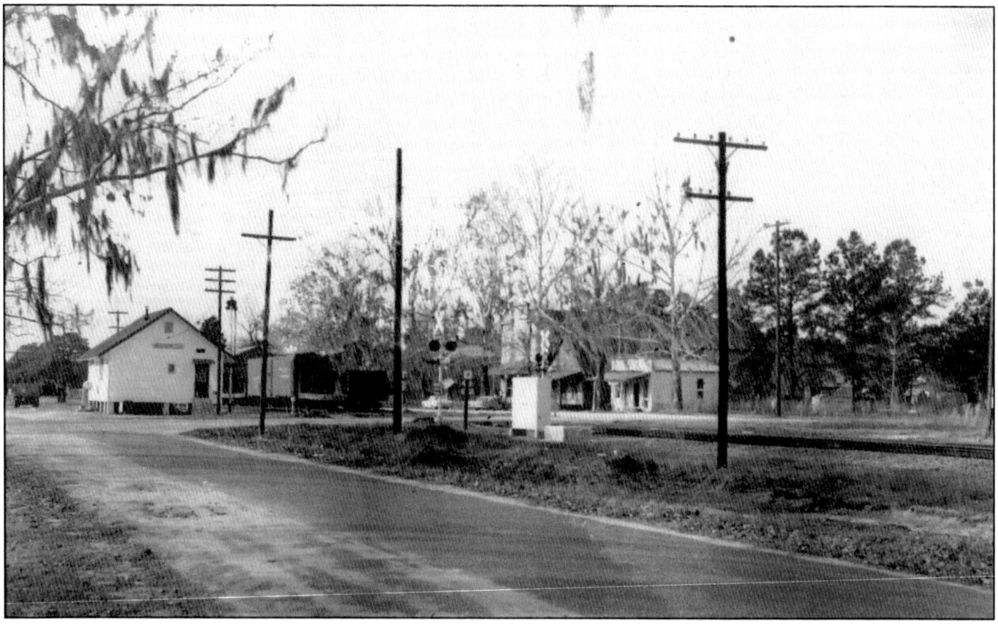

Wellborn is still one of the larger communities in Suwannee County, and until 1928, it boasted a town council and mayor. As one of the larger communities and a stop along a major railroad, Wellborn had several businesses and also a train depot. The picture above shows the train depot and post office around 1965–1966. The first post office and railroad depot had been established more than 100 years before, when Wellborn was named in 1860. The McLeran Store and Cash Store, both still existing structures, can be seen in the center background. The photograph below, taken some 15 years later, shows the Wellborn Cold Storage and Garage. Notice the brick road in the foreground; it was supposedly the first brick road in all of Suwannee County. (Both, Kenneth Thrower.)

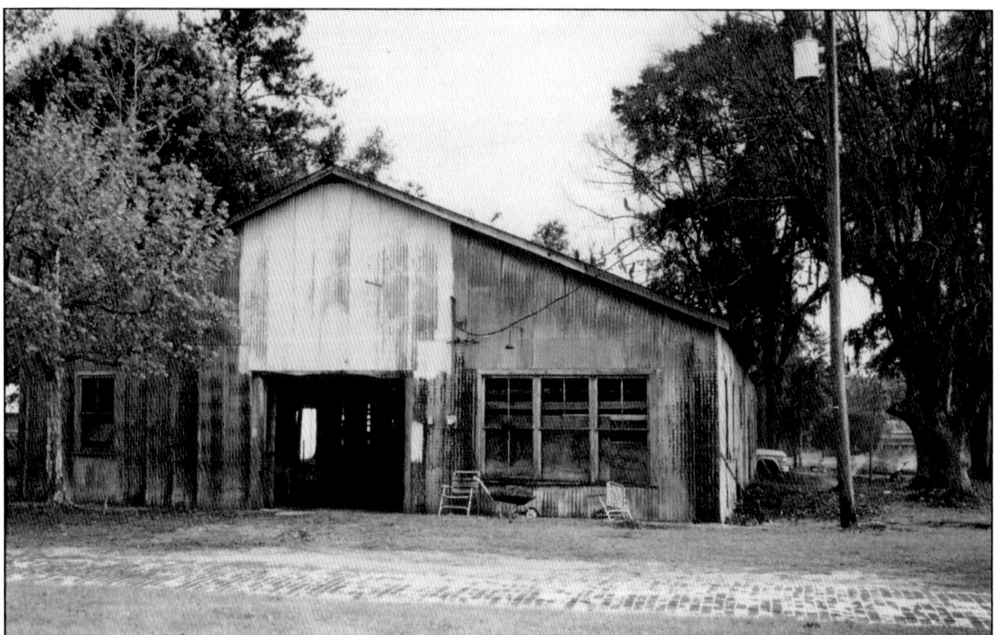

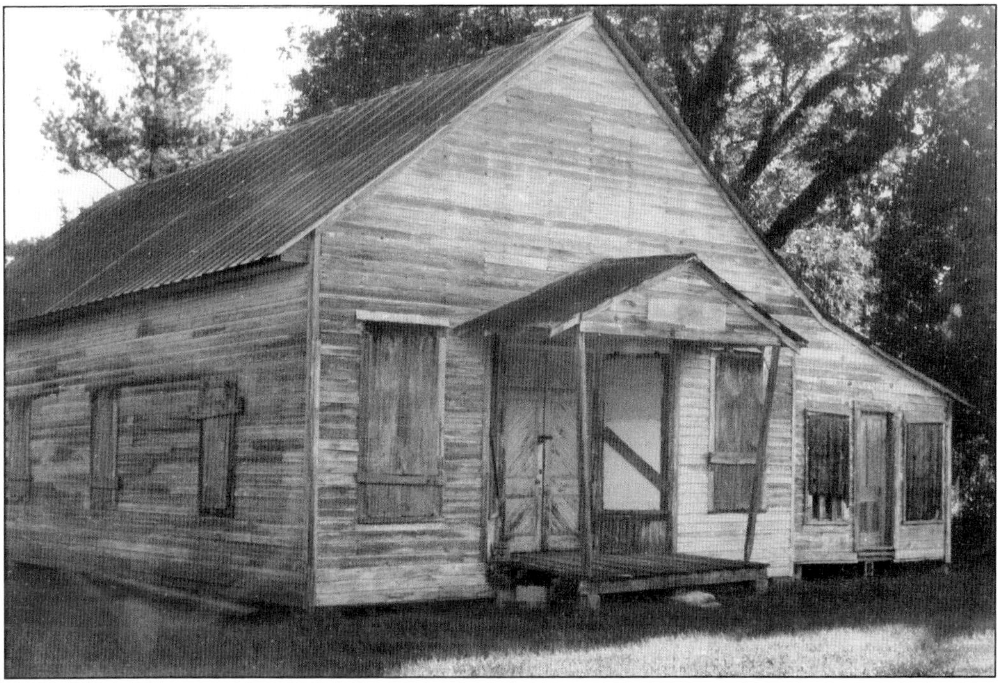

In the photograph above, Wellborn's C.A. Knight store stands forlorn and neglected around 1980. It has since been remodeled. The postcard below shows Suwannee Springs, one of Suwannee County's most famous springs. Native Americans visited the sulphur springs there for their healing powers, and early American settlers were drawn to the same waters. A small community had been established there by the Second Seminole War of 1835–1842, and soldiers were periodically stationed there until the threat of Seminole attacks had ended. After the Civil War, thousands of people visited the springs and related hotel facilities (seen through the trees in the background), where advertisements touted healing powers for everything from arthritis to diarrhea to "female problems." The stone structure surrounding the springs still draws visitors today. (Above, Kenneth Thrower; below, SCCC.)

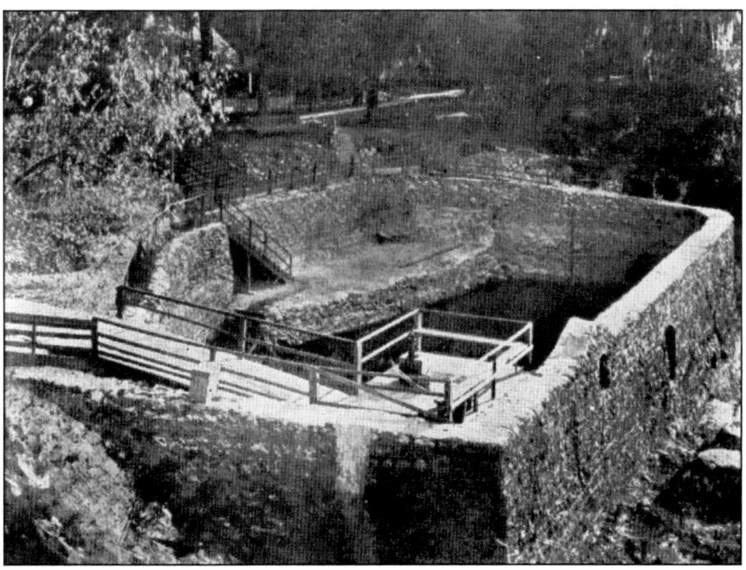

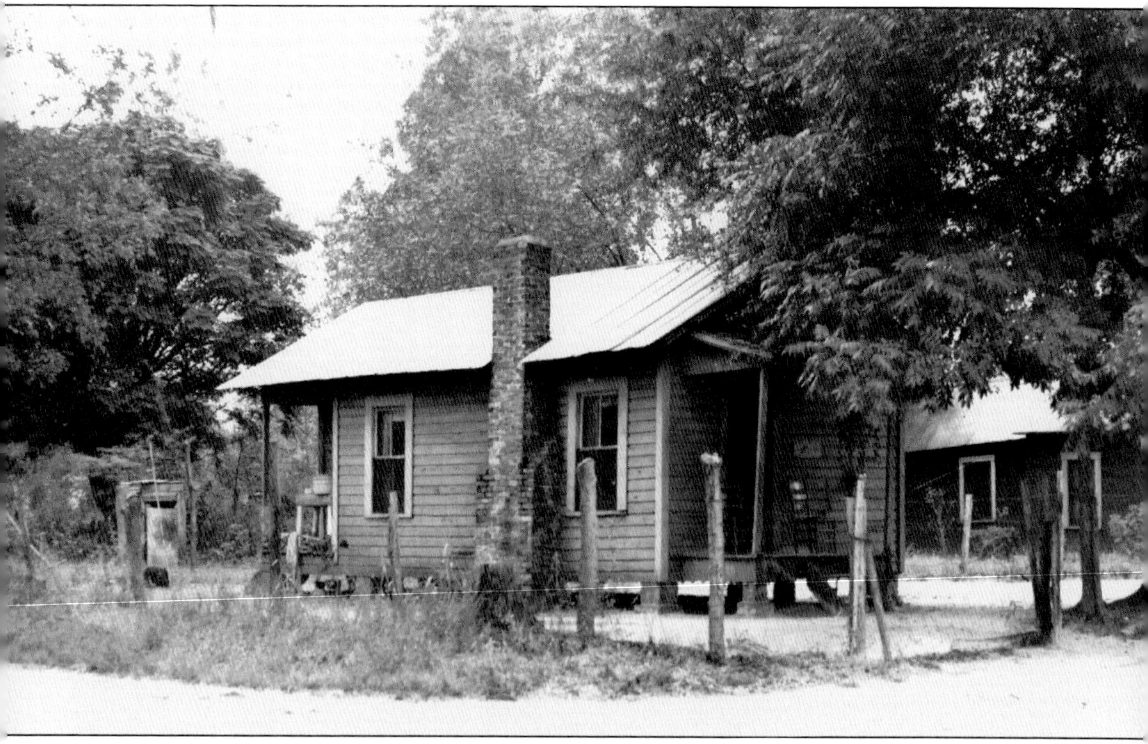

This unidentified home is representative of many houses built in the early years of the 20th century. Although no one knows where the house was located, the fact that there is a house to its right would indicate a built-up area, such as Live Oak or Branford. The porches at the front and back are to catch the winds. Other visible features include the double-hung windows, a fireplace for warmth and cooking, and the metal roof. Keen observers will no doubt notice, perhaps with a chuckle, the privy in the left background for the owners' calls of nature. It appears that the privy's construction is more haphazard than the rest of the home, but then again, its use was more specialized and private. Fences were also common during this period to keep in or exclude livestock, as this was the time of free roaming.

Four

Activities

As with all thriving communities, the residents of Suwannee County have always had a multitude of activities in which to participate. The early American settlers spent much of their time clearing land for farming, constructing homes, and fighting off Native American attacks, but they still found time for important events, such as holding church services and family gatherings. Other activities included swimming in the famed Suwannee River or hunting the many animals found in the abundant woods.

As time went on and industry progressed, Suwannee County's residents branched out into more involved and "civilized" activities. Whether it was visiting the circus or opera or relaxing in a game room, a bowling alley, or one of the newfangled motion picture theaters, Suwannee County had it all. After the decline of the county during the Great Depression, activities were usually more limited because of economics, but the residents still found time for relaxation.

There were a number of schools within the county, many times also serving as church buildings. In fact, at one time in its history, the number of schools in Suwannee County numbered well over 140. As better roads and automobiles allowed easier travel, these schools were gradually consolidated and either torn down or allowed to deteriorate.

The establishment of state parks before World War II gradually allowed all residents access to a variety of springs and natural wonders that had made the area popular a generation or two before. Religion continues to be, as it always has been, an important part of the majority of the citizens' lives, as evidenced by the number of church buildings found in this chapter. It has been said, with some merit, that Suwannee County has more churches per capita than any other county in Florida.

Farris Meeks was a Suwannee County resident and avid amateur photographer. Between the 1940s and 1960s, he photographed a variety of buildings within the county, most of which are now long gone. Many of the pictures contained in this chapter were originally taken by him and later donated to the Suwannee County Historical Museum.

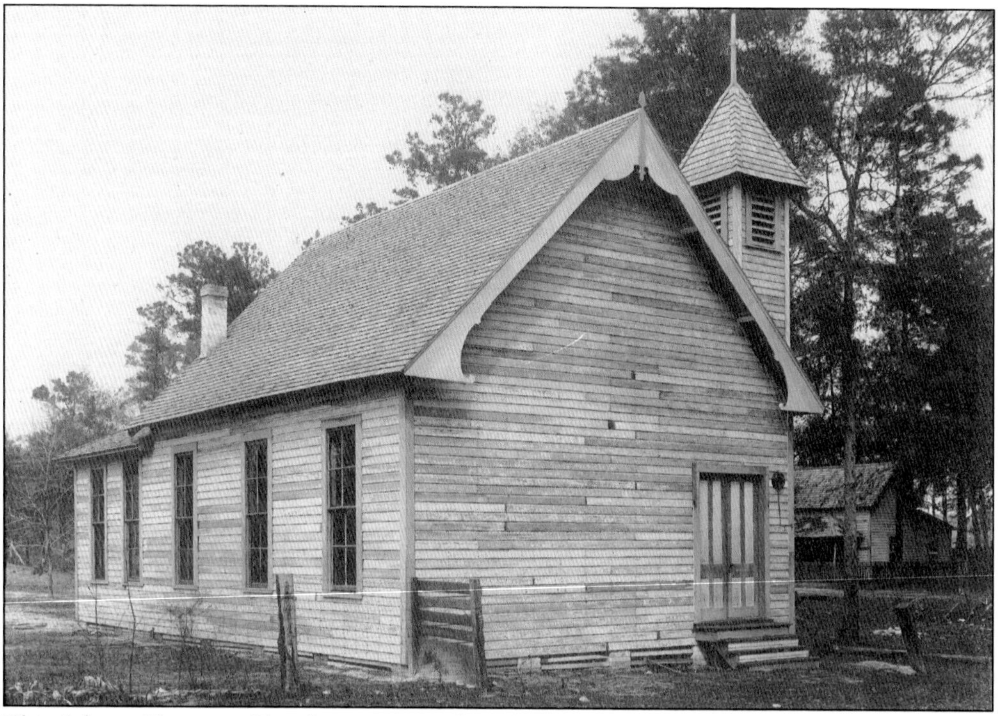

This Advent Christian Church, seen around 1915, was one of several churches built in Dowling Park after 1900. It was also used as a schoolhouse and finally as a dining room and kitchen for Camp Suwannee until the late 1960s. It stood on or near the site of the current First Federal Savings Bank. A millworker's home sits behind and to the right of the church. (ACV Archives.)

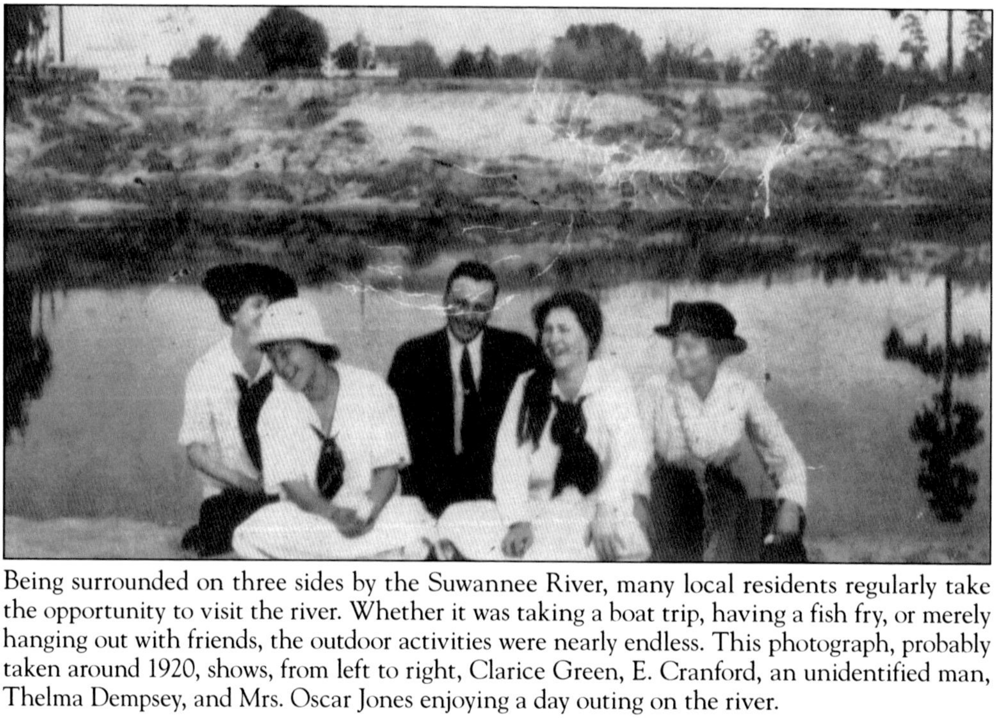

Being surrounded on three sides by the Suwannee River, many local residents regularly take the opportunity to visit the river. Whether it was taking a boat trip, having a fish fry, or merely hanging out with friends, the outdoor activities were nearly endless. This photograph, probably taken around 1920, shows, from left to right, Clarice Green, E. Cranford, an unidentified man, Thelma Dempsey, and Mrs. Oscar Jones enjoying a day outing on the river.

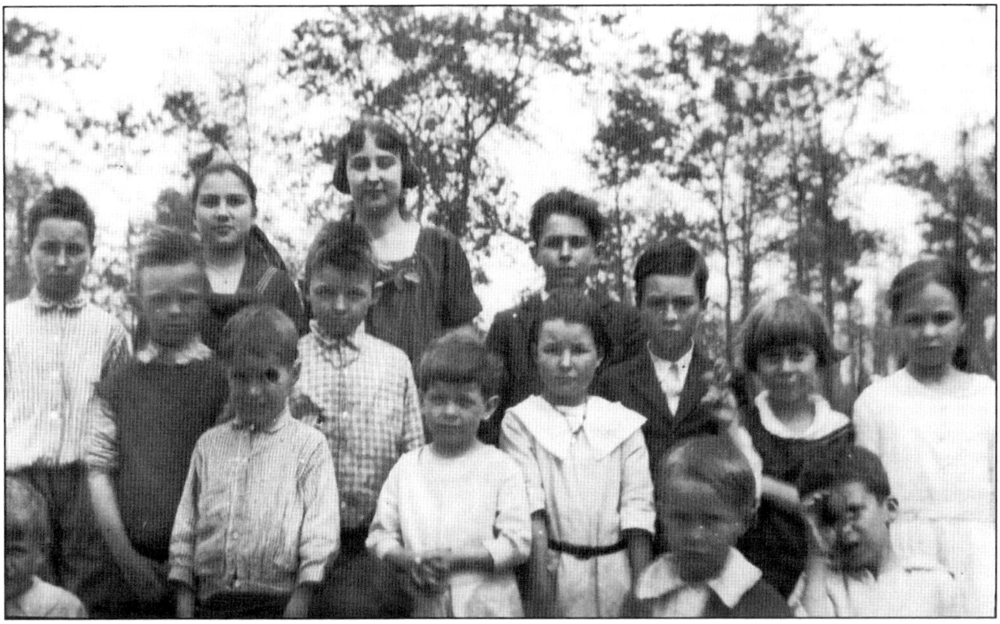

The community of Beachville lies in the southern portion of Suwannee County, a few miles northeast of Branford. During its heyday of the early 20th century, it boasted a school for multiple ages as well as several businesses. These two pictures show the children of the Beachville School during the school year of 1921–1922; the photograph above is a period postcard advertising Suwannee County. In the photograph below, most of the children have no shoes, and by the looks of some of the poses, the photographer seems to have caught the children off-guard. The Beachville School eventually consolidated with larger schools, and little remains of the community except for scattered houses and churches.

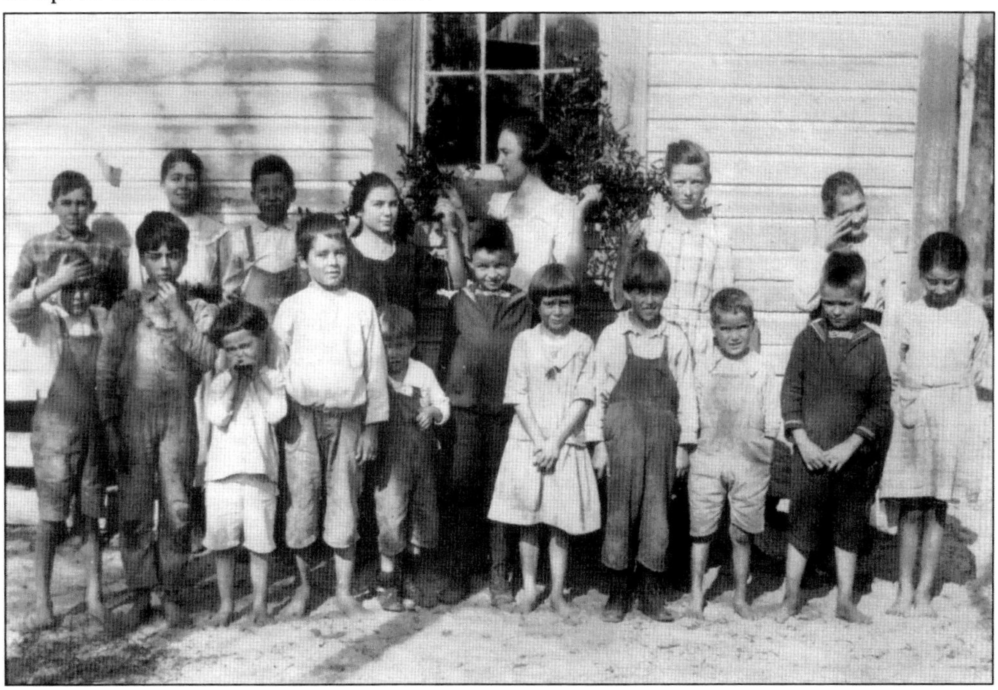

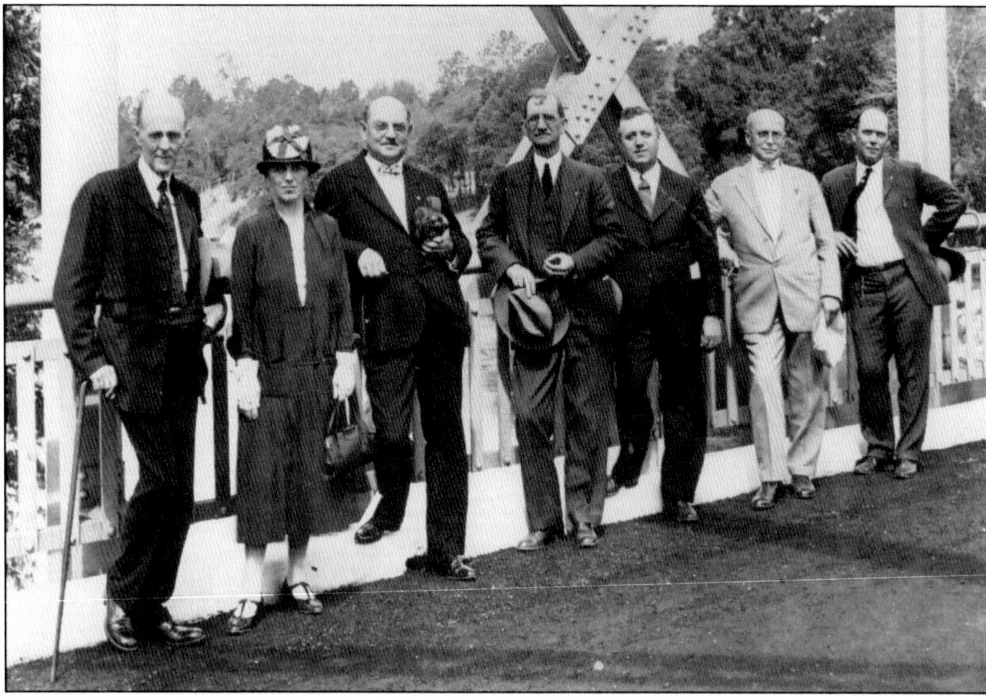

The Rotary Club of Live Oak, founded in 1921, is one of the oldest chapters of the organization. In 1925, Paul Harris, founder of Rotary International, visited the Live Oak club and had his picture made on a bridge above the famous Suwannee River. From left to right are Paul Harris, Jean Harris, George W. Clark, Chapman H. Tedder, Clarence Williams, Charles A. Clark, and John F. Harrell. The Clarks were from Jacksonville, and the others were from the Live Oak club. (ACV Archives.)

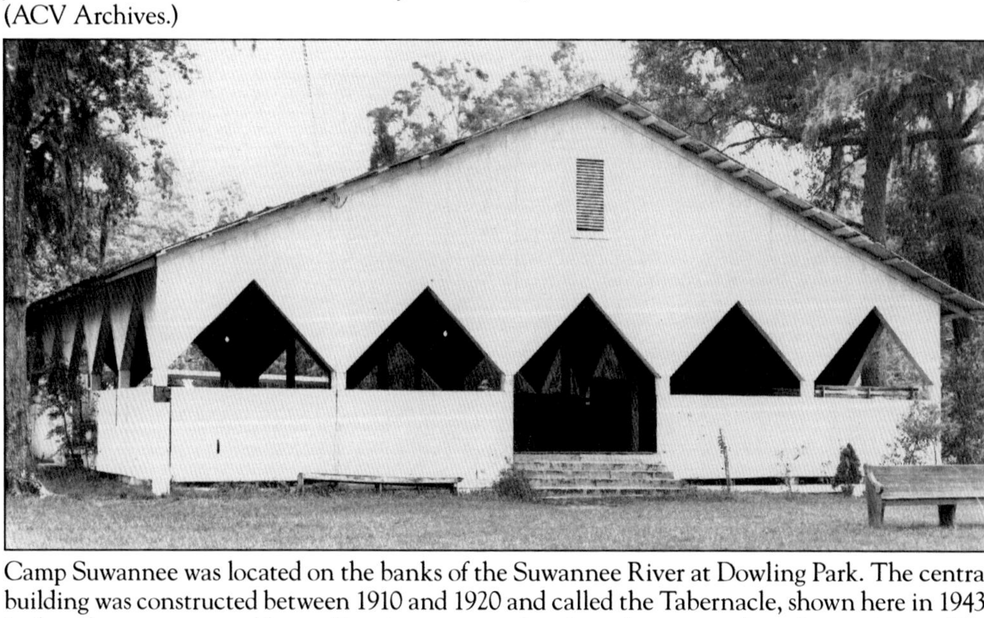

Camp Suwannee was located on the banks of the Suwannee River at Dowling Park. The central building was constructed between 1910 and 1920 and called the Tabernacle, shown here in 1943. Its benches were moveable to allow its use as a church, a theater, or for other activities. The building was finally torn down in the late 1960s, and the location is now occupied by the Village Square Parking Lot. (ACV Archives.)

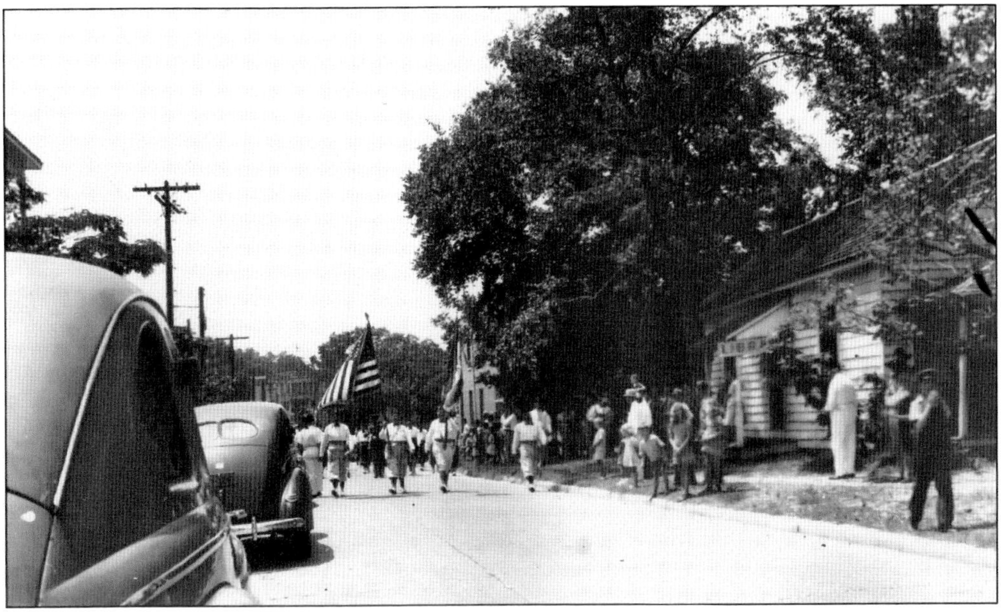

The Ancient Arabic Order of the Nobles of the Mystic Shrine, more commonly called the Shriners, has long been a part of Suwannee County history and is most famous for supporting children's hospitals and for the miniature cars they drive in parades. These two photographs show a Shriners parade along Live Oak's Wilbur Street in 1941. In the picture above, residents watch as Shriners march past the old library (right foreground) on their way to the courthouse. In the center background, at the end of Wilbur Street, is the junior high school building, and mostly obscured by trees closer to the library is the high school and R&V Furniture building. In the picture below, the parade moves past the old armory, which according to the sign served as the Shriners' headquarters.

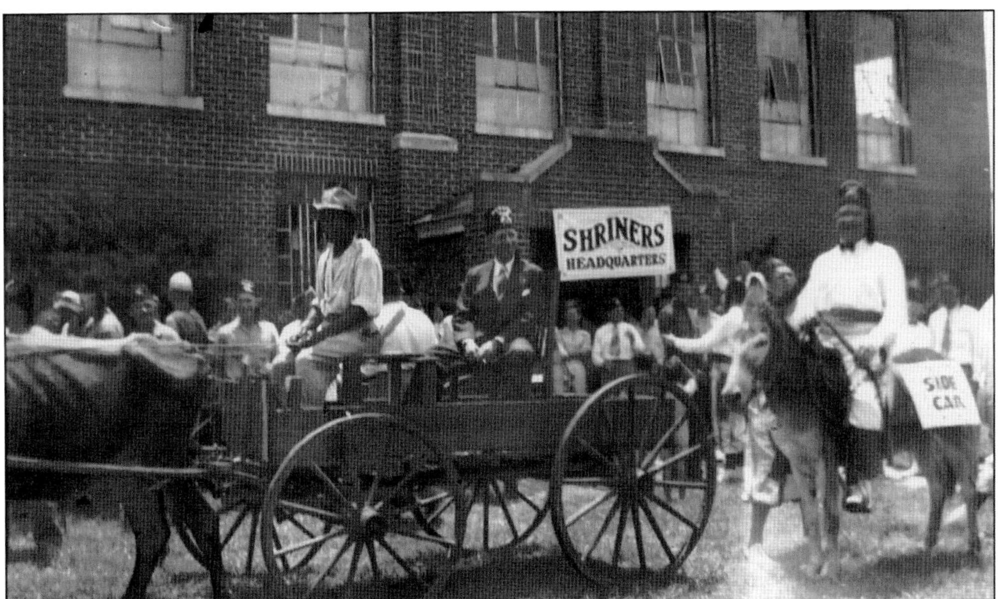

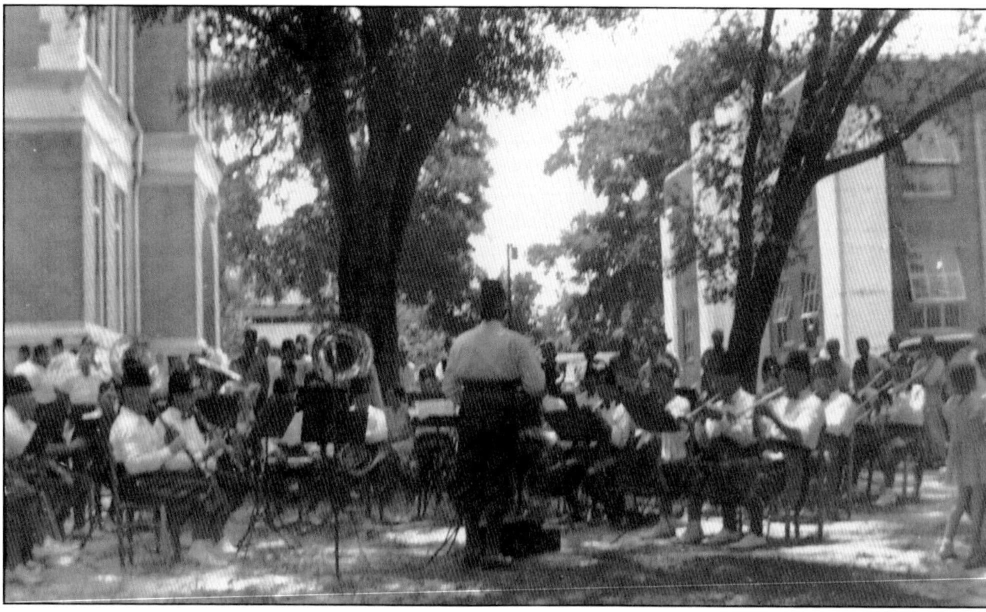

Among the activities of the Shriners was a band, which in 1941 had some three dozen members. These two photographs show the Shriners at the end of the parade on the preceding page, at which time they performed a concert for the residents of Live Oak. In the picture above, looking to the south, the courthouse stands in the left background, and the jail is to the right background, as the band strikes up a tune in the downtown commons area. This location is now the site of the 1964 courthouse addition and parking. In the photograph below, looking north, a large group has assembled to listen. In the background stands part of Live Oak's business district.

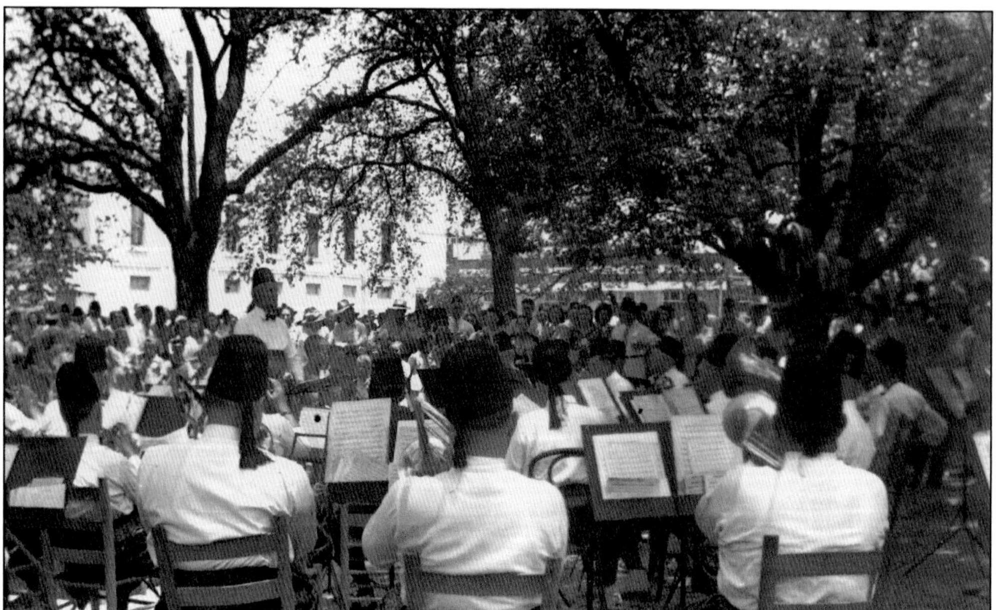

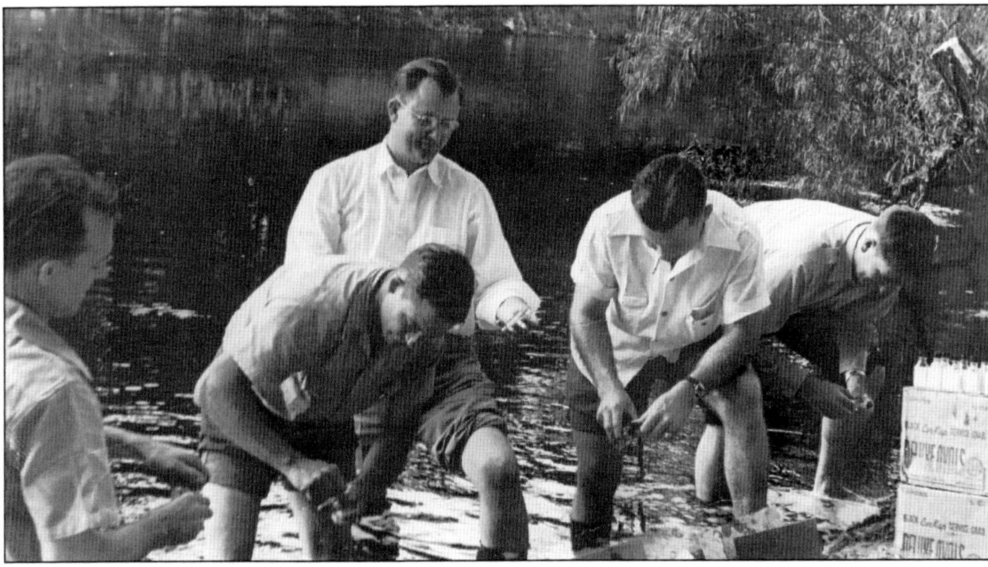

The US Junior Chamber of Commerce (popularly called the Jaycees) was one of many national and international organizations that found a following in Suwannee County. Tasked with improving the community and growing personally, the Live Oak Jaycees was organized in 1942 by J.L. McMullen. Here, from left to right, Ottis Brown, Fred Glass, J.L. McMullen, Charles Green, and Horry Hair bottle some of the famed Suwannee River water for presentation to the Jaycee's Convention in Milwaukee, Wisconsin, in 1946.

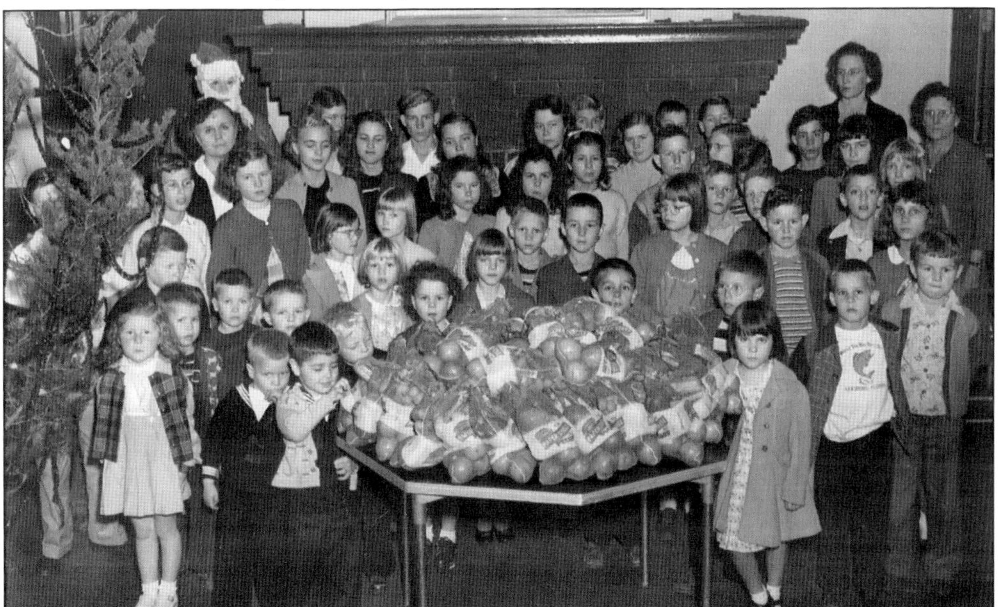

The Live Oak Elks Club gave an annual Christmas party to the orphans of the Advent Christian Home and Orphanage for many years. Oranges were always among the gifts for the children. This photograph, probably taken in DeLong Hall in 1948, shows one such event. The names of many of the children are unknown, but some of the adults include Fay Agner, Mrs. Phillip Griffen, Martha Strange, Joanne Richardson, and Florence Tiffen, resident manager and sister of Burr Bixler. (ACV Archives.)

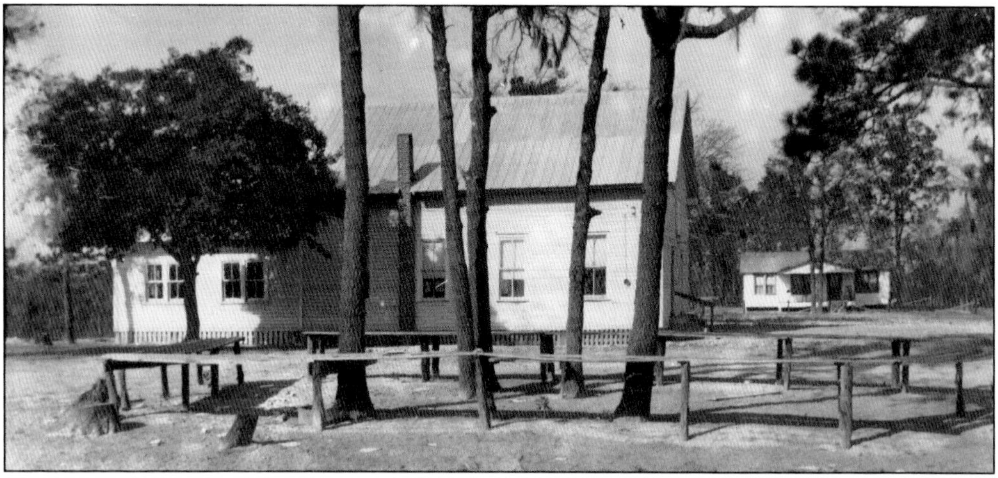

Mount Pisgah Baptist Church was established on April 21, 1878, about seven miles southeast of McAlpin. This photograph, taken in 1948, shows both the church building and the preacher's home. Notice the tables in the forefront, presumably for "dinner on the grounds." The congregation continues today in a newer brick building. (Suwannee County Historical Commission.)

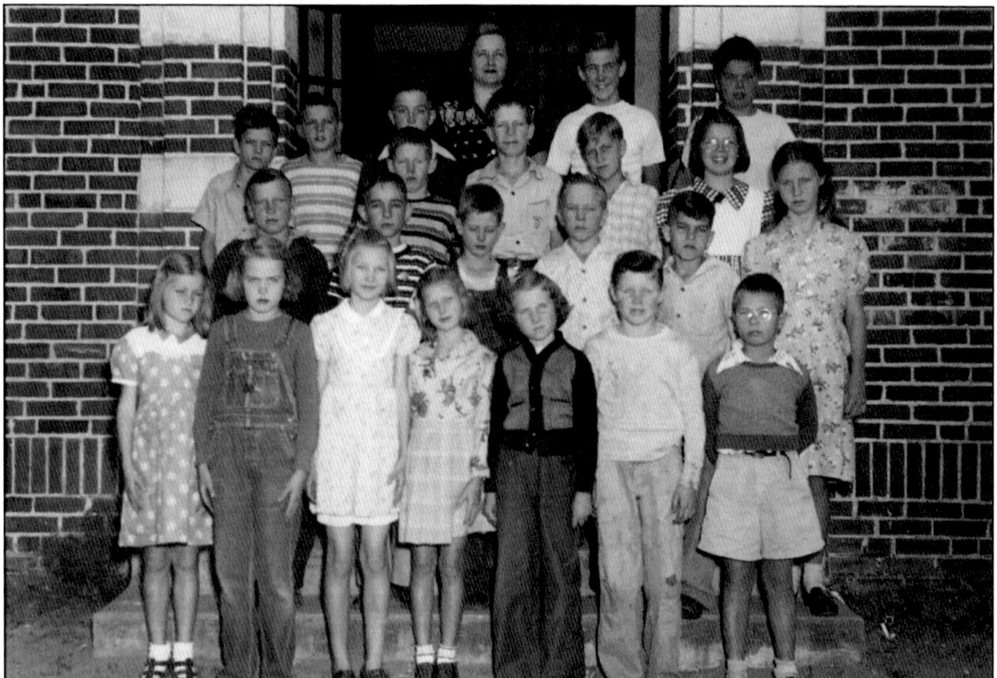

One of the long-running rural schools in Suwannee County was the one at Dowling Park, which taught children of staff as well as the orphans of the Advent Christian Village. This 1949–1950 photograph shows the fourth, fifth, and sixth grade students of Ruth Taylor. From left to right are (first row) Joyce Wilder, Glenda Mosley, Carolyn ?, Kathryn Lyons, Shelby Jean Clark, Danny Powers, and Sammy Foster; (second row) Mack Brown, Raymond Wilder, Herbert Baxter, Junior Baxter, Bill Daye, and Connie Lee; (third row) Walter Shankler, Earl Gann, Douglas Parker, Cecil Powers, Lewis Williams, Harold Lee, and Glenda Ruth Markiton; (fourth row) Mrs. Taylor, Harold Cosner, and Billy Peterson. (ACV Archives.)

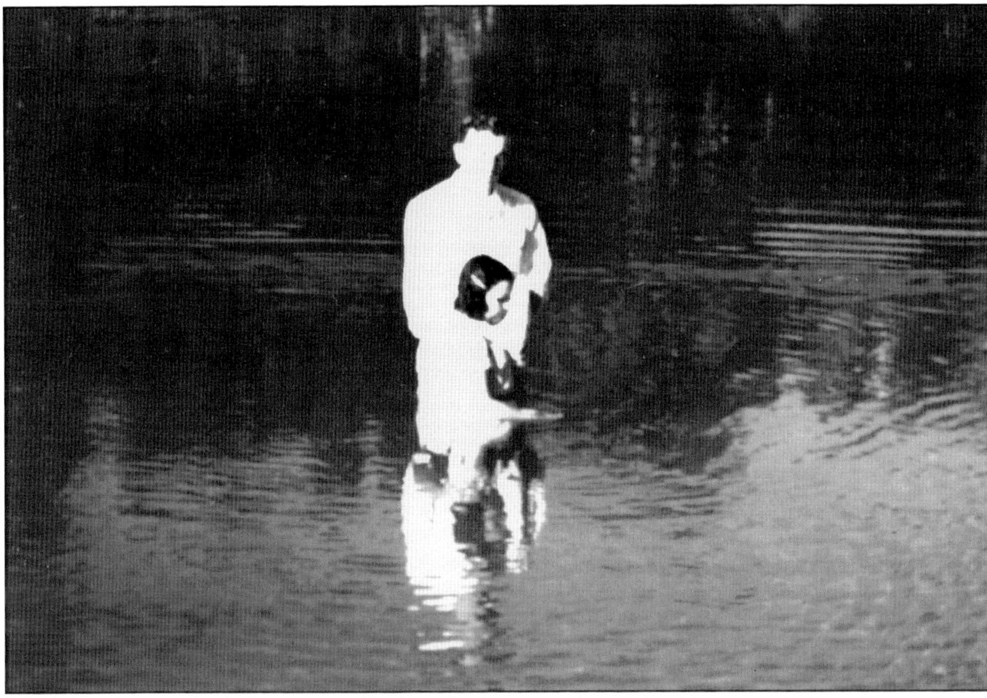

The Suwannee River makes a scenic location for baptisms. This 1950 photograph shows Travis Carter, minister of the Live Oak Advent Christian Church and director of Camp Suwannee from 1954 to 1961, baptizing Josephine Johnson at the old "cow drink" at Dowling Park. Carter also hatched the idea to have a floating raft at the camp's popular swimming hole. (ACV Archives.)

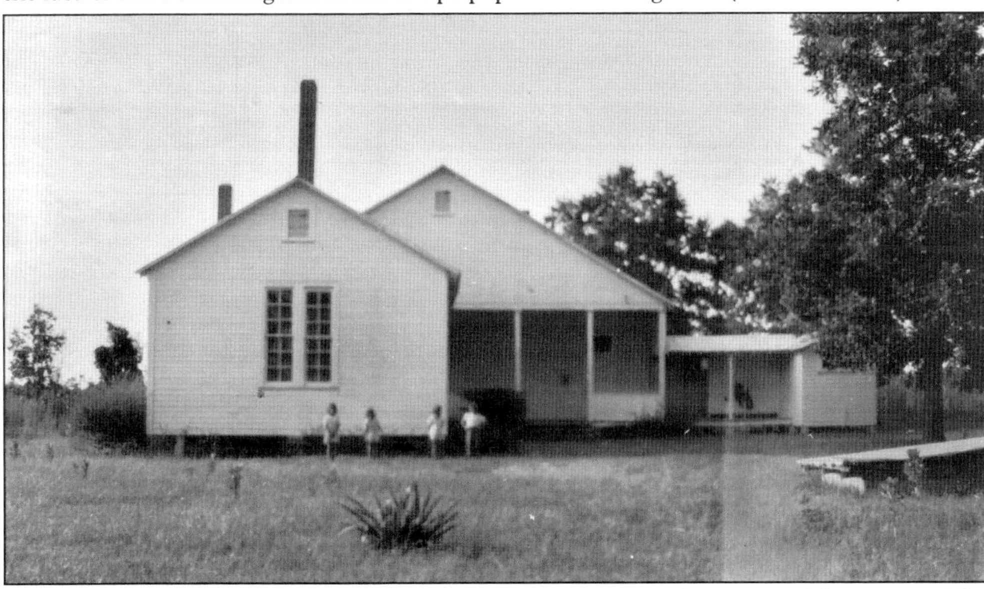

The aptly-named Central School was located near McAlpin, in the center of the county. After its students were consolidated with other schools, the building was bought by the Evergreen Church of Christ and became the Central Church of Christ, apparently much to the chagrin of some of the neighbors. This photograph shows the school in July 1950, before it burned down under mysterious circumstances.

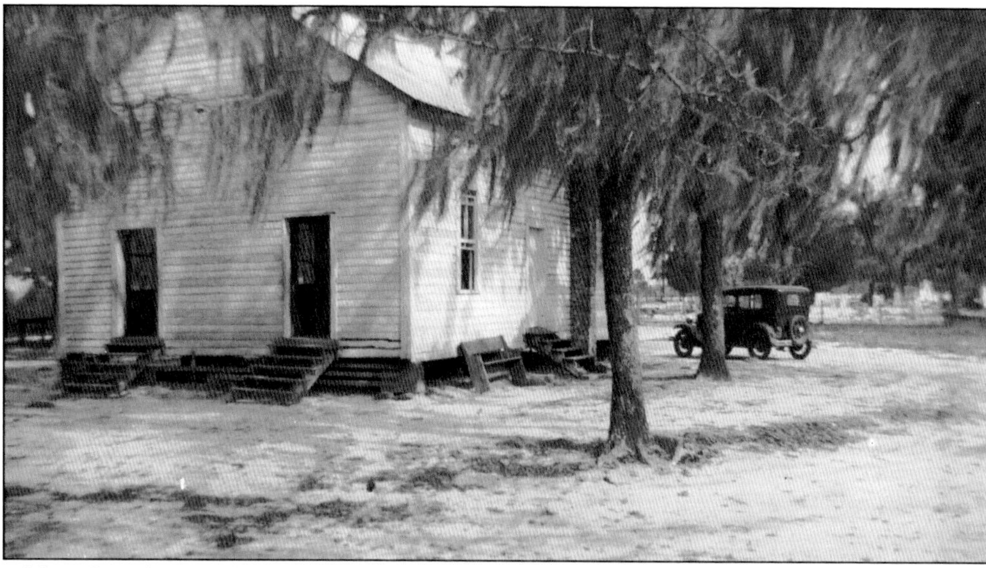

Although early records are unclear, Rosemary Baptist Church had been established by 1878, when the first baptisms were recorded. The church, located about 12 miles northwest of Live Oak, continues to hold services today. This photograph was taken on January 20, 1952, and shows the old building, since replaced by one of brick.

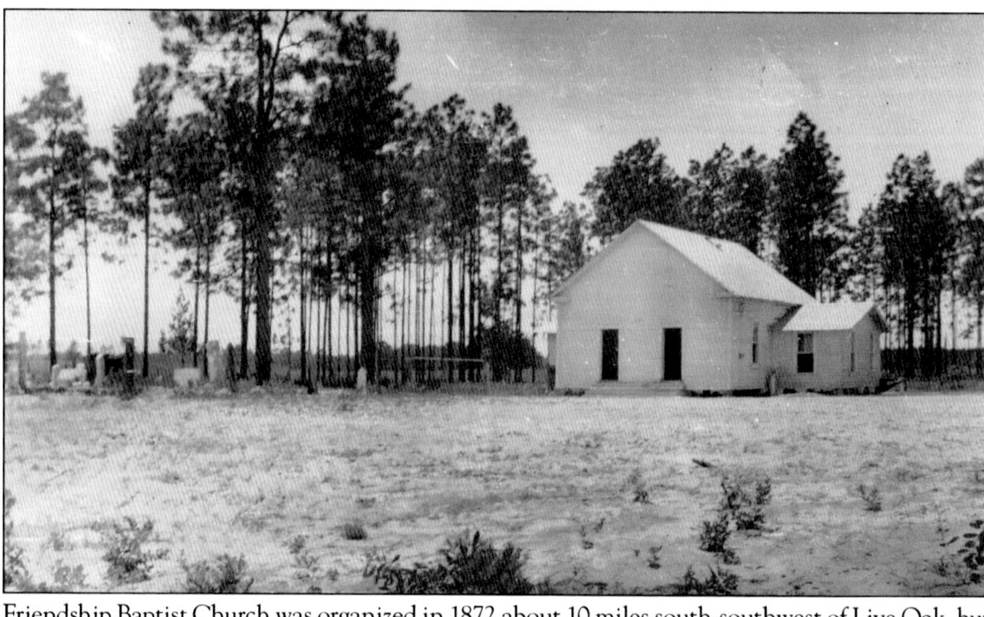

Friendship Baptist Church was organized in 1872 about 10 miles south-southwest of Live Oak, but it closed between 1928 and 1934. Reopened in 1934, it continues today. This photograph, taken on May 23, 1953, shows the old building. A note on the back of the photograph says that Augustus Smith was buried in the cemetery to the left a few minutes before the picture was taken.

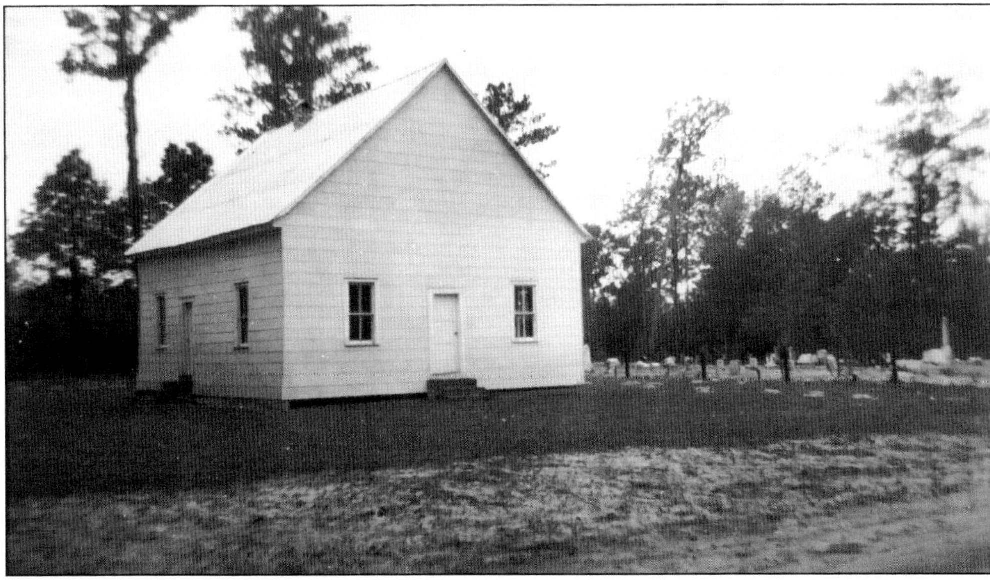

Crawford Lake Primitive Baptist Church was organized with 10 members on October 2, 1893, about two miles east of the community of Pinemount. The photograph above, taken on Thanksgiving Day, 1953, shows the church building. The congregation continues to hold services on County Road 252. The Live Oak Church of the Nazarene first held services in 1947. Within a few years, the old Presbyterian church by the post office on Ohio Avenue had been purchased, only to be replaced by a new building shortly thereafter. The photograph below was taken on May 25, 1958, and shows the second building on Ohio Avenue; it was eventually replaced by parking.

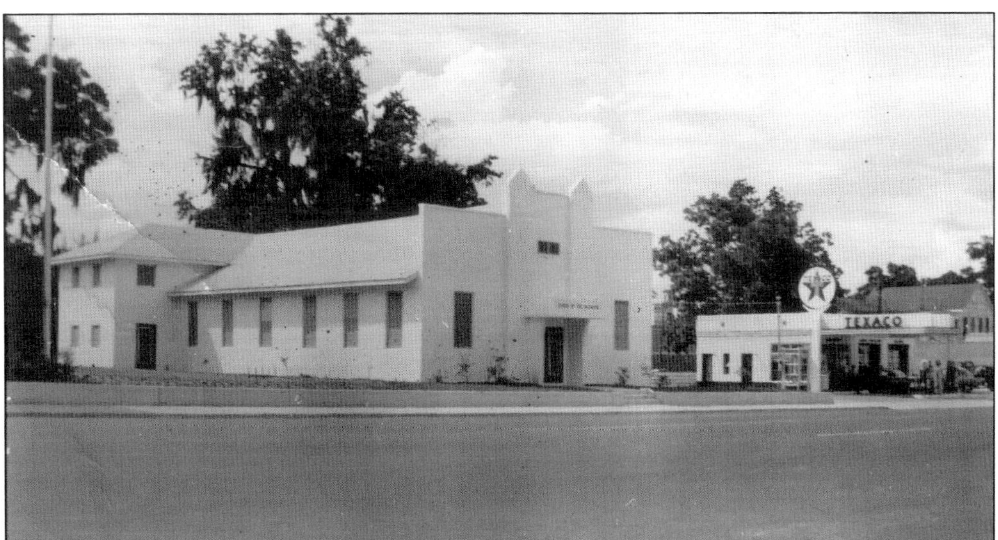

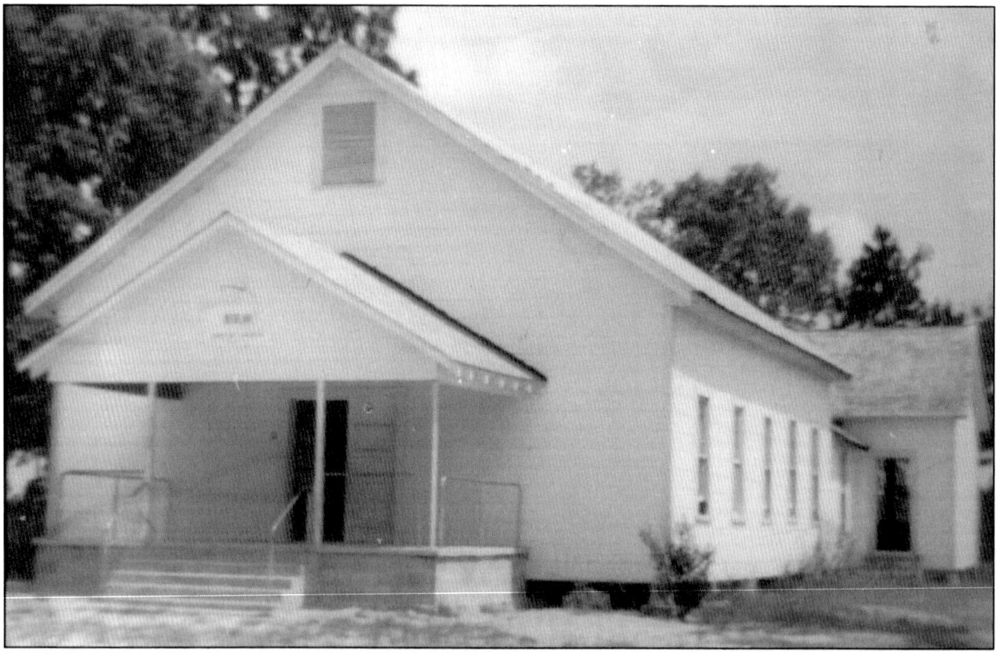

Beulah Baptist Church was organized in 1897 about 15 miles southwest of Live Oak. Built of roughly hewn wood, the building still stands today but has been replaced by a newer structure. The photograph above shows the church building on June 15, 1958. When the public school system was founded in 1869, one of the first schools on the list was the New Harmony School. The photograph below shows the school building on June 15, 1958, by which time the school had been consolidated with the larger schools at Live Oak and Branford. Neglect can already be seen in the building, and it appears that part of the front porch has rotted away.

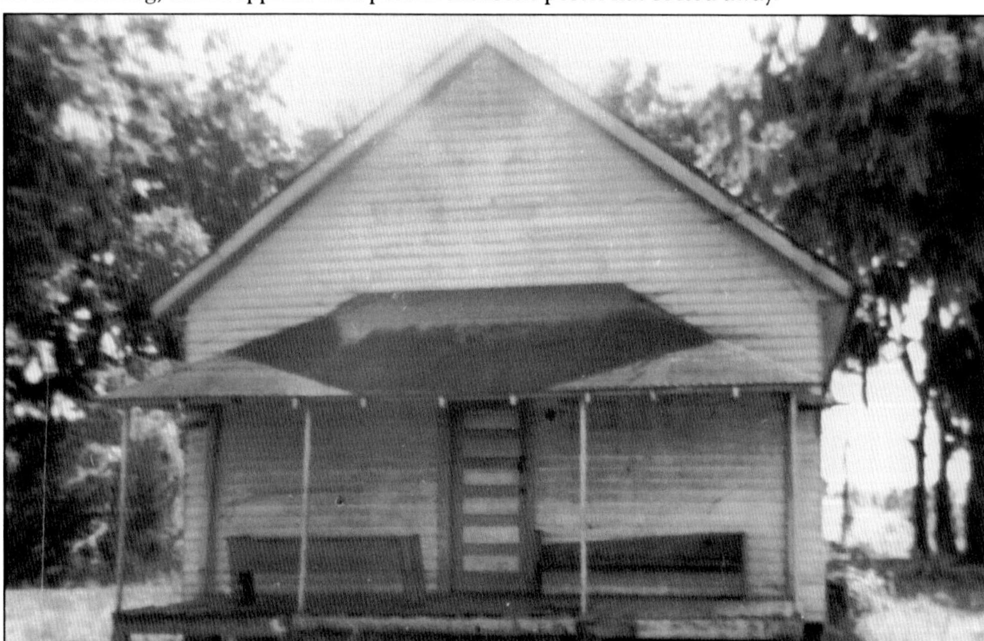

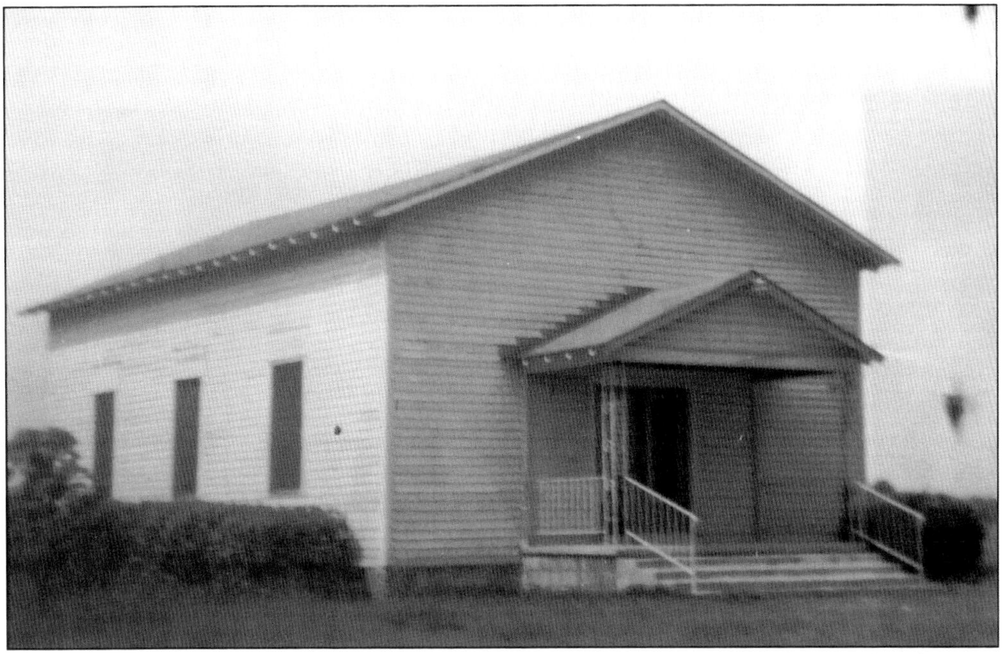

New Harmony Methodist Church was organized in 1872 as Harmony Methodist Church, using a log schoolhouse for its meetings. In 1874, a church building was constructed that served for many years. In 1974, the word "new" was added to the name, and a new building was constructed nearby. This photograph shows the old building on June 15, 1958.

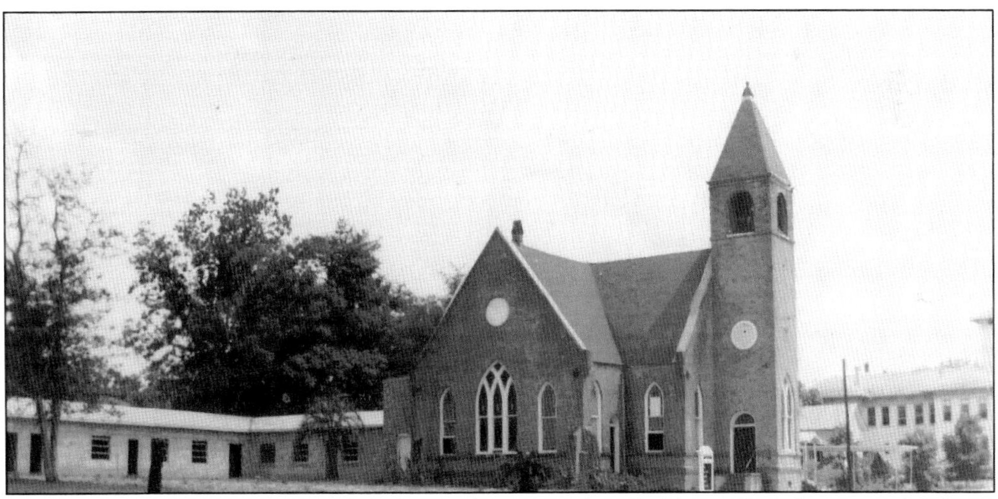

Established in 1896, the original Advent Christian Church (also called the Second Advent Christian Church) was constructed near the corner of Ohio Avenue and Duval Street. A fire destroyed the building in 1904, but it was rebuilt with the help of Thomas Dowling. This structure remained in use by the church until 1969, when the congregation moved to Pinewood Way. This photograph was taken on June 29, 1958.

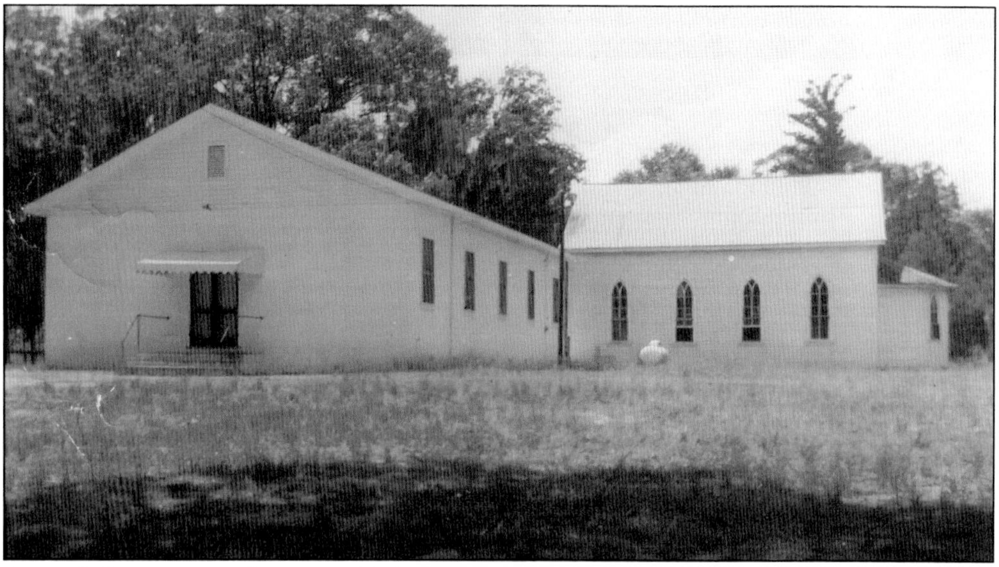

Antioch Baptist Church was established approximately five miles north of Live Oak prior to 1851, when family records first indicate its existence. This photograph was taken on August 10, 1958, and shows the new building, constructed in 1953, along with the old building, constructed in 1909 and then used for classrooms.

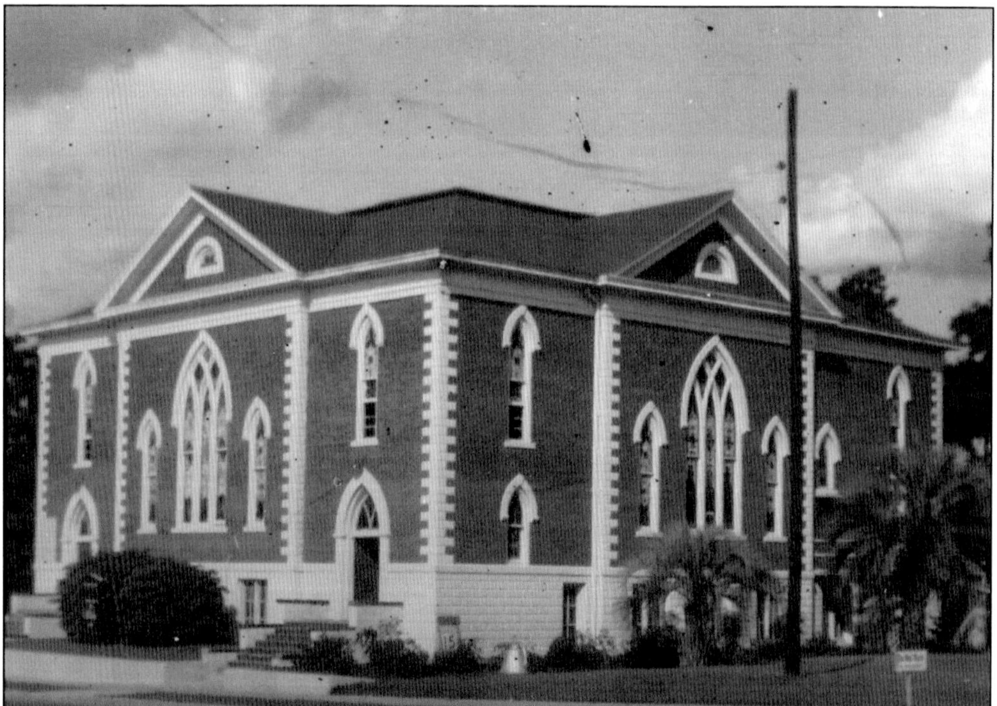

First Methodist Church of Live Oak was organized in 1865 in a frame building constructed by John Parshley and Nathan Walker. A new structure was completed in 1885 at the corner of Duval and Houston Streets, but it was condemned in 1921. A new church was built on Ohio Avenue in 1923 and stands today. This photograph shows the current building on August 10, 1958.

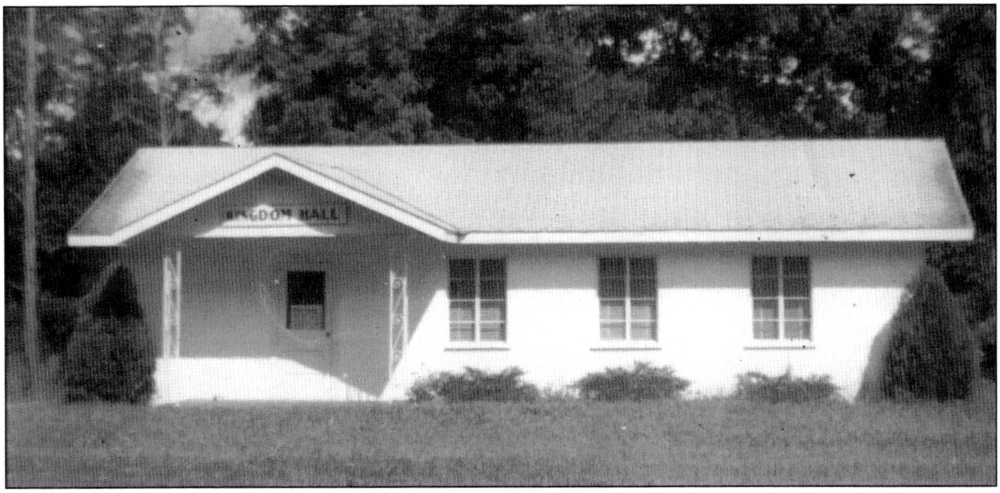

The Jehovah's Witnesses are yet another group of religious people that can be found in Suwannee County. This photograph shows the Kingdom Hall of the Jehovah's Witnesses on North Houston Street on August 10, 1958. In recent years, this building was sold and a new one erected north of Live Oak on US Highway 129.

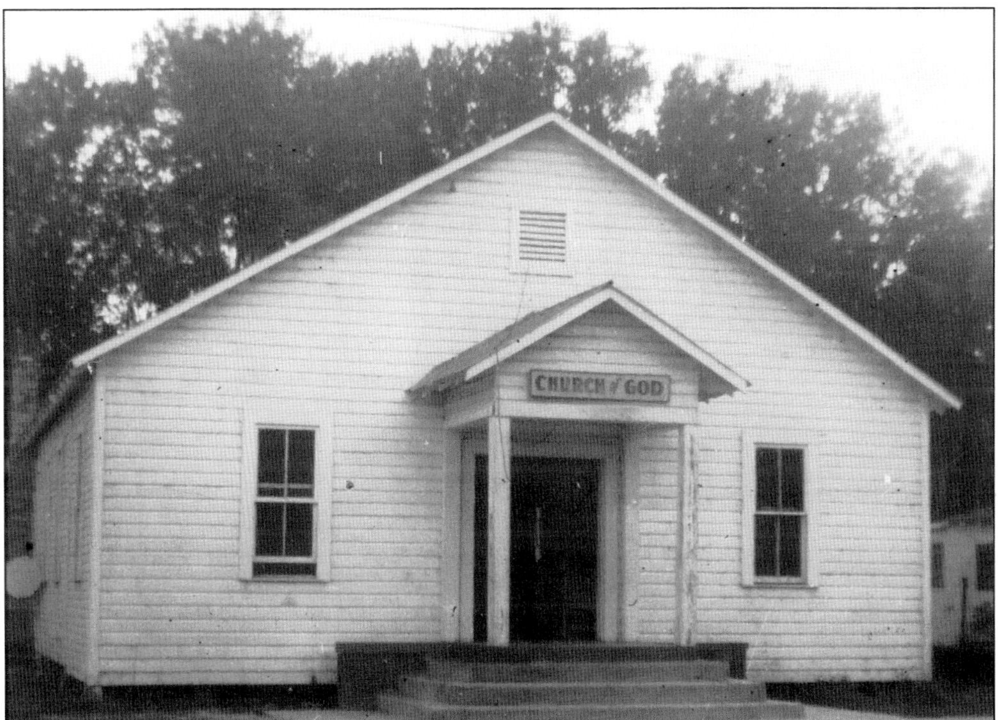

The Live Oak Church of God originally met in the Old Salem community, about eight miles southwest of Live Oak, when it was established in 1919. In 1939, the church moved into Live Oak and constructed a building on East Duval Street. This photograph shows that structure on August 10, 1958. It has since been replaced with a more modern structure on US Highway 129.

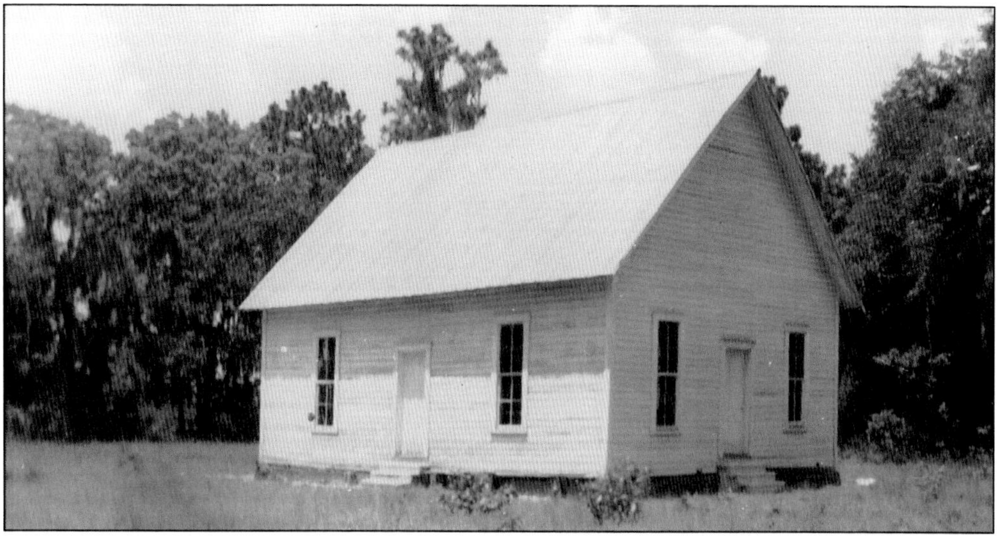

Rixford Primitive Baptist Church was established in the community of Rixford, a few miles north of Live Oak. The photograph above was taken on August 10, 1958, and shows the simple building used by the congregation, which has since disbanded. The Rocky Sink Baptist Church was established in or prior to 1893, at which time the church met on the first floor of the building below and the Rocky Sink Masonic Lodge met on the second. The building was replaced in the late 1960s with two separate structures for the church and lodge. The photograph below shows the original structure on August 10, 1958.

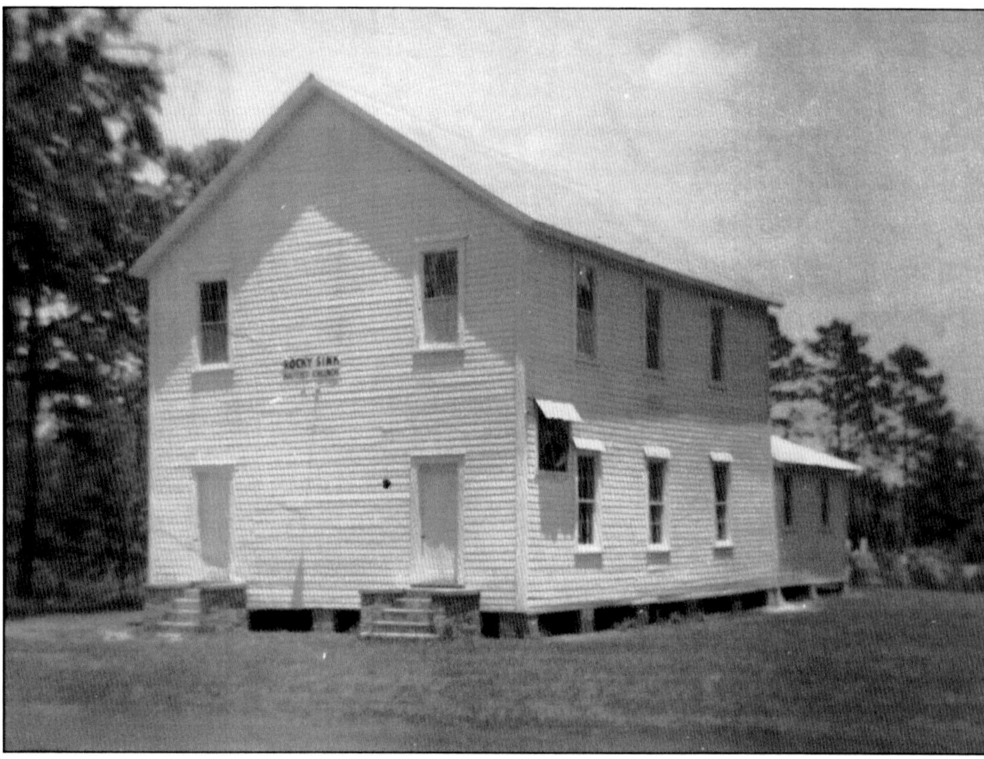

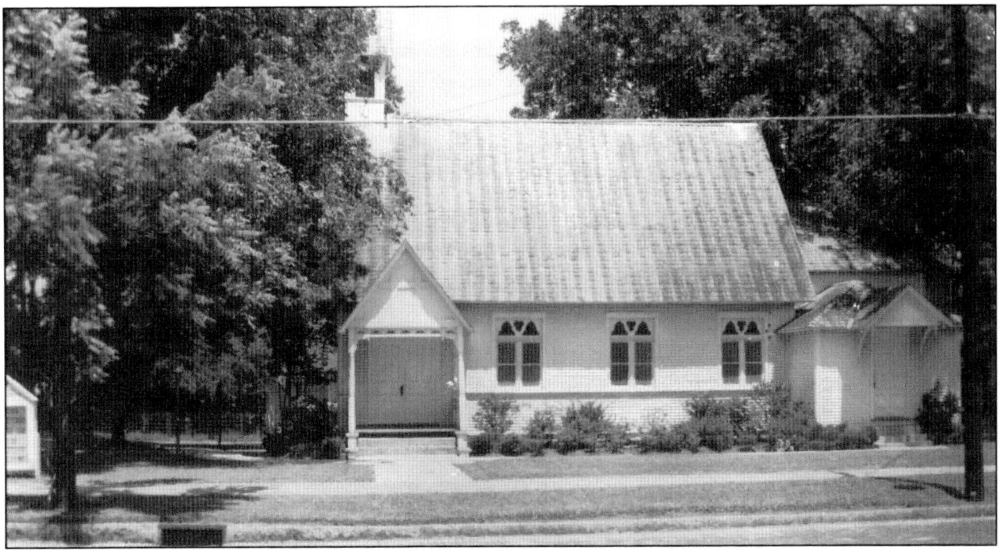

St. Luke's Episcopal Church was organized in 1900, although services had been held in various homes for 10 years prior to that. The church's building was originally on West Duval Street, where it served for a number of decades. In 1971, the building was moved to a location on Newbern Road across from the coliseum and thoroughly renovated, and it continues to serve there today. The photograph above shows the building in its original location on August 10, 1958. Leona Methodist Church was one of the many churches that did not continue to thrive through the 20th century, and eventually, the congregation disbanded. The photograph below shows the building on August 17, 1958.

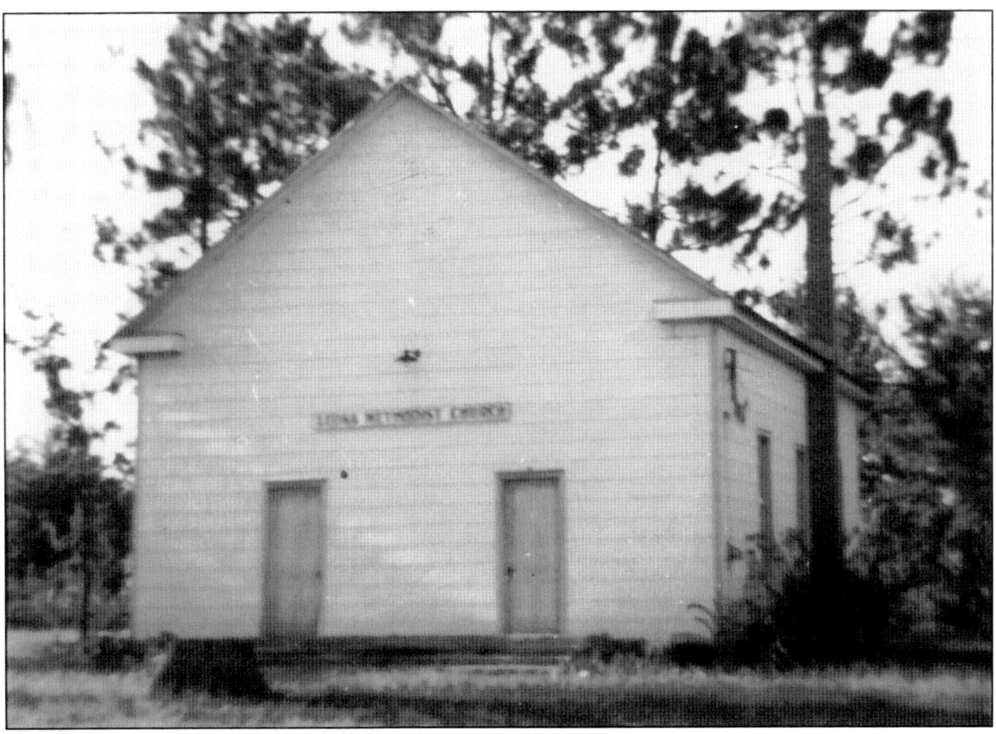

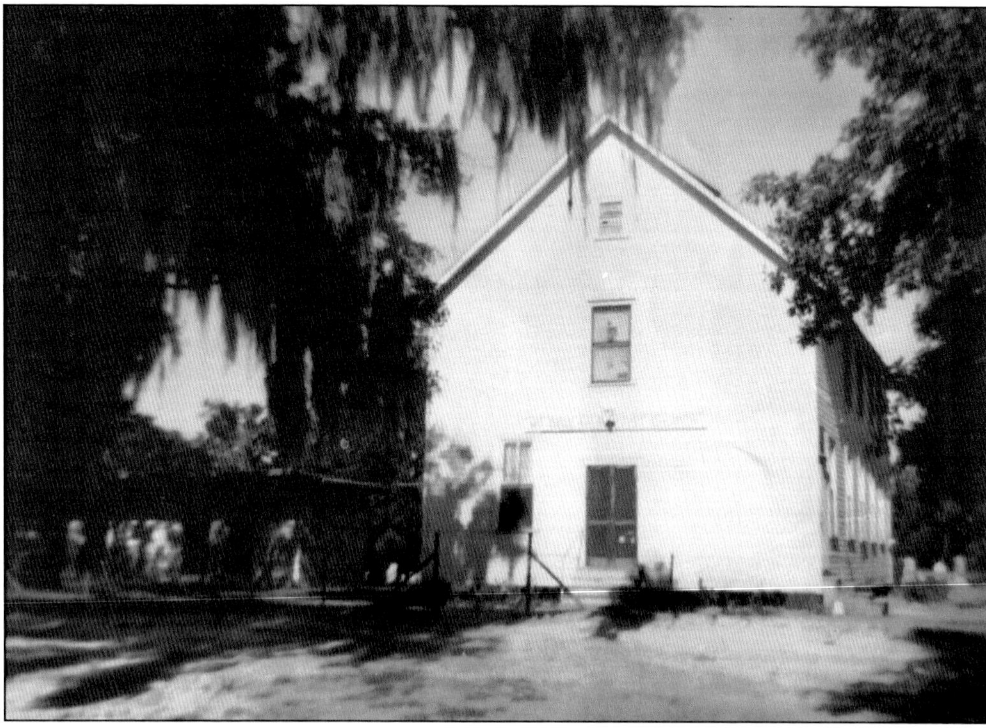

Mount Beulah Baptist Church was one of the many congregations established in the late 1800s and early 1900s. The photograph above shows the two-story church building on August 17, 1958; closer inspection shows the cemetery in the right background. The congregation continues to meet on Forty-fifth Road near Live Oak. Mount Olive Baptist Church was organized in 1892 near Wellborn on land donated by John and Sallie White; the congregation had met as a Methodist church for at least 13 years prior to becoming a Baptist church. The congregation continues to meet today and is located on Ninety-eighth Terrace. This photograph shows the simple block church building on August 17, 1958.

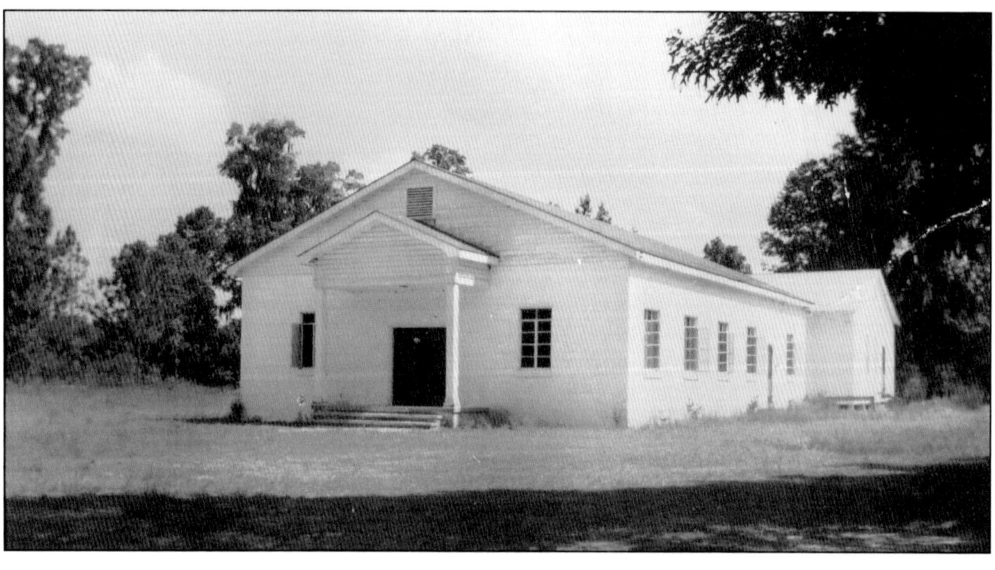

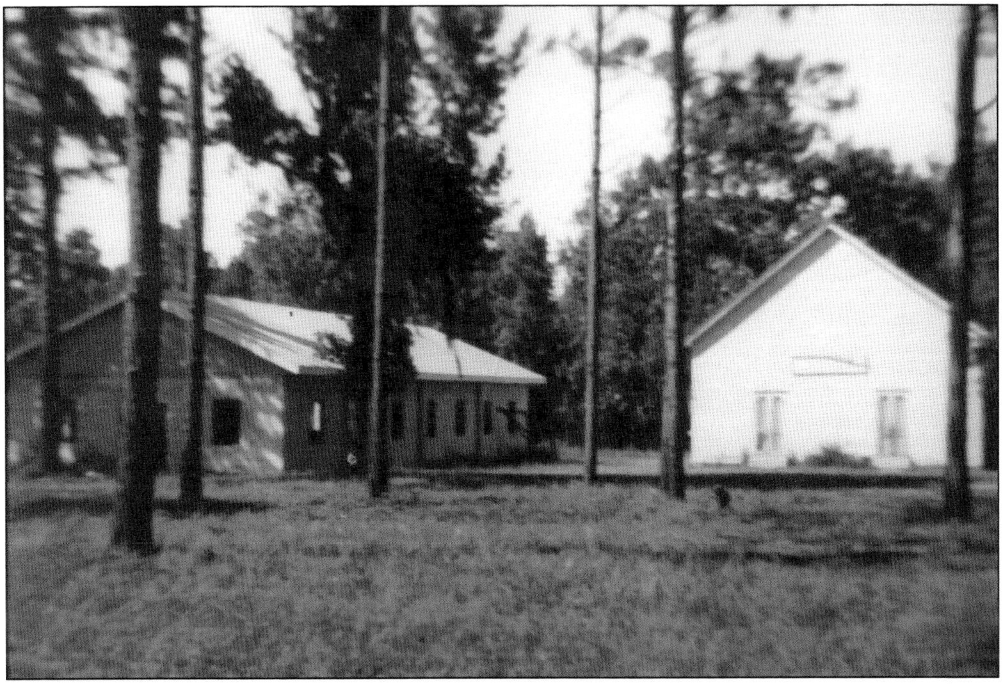

The founding date for the Mount Pleasant Baptist Church is not known with any certainty, but it is known that the church building was reconstructed in 1943 on County Road 10A near Wellborn after a windstorm destroyed the original building. This photograph from August 17, 1958, shows the reconstructed building. The congregation continues to meet today.

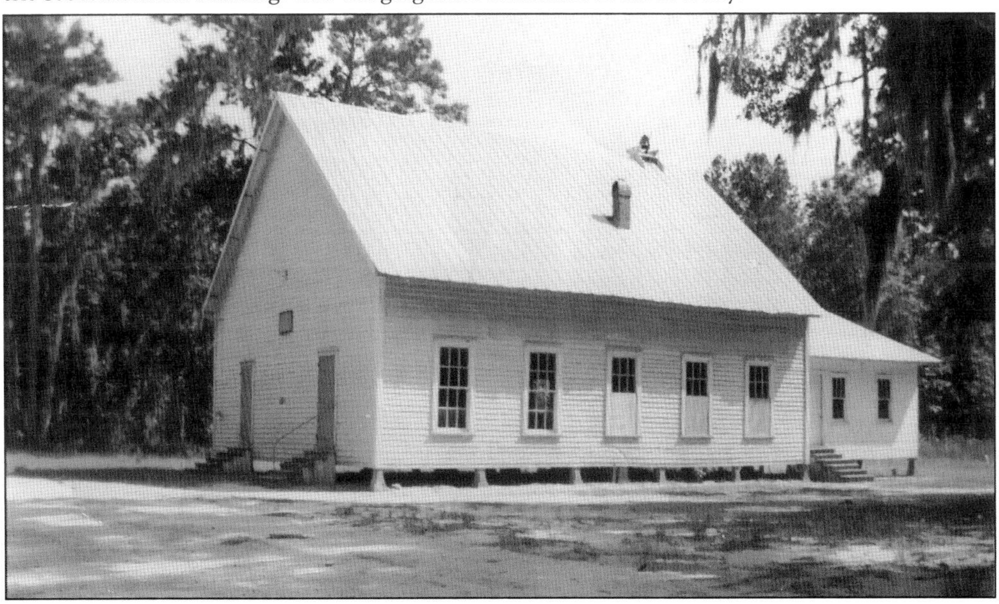

Suwannee County's history would not be complete without mentioning the Pine Grove Methodist Church, the oldest existing church in the county. It was established in 1822 northwest of what is now Live Oak, and men originally stood guard outside the building during services as protection from sporadic Indian attacks. This photograph was taken on August 17, 1958, and shows the fifth church building; it has since been replaced by yet another.

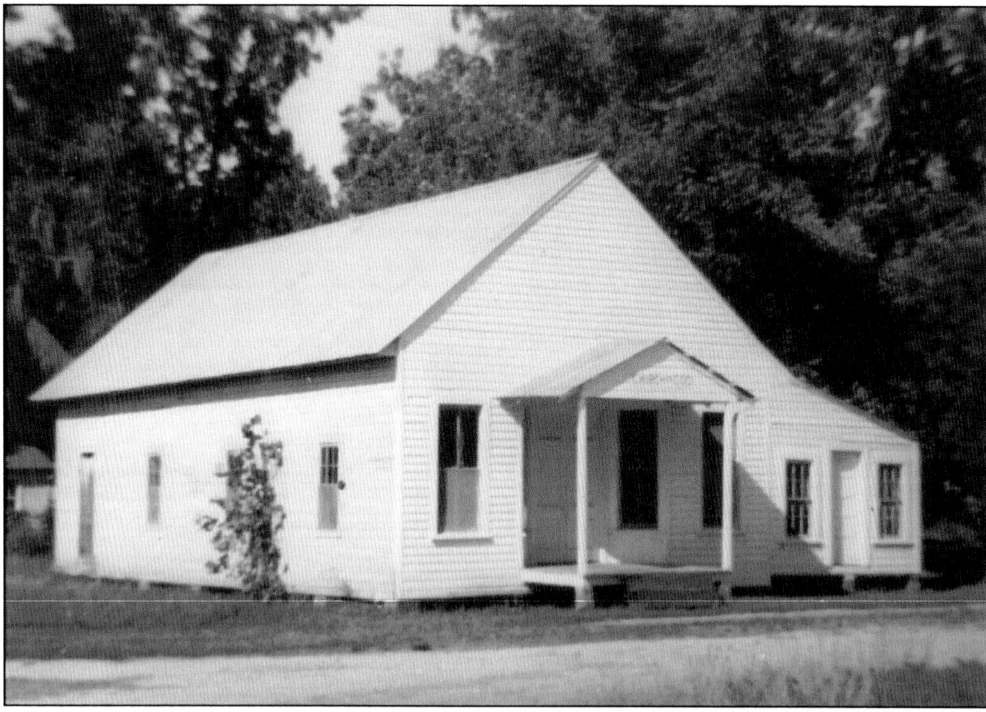

At one point in its history, the Wellborn Church of God worshipped in the old C.A. Knight store, but eventually it built a new structure on US Highway 90, where it worships today. This photograph shows the old church building on August 17, 1958. This photograph can be compared with one of the same building from about 1980 on page 65.

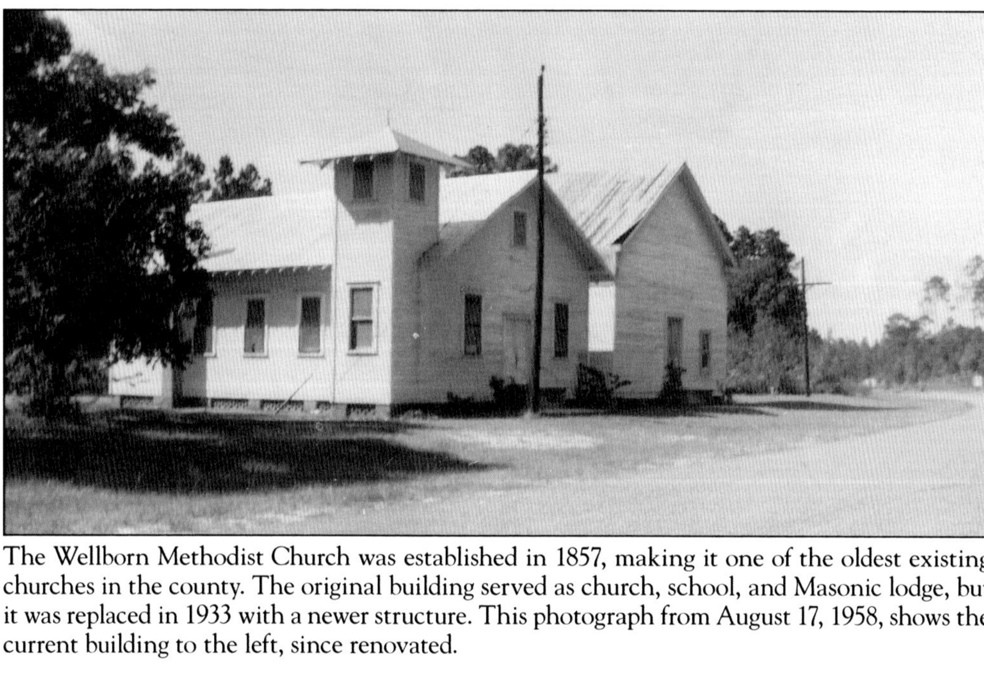

The Wellborn Methodist Church was established in 1857, making it one of the oldest existing churches in the county. The original building served as church, school, and Masonic lodge, but it was replaced in 1933 with a newer structure. This photograph from August 17, 1958, shows the current building to the left, since renovated.

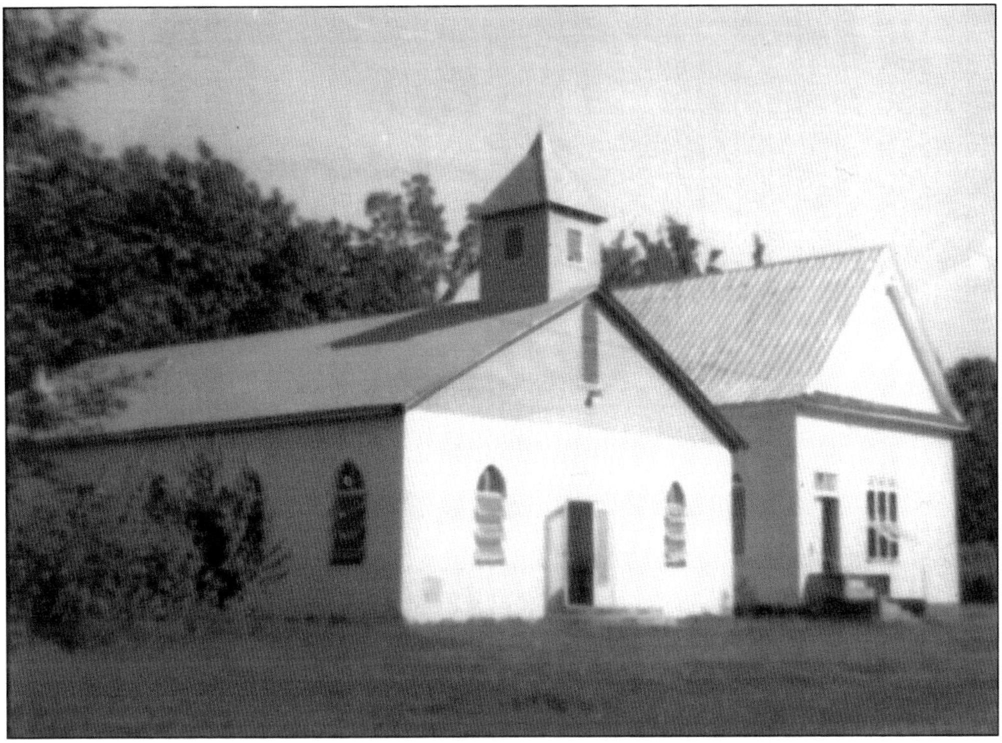

Wellborn Baptist Church was chartered on May 22, 1910, as the First Baptist Church of Wellborn. A new building was constructed in 1954 on County Road 137, but it burned down in December 1999. It has been replaced by a large modern building on US Highway 90. The photograph above shows the old building on August 17, 1958. Luraville Missionary Baptist Church was organized in 1946 with 13 members. A structure was completed that continues to serve today, although it has been modified with a steeple and bricked in. The photograph below, taken on August 31, 1958, shows the church building in its original form.

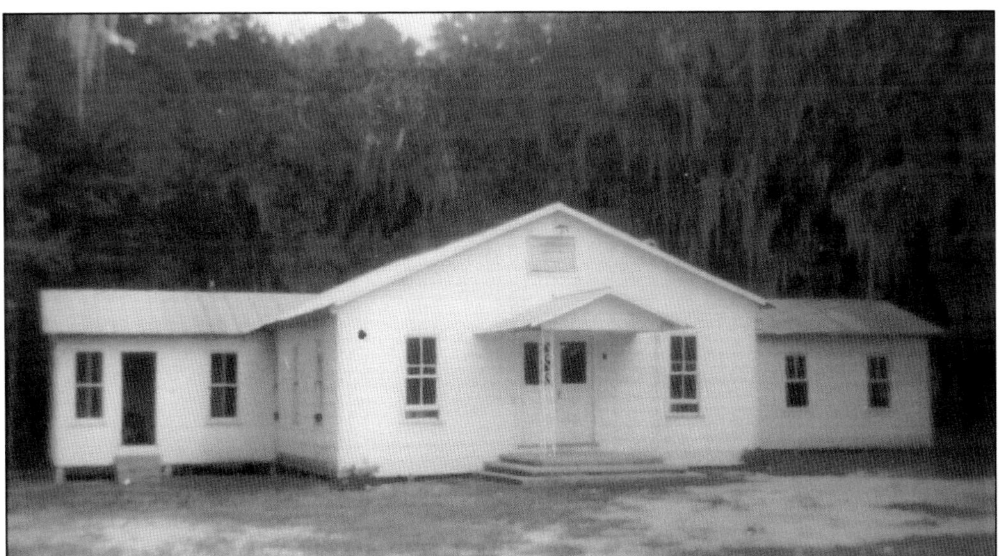

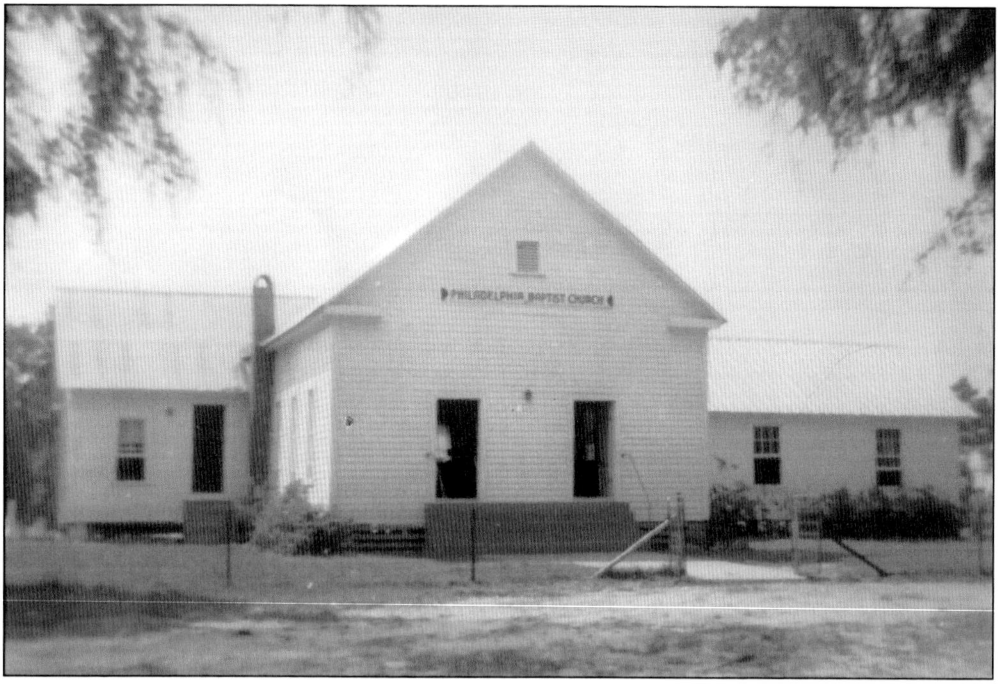

Philadelphia Baptist Church was organized on September 28, 1876, at Irvine's Ferry in Luraville. The original log structure was replaced by a rough-sawed lumber building in 1903, and in October 1964, a new building, which still serves the congregation today, was constructed. The photograph above, taken on August 31, 1958, shows the second wooden building. Pine Grove Church of God was established during a brush arbor revival meeting in 1932, and the congregation continues to operate today on 180th Street, one mile east of Peacock Springs near Luraville. The photograph below shows the block church building on August 31, 1958.

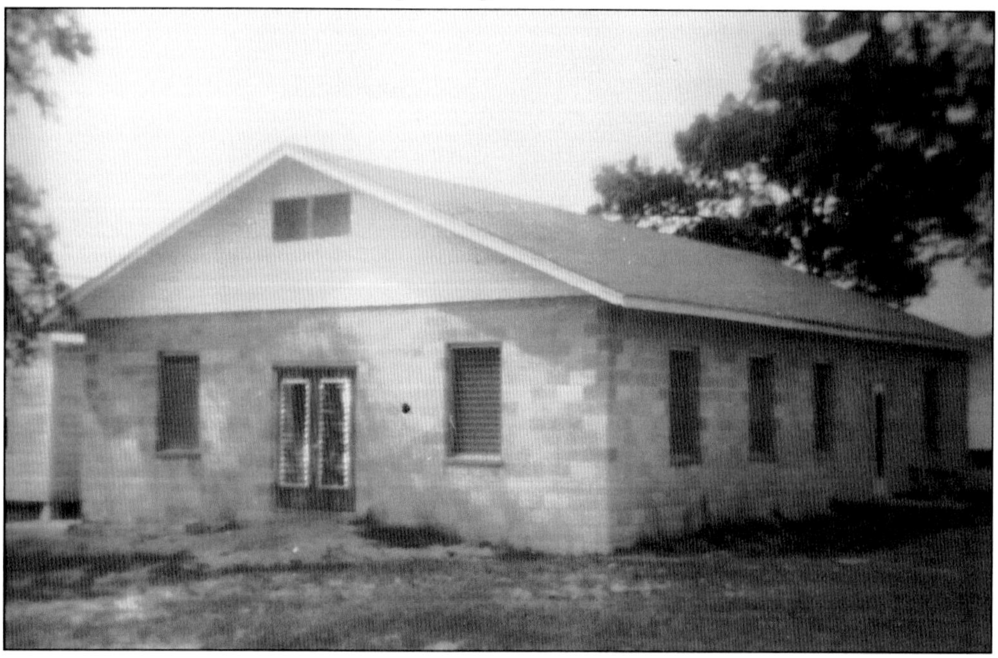

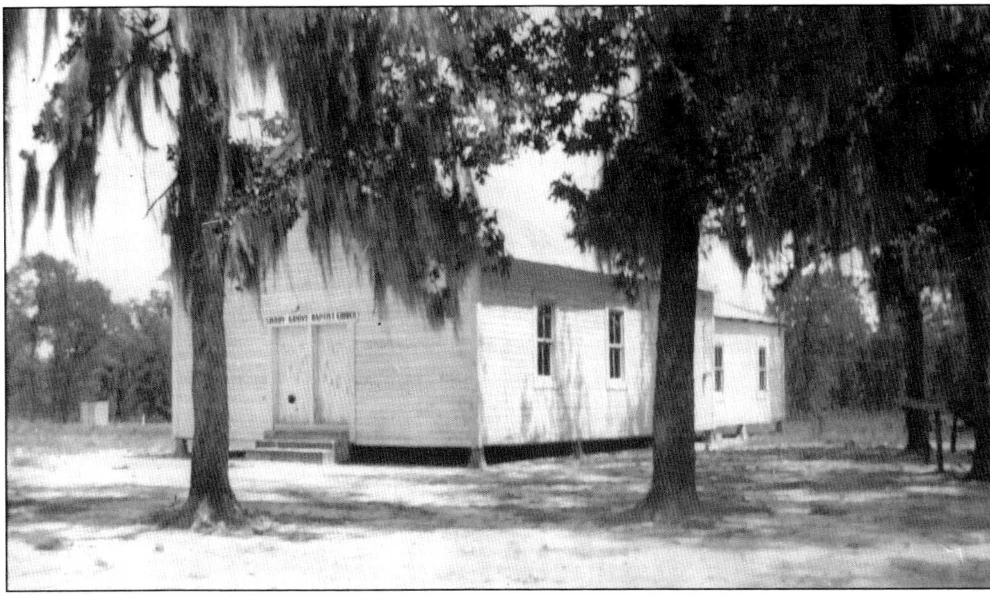

Shady Grove Baptist Church was organized between Falmouth and Dowling Park, approximately 12 miles west of Live Oak. The photograph above shows the old building on August 31, 1958; it has since been replaced by a newer structure on River Road. The congregation continues to worship today and holds an annual "Old Timey Day" to commemorate the days before electricity. Mount Zion Christian Church was organized in 1904 by A.J. Bass Sr. and Samuel J. White in the Macedonia or Bass community on what is now Bass Road, just south of Live Oak. The charter members included the Bass and Hurst families. The photograph below shows the church building on May 24, 1959.

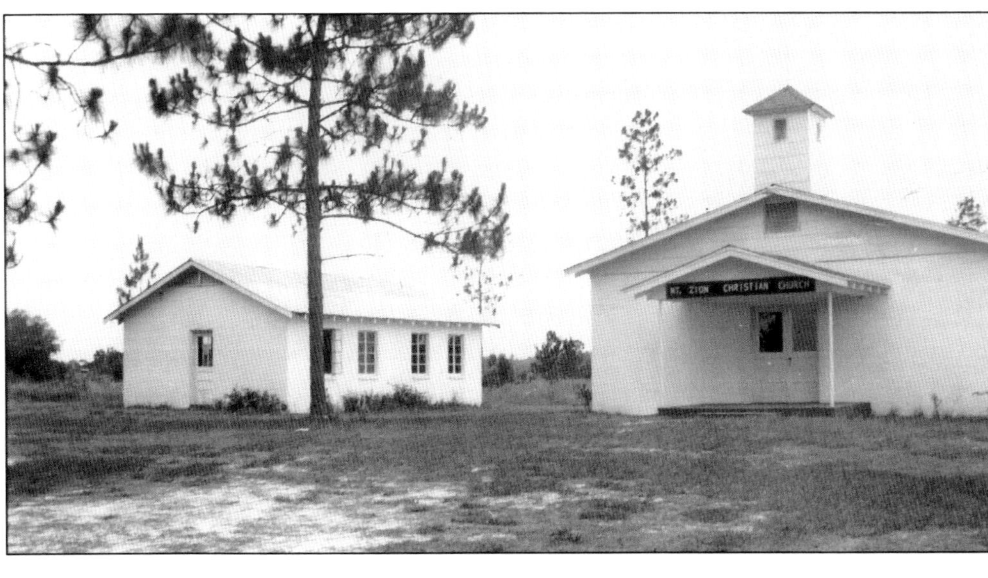

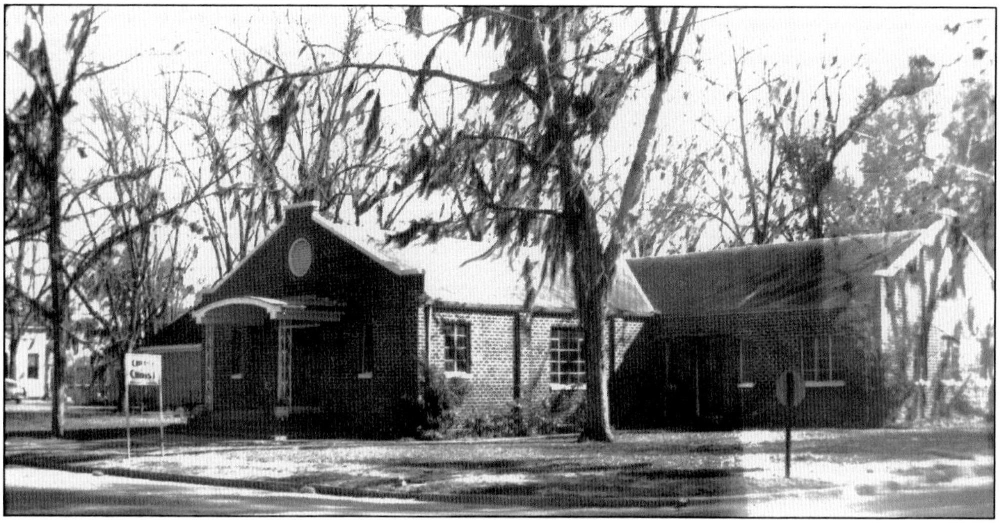

The Live Oak Church of Christ was established in 1940 and first met in the Suwannee County Courthouse. Later, the congregation met in the Magnolia House on Wilbur Street before moving to Walker Street. A brick building was constructed on the corner of Duval and Walker Streets in 1954, shown here in March 1960. The congregation moved to a new building on Highway 51 South in 1986.

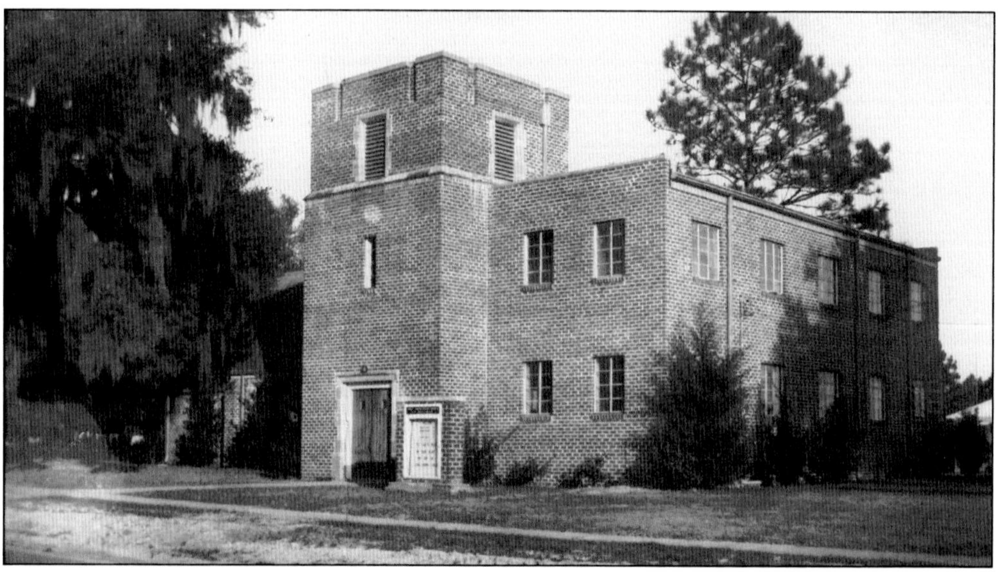

First Presbyterian Church of Live Oak was organized in 1870 in a vacant store on the west end of town. In 1880, a wooden frame structure was completed on Pine Avenue that served many years. In 1951, a new Old English Norman structure was occupied, and it is shown here in March 1960. After 140 years, the congregation disbanded on the last Sunday of December 2010.

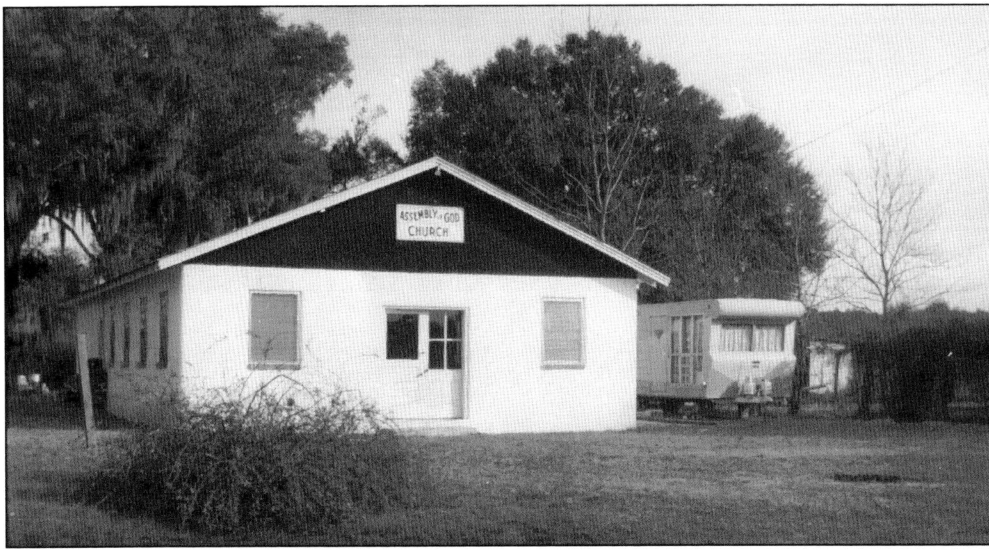

The Assembly of God was established on Duval Street in Live Oak some time during the 20th century. The photograph above shows the block building in March 1960. What is now known as the Beachville Advent Christian Church was established prior to 1896. In 1915, property northeast of the town of Branford on County Road 49, near its intersection with State Road 247 was donated for use by the church, and the name was changed to the Second Advent Christian Church of Beachville. The photograph below was taken on July 4, 1960, showing the building that was constructed in 1948 and that is still used today.

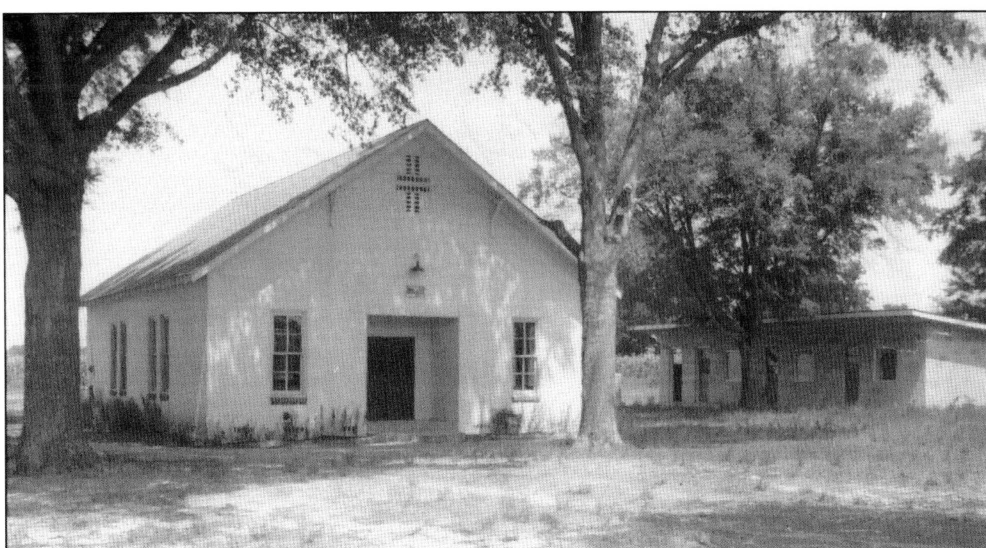

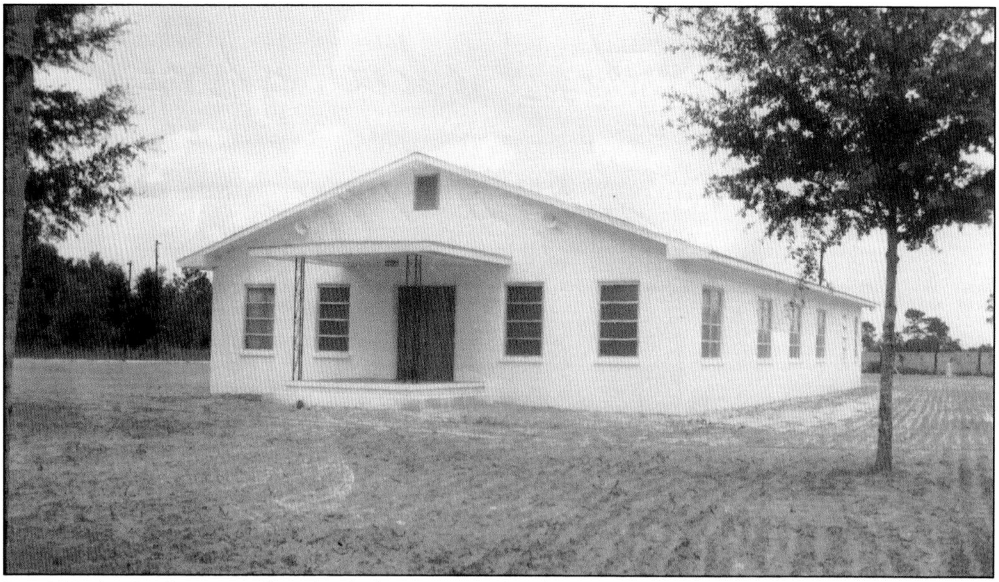

In 1959, the Burlington Church of Christ merged with the Santa Fe Church of Christ to become the Burlington–Santa Fe Church of Christ. The following year, a new building was constructed on US 27 east of Branford. This photograph, taken on July 4, 1960, shows the newly constructed building, which served the congregation for over half a century.

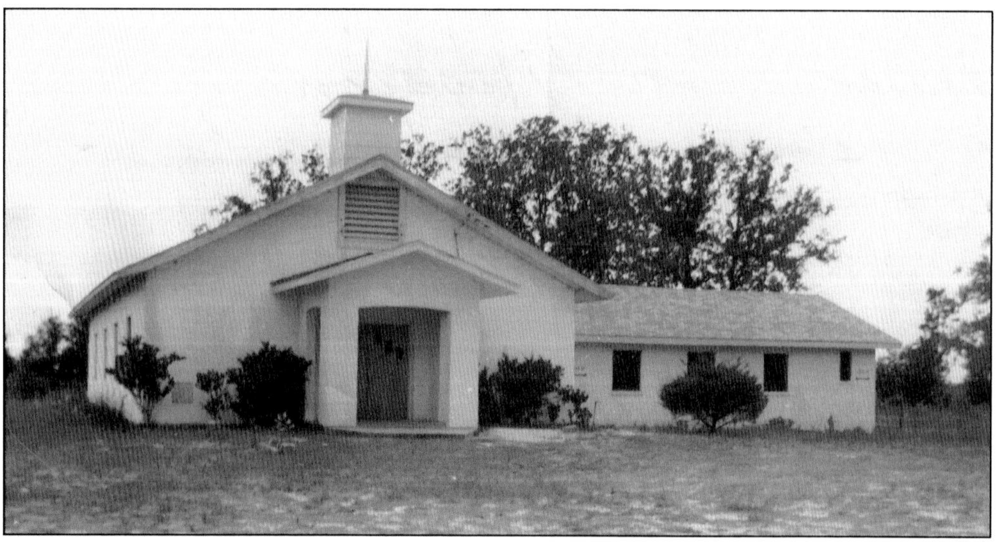

Magnolia Baptist Church was founded in 1924 and was made up primarily of members of the Aderholt family. Its first five years were spent meeting in the old wood-frame home of "Granny" Aderholt, but in 1929, a church building was constructed on land near Branford, donated by the Mellette family. This photograph shows the church building on July 4, 1960.

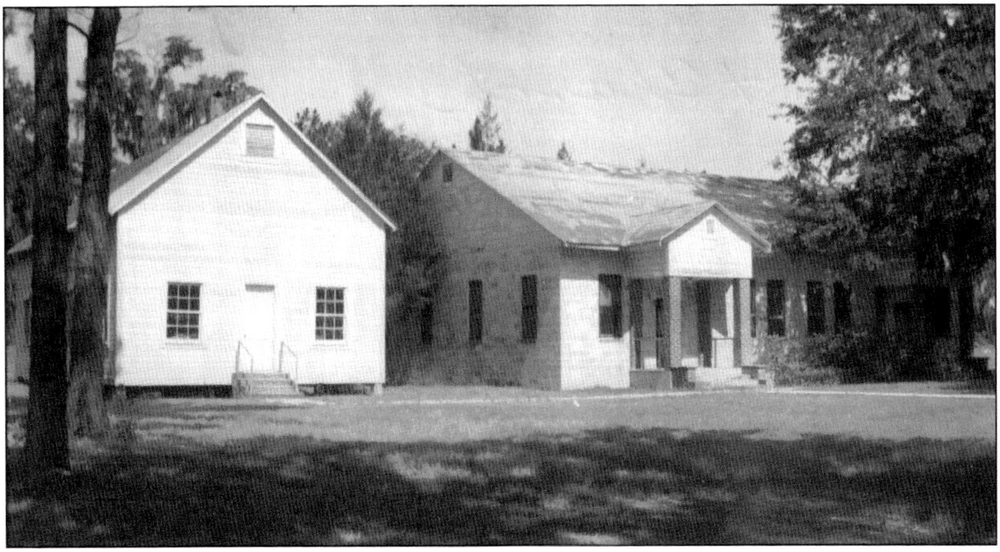

Tiger Lake Missionary Baptist Church was established in June 1883 with nine members. The congregation met in a log schoolhouse until 1886, when a new wooden building was constructed on what is now County Road 49. This structure was replaced in 1947 by a block structure that is shown in the photograph above on July 4, 1960, alongside the older structure. Union Baptist Church was established in the community of Houston, once the county seat of Suwannee County, some time after the end of the Civil War. The photograph below, taken on July 4, 1960, shows the block structure that continues in use today.

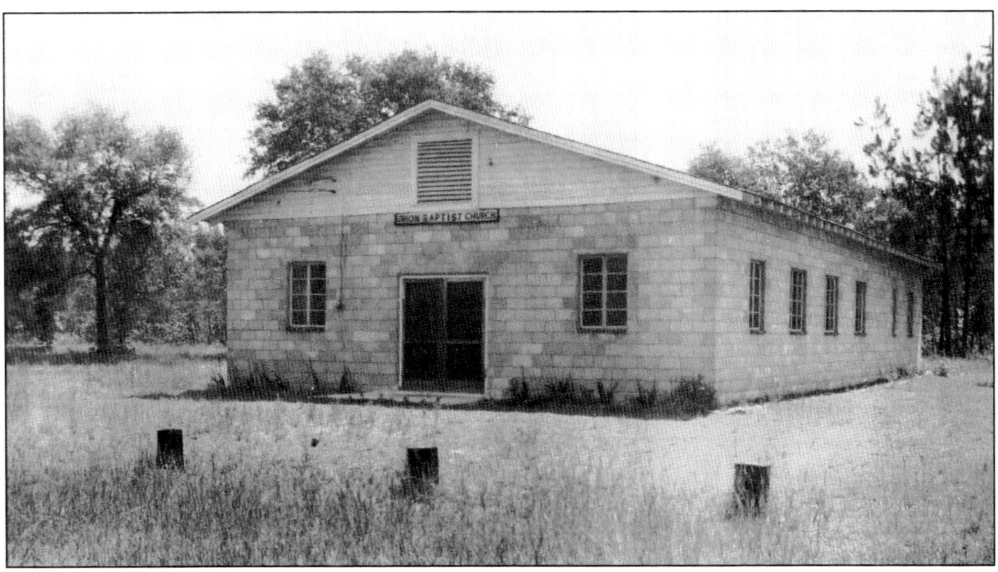

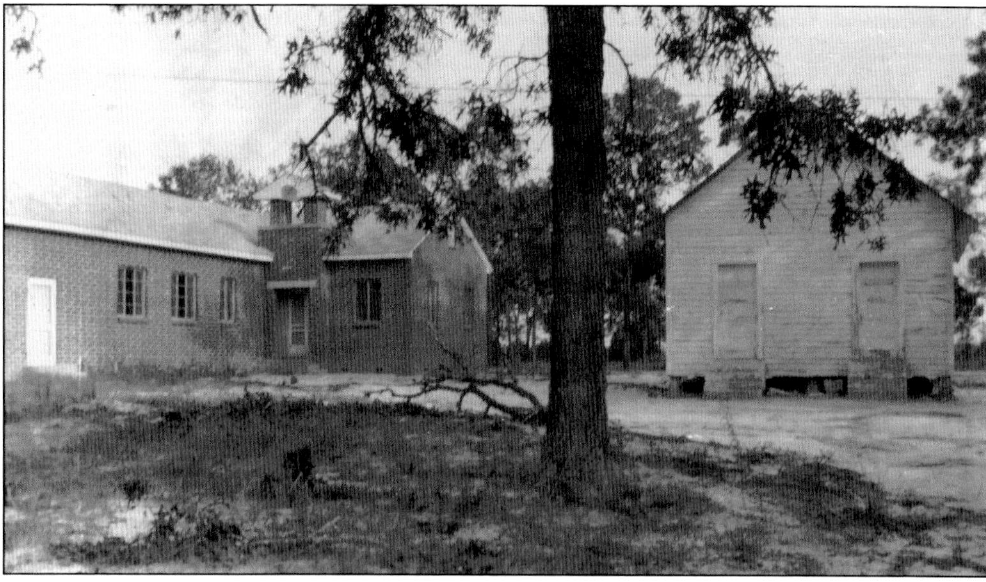

The McAlpin Advent Christian Church was established in 1905. The first meetings were held in a local schoolhouse, but a wooden church building was constructed in 1907 and was used for many years. In 1953, a new building was constructed that continues to serve the congregation today on Eighty-ninth Road. The photograph above, taken in 1960, shows both old and new buildings. McAlpin Baptist Church was established during the heyday of country churches in the late 1800s and early 1900s. The lower photograph shows the newer block church building, which had replaced an earlier two-story wooden structure, on September 5, 1960.

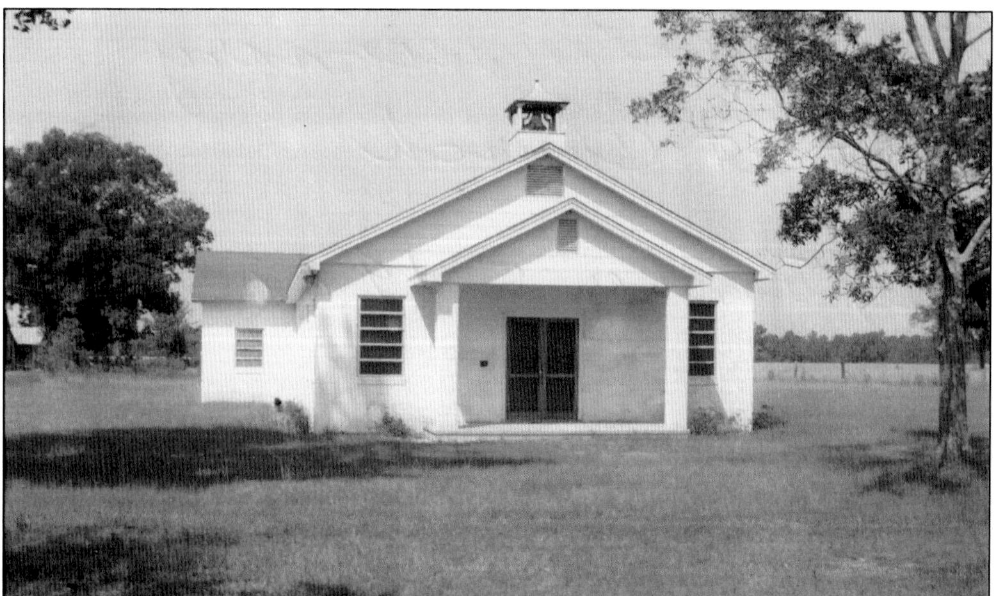

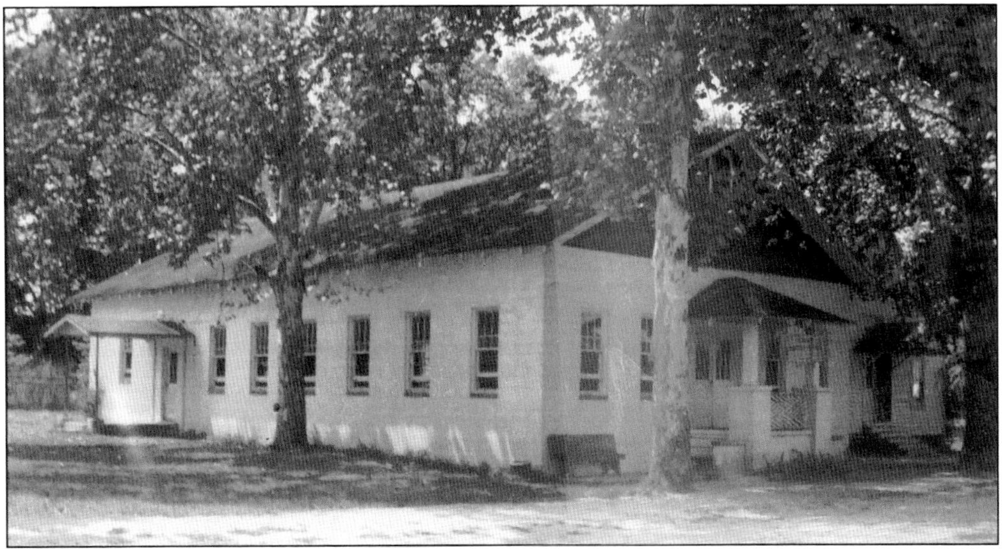

O'Brien Baptist Church was established in the 1870s near Troy Springs. A simple one-room log structure was eventually replaced by a newer building. A concrete block building was constructed in 1948 along County Road 349, approximately one-quarter mile from O'Brien. The original wooden building was relocated there as well four years later. This photograph shows the block structure, with the old wooden structure to the right, on September 5, 1960.

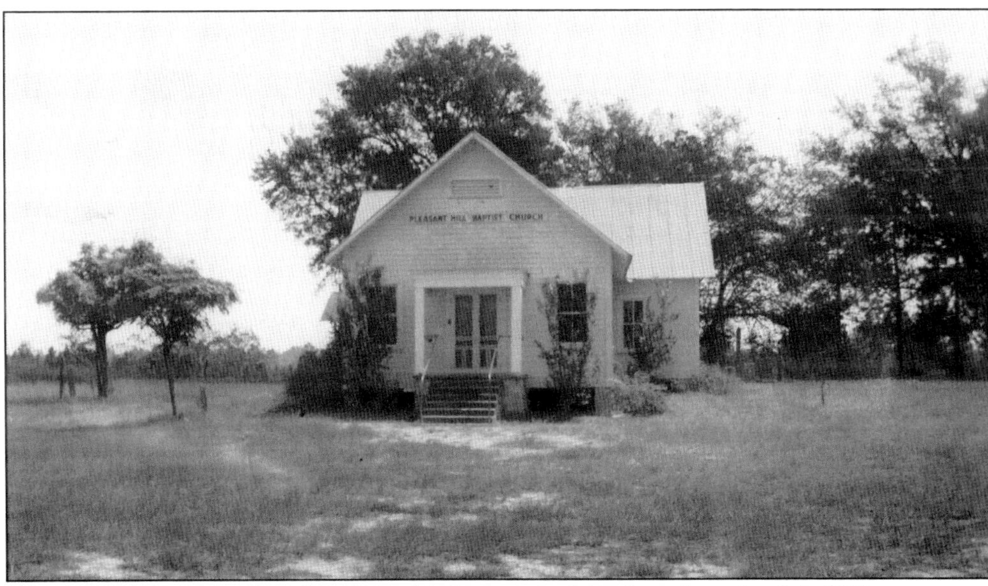

Pleasant Hill Baptist Church was established around 1890, and on April 7, 1892, prominent businessman C.K. Dutton and his wife sold two acres of land to the church. The original building was replaced by a newer wooden structure, which itself was remodeled in 1950 for further service. This photograph shows that building on September 5, 1960; it looks much the same today.

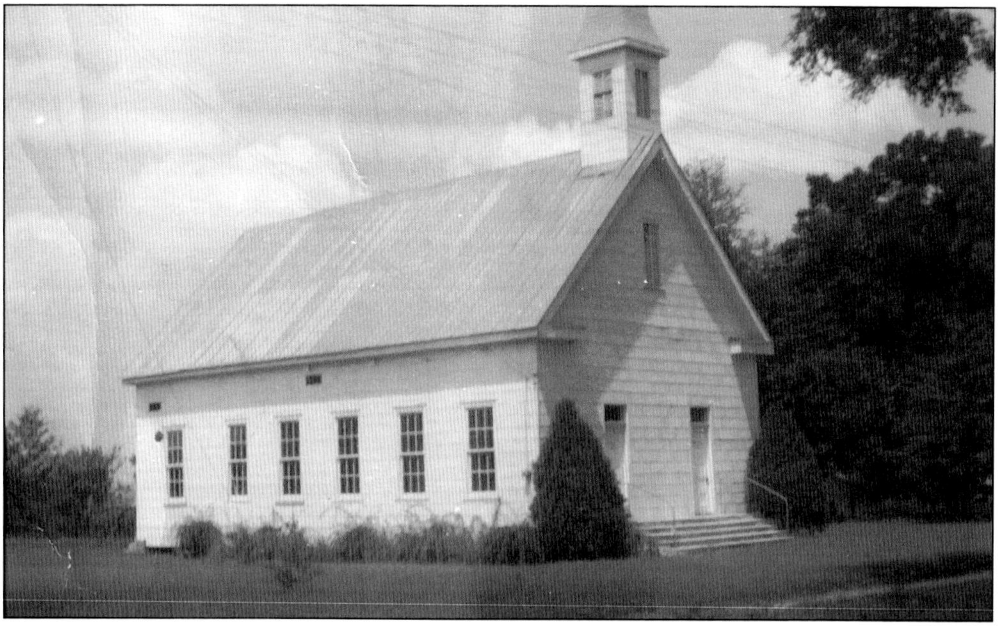

The photograph above shows the O'Brien Methodist Church in March 1961, one of the many congregations that no longer exist. After the congregation became too small to support the building and its upkeep, the remaining members decided to merge with the Branford United Methodist Church. The Florida Sheriffs' Boys' Ranch was established in 1957 north of Live Oak on the Suwannee River, and accepted its first boys the next year. Tasked with helping troubled boys, it is one of four such facilities in Florida. Among other structures completed in the Boys' Ranch's first decade was a chapel, shown in the picture below on December 27, 1964.

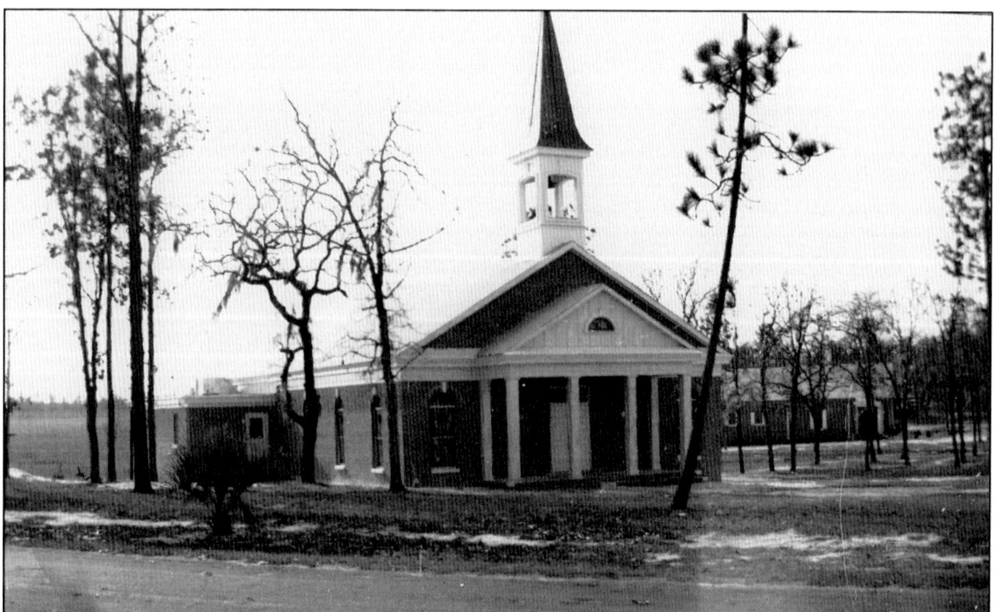

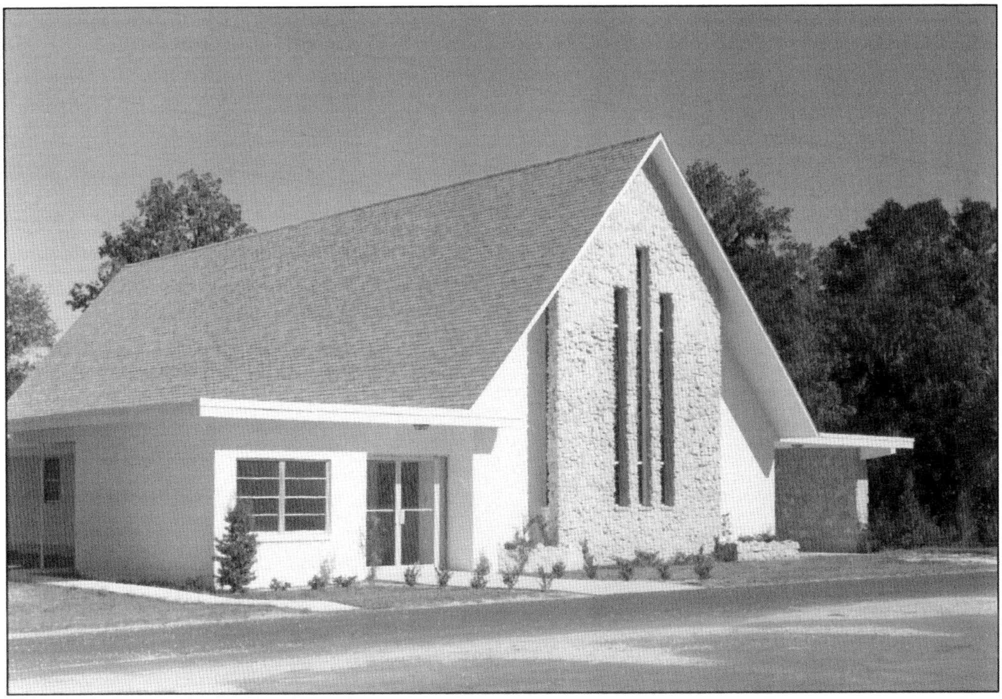

In 1963, a campaign was launched to build the Bixler Memorial Chapel at the Advent Christian Village in honor of Dr. Burr Bixler, who had passed away in 1950. Cochairmen of the fundraising campaign were Dr. Robert Preston and Roy Hunter, a Live Oak pharmacist. The chapel was completed in 1965 and is shown here shortly thereafter; it continues to serve the Dowling Park community today. (ACV Archives.)

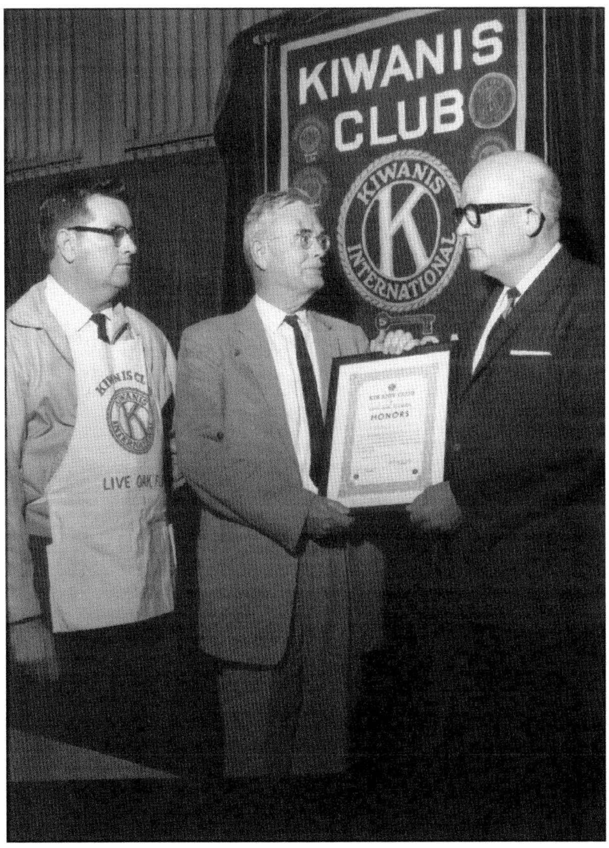

Suwannee County residents have a long history of service to their community. One of the longest serving organizations is the Kiwanis Club of Live Oak, chartered on July 18, 1924, with 36 members. Kiwanis International is primarily focused on serving the children of the community and world. This photograph, taken around 1965, shows president Garth Nobles (left) with Marvin O'Hara (center) and Reese Brown.

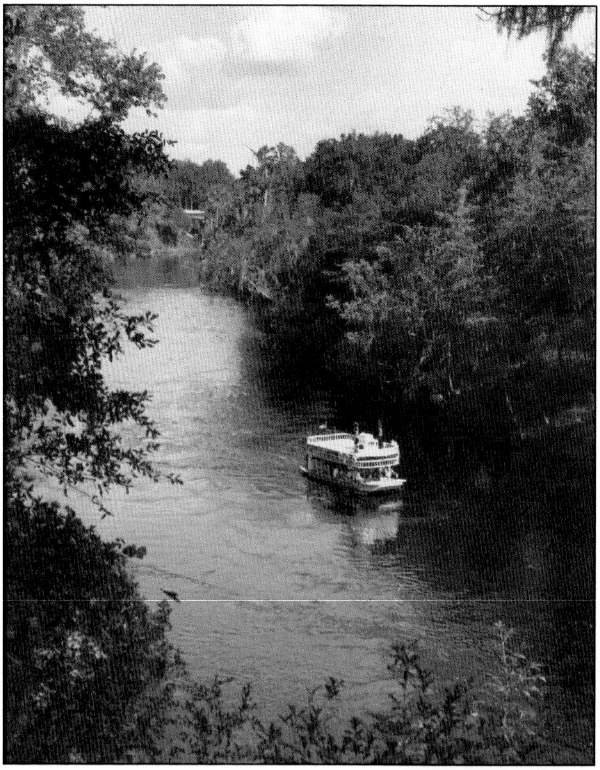

The Stephen Foster Folk Culture Center State Park was established in 1950 in White Springs, across the Suwannee River from Suwannee County in neighboring Hamilton County. Among its early attractions was a small-scale replica steamboat of the type that steamed the Suwannee River during their heyday, aptly named *Belle of the Suwannee*. These two photographs, taken in the 1960s, show the replica plying the Suwannee River near White Springs. The photograph below also shows a Radcraft wooden-hulled motorboat in the foreground, built by the Live Oak–based Thomas H. Radford Construction Company until going out of business in the last half of the 20th century. The replica steamboat outings were eventually discontinued.

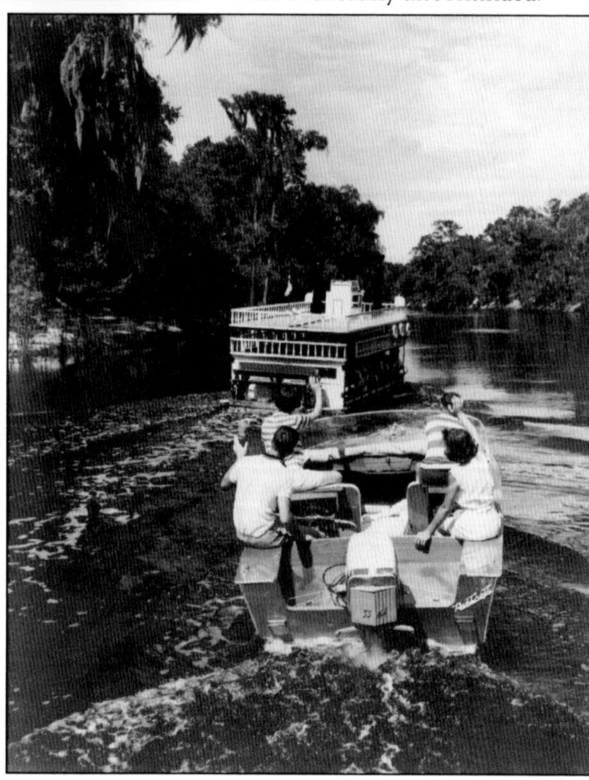

Five

DISASTERS

It is said that "You cannot change or hide history; it is what it is." Nowhere in this book is that plainer than in this chapter, where the reader is invited to stroll through a variety of disasters that have overtaken the county. Disasters, whether they are international, national, or even local, seem to elicit memories from those who were alive when it happened. Take national tragedies, such as the assassination of Pres. John F. Kennedy, the attacks on September 11, 2001, or a host of other events: those alive can remember exactly where they were and what they were doing. For some of the pictures in this chapter, it may be much the same. Either way, browsing through photographs of disasters holds a certain fascination for many people.

The source of the county's greatest pride and recognition is also the source of many of its disasters: the Suwannee River. Normally, it is a beautiful and peaceful waterway, lazily meandering to the Gulf of Mexico; from time to time, however, heavy rains or tropical storms cause it to rise up and inundate the surrounding area, turning farmlands into swamps and destroying thousands of acres of crops. Some of the pictures in this chapter show the Suwannee River at its worst.

The majority of this chapter is made up of what is most probably the greatest natural disaster in Suwannee County's history: the destruction wrought by Hurricane Dora in September 1964. Damages totaled millions of dollars, and Suwannee County was not spared by the deluge of rain that accompanied the cyclone. Particularly hard hit was the center of Live Oak, which was inundated with flooding that its drainage ponds could not handle. Store inventories were ruined, records destroyed, and foundations shifted, as much of the central business district was covered in several feet of water. Gov. Farris Bryant made his way down Howard Street in a boat, surveying the damage before declaring Suwannee County a disaster area; Pres. Lyndon Johnson called to add federal aid to the recovery. This chapter shows that even during the best times, bad events can happen.

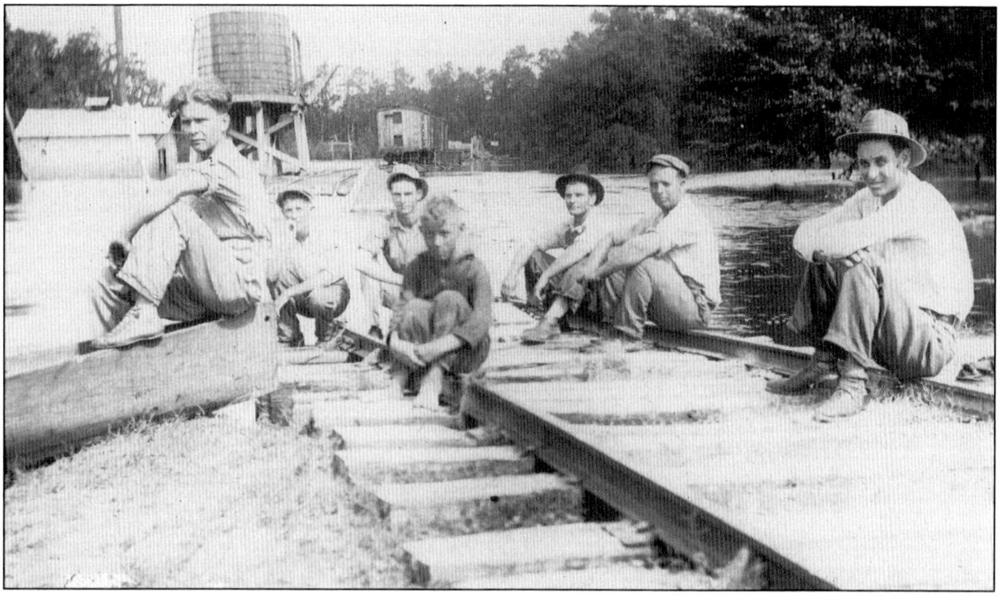

Suwannee County has had its share of floods. One of the worst floods occurred in 1928, impacting the riverside communities of Suwannee Springs, Ellaville, Dowling Park, and Branford. This photograph shows men and boys sitting on the Live Oak, Perry & Gulf Railroad tracks on the south side of the Suwannee River at Dowling Park. The water tank in the background was used to refill the engines. (ACV Archives.)

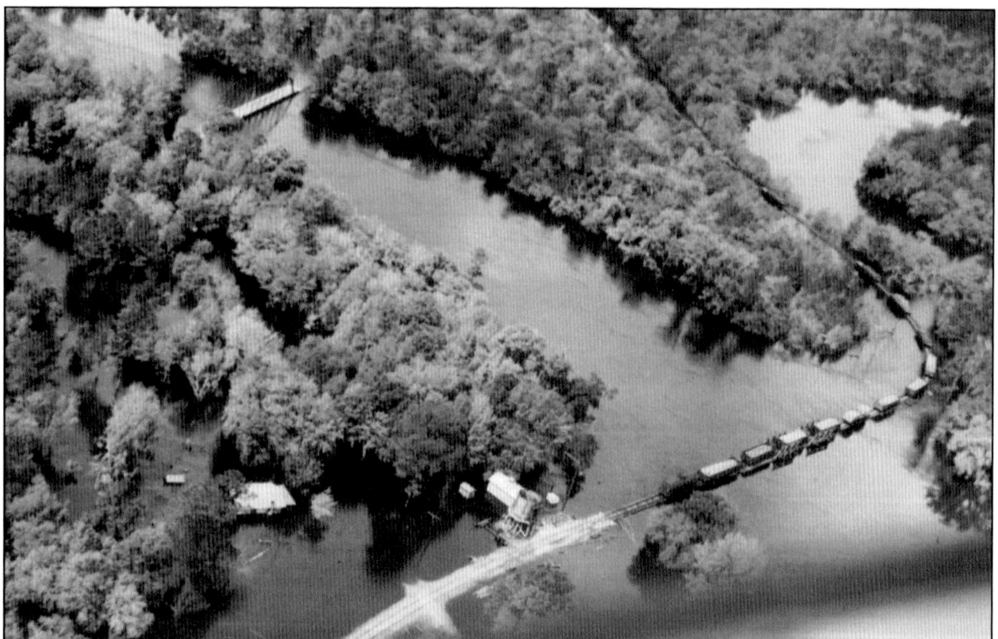

The year of 1948 saw another major flood affect Suwannee County. This aerial photograph shows the Suwannee River at Dowling Park during the flood. Railroad cars have been placed on the railroad bridge to keep it from being washed away. The vehicle bridge on the left side of the photograph was known as the Stagecoach Bridge; it is now the location of a county boat ramp. (ACV Archives.)

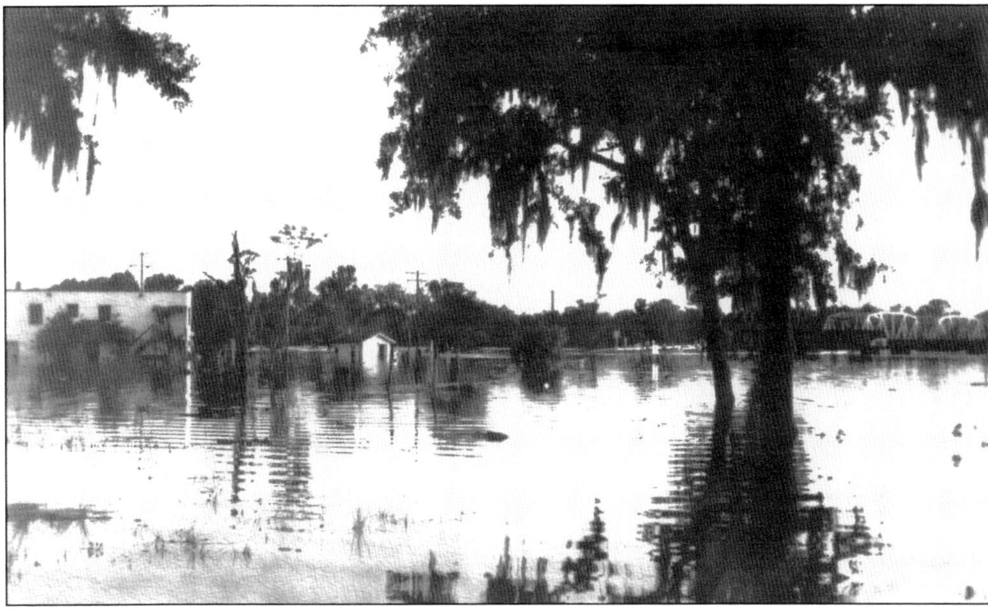

Dowling Park was not the only Suwannee County community that suffered during the flood of 1948. The community of Branford was also inundated by the waters of the nearby Suwannee River, and streets became fast-flowing canals. These two photographs, both taken on April 11, 1948, show some of the devastation. In the photograph above, the bridge crossing the Suwannee River is in the right background; the small fruit inspection station sticks out in the left center, and a filling station is at the far left. In the picture below, one of the streets and some of the residences of Branford are shown near US Highway 129, a few feet south of Fletcher's Garage.

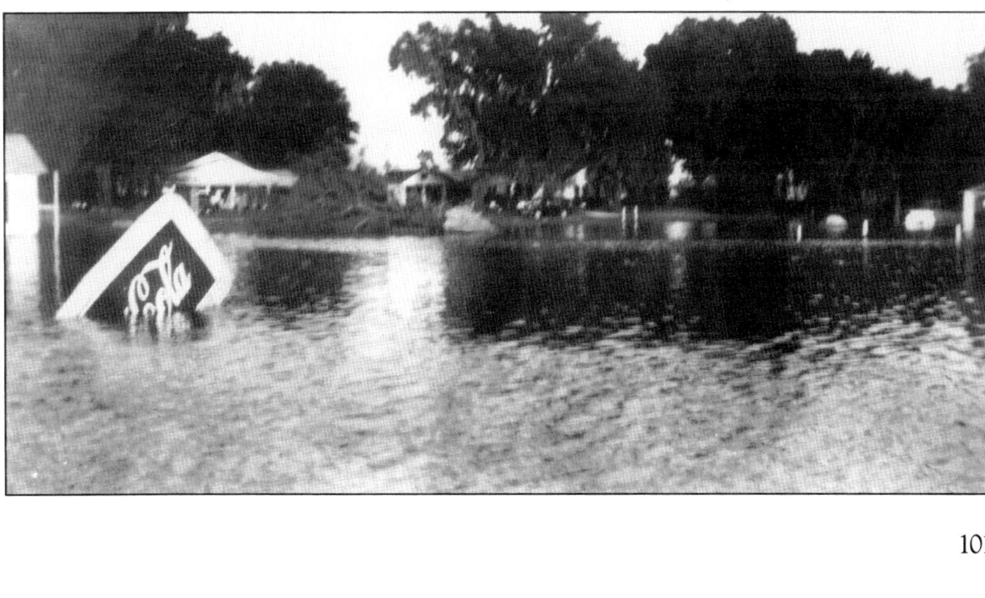

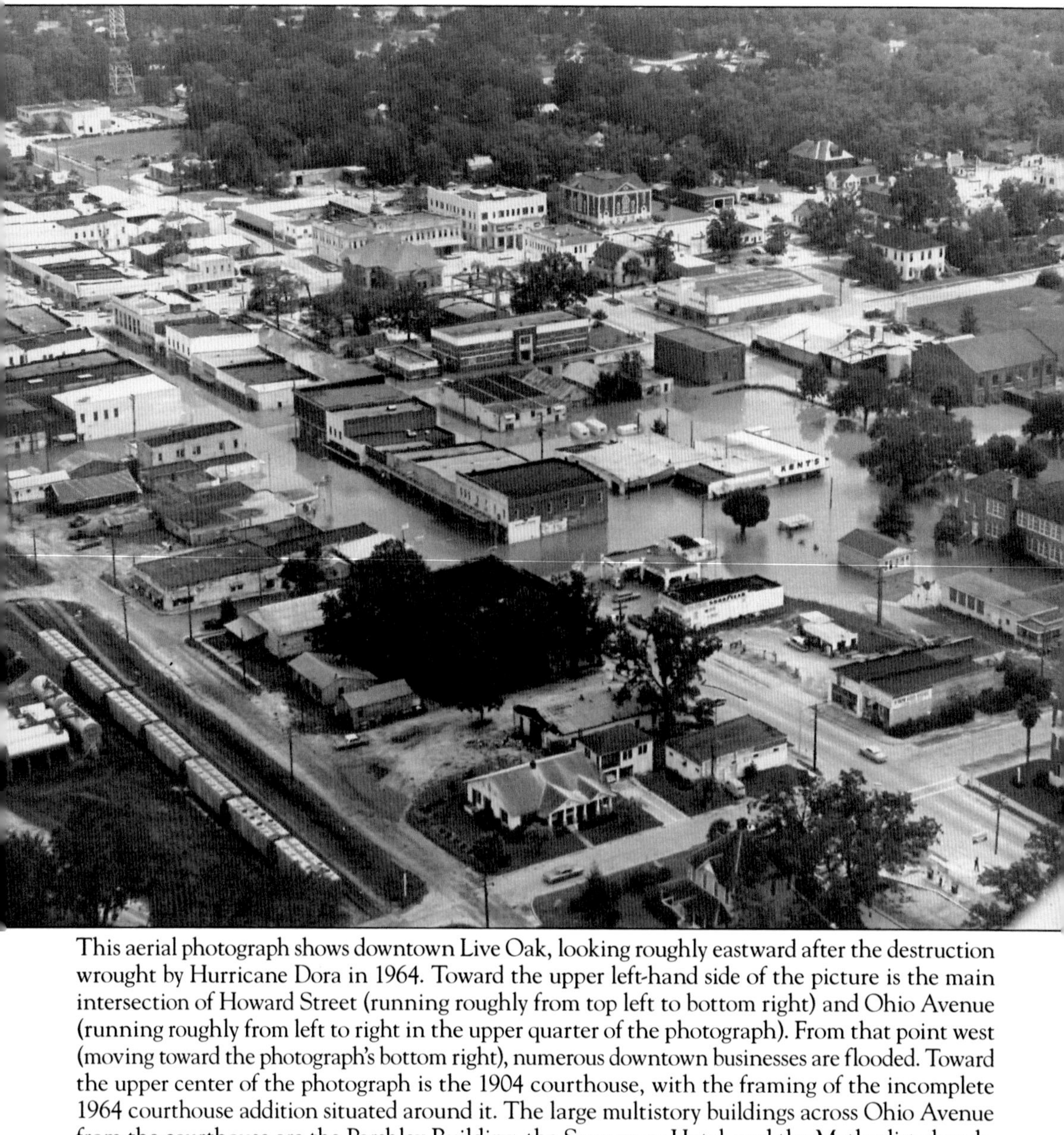

This aerial photograph shows downtown Live Oak, looking roughly eastward after the destruction wrought by Hurricane Dora in 1964. Toward the upper left-hand side of the picture is the main intersection of Howard Street (running roughly from top left to bottom right) and Ohio Avenue (running roughly from left to right in the upper quarter of the photograph). From that point west (moving toward the photograph's bottom right), numerous downtown businesses are flooded. Toward the upper center of the photograph is the 1904 courthouse, with the framing of the incomplete 1964 courthouse addition situated around it. The large multistory buildings across Ohio Avenue from the courthouse are the Parshley Building, the Suwannee Hotel, and the Methodist church. The white, two-story frame building toward the top right of the photograph is the old 1873–1874 courthouse, moved to this location and serving as an apartment complex. In the middle of the right edge of the picture is the high school, with its many windows; it was totally flooded and rendered unusable. Just above the high school is the old, two-story brick armory. (SCCC.)

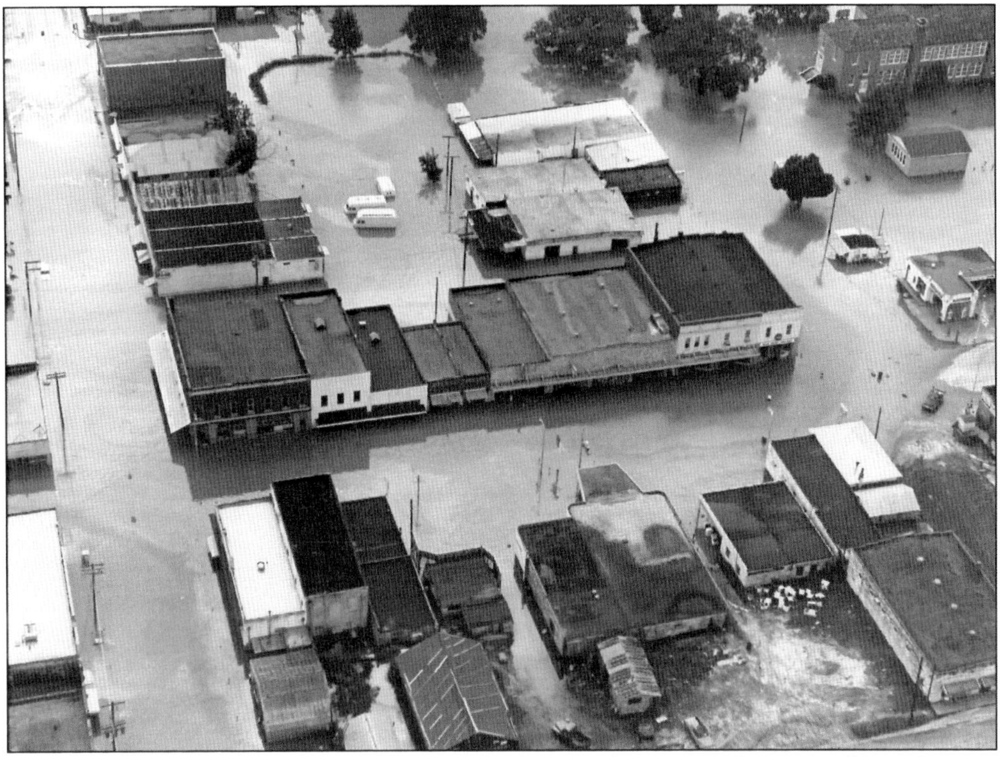

These two photographs show a closer view of the damage along Howard Street and Pine Avenue. In the above picture, looking roughly south, the western half of the Howard Street business district is shown. At the top right of the photograph is the high school. The half-circle hedge near the top center of the picture was the area's retention pond, which was totally inadequate for the deluge that transpired. The photograph below is taken from roughly the same location, but this time looking to the southeast. The 1904 courthouse and the frame of the 1964 addition stand out in the upper left, with the jail and health department to the right (west) of them. (Both, SCCC.)

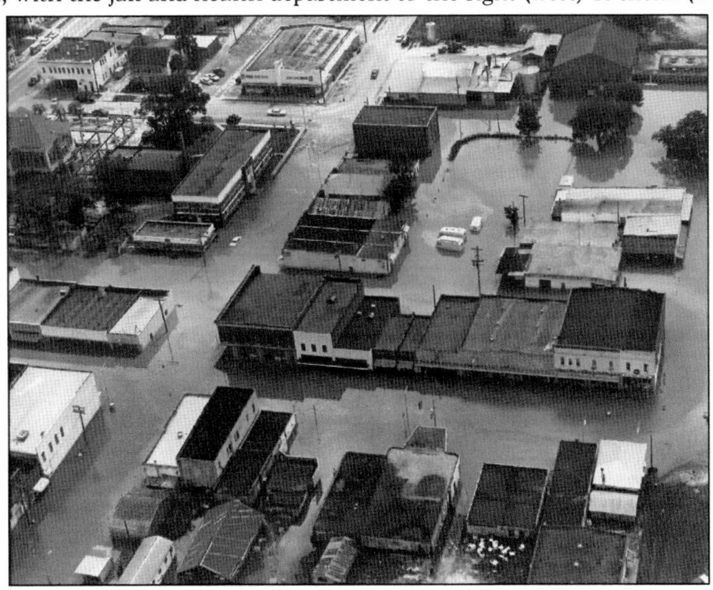

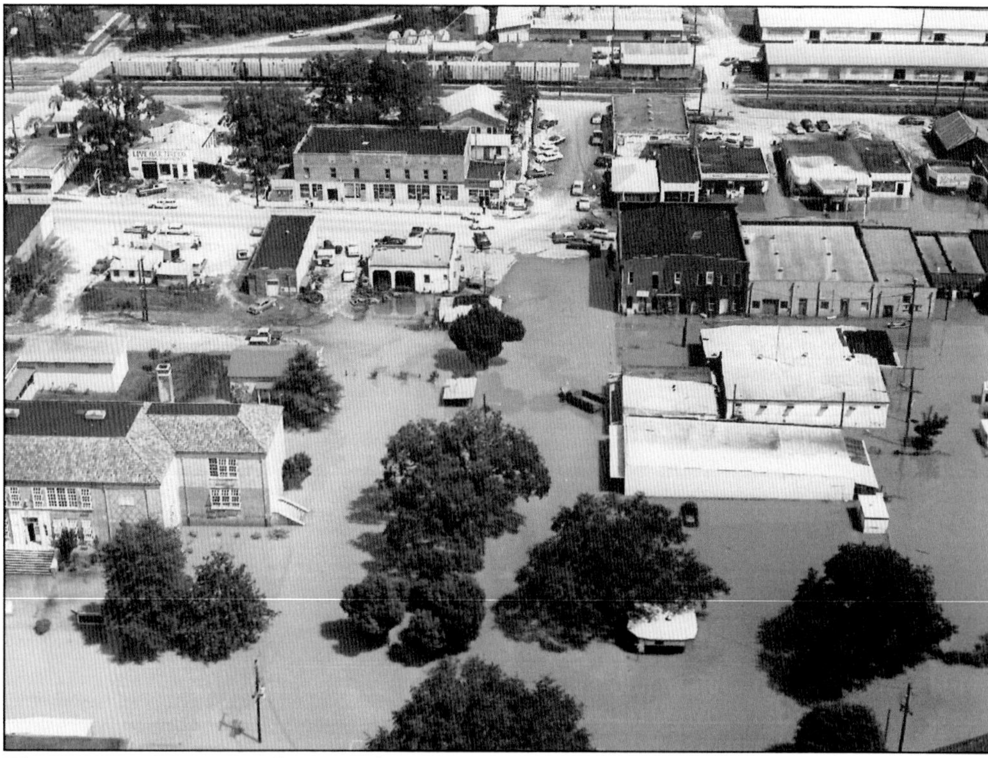

These are two more aerial views of Hurricane Dora's devastation. In the upper photograph, looking north, the high school stands in the middle left of the picture. Near the top center is the African American business section of town, called the "Hill" in politically correct circles today. The lower photograph shows the eastern city limits a few days after the flood. Rising in the top background are Thomas Dowling's original water tower (right) and a newer water tower to augment it. To their left are the passenger and freight depots as well as city hall. The area in the center and foreground had once been the site of several manufacturing and sawmill plants in Live Oak. In the top right can be seen the cleared land of the Suwannee County Recreation Department baseball fields. (Both, SCCC.)

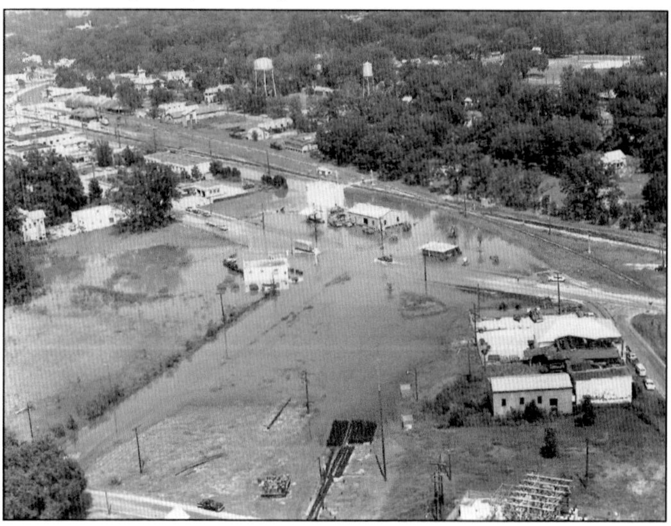

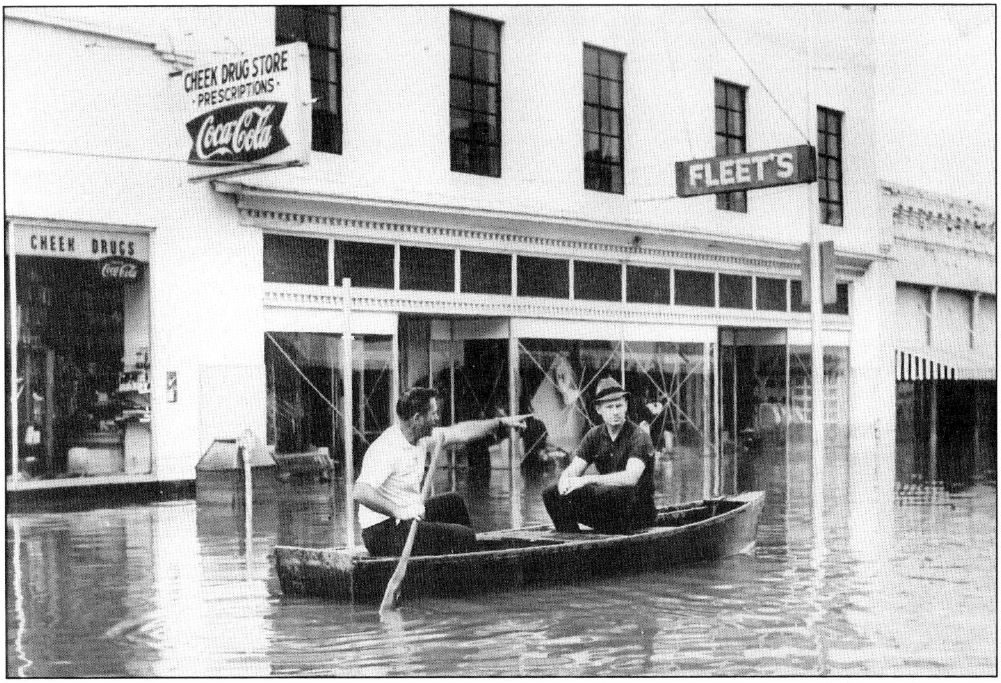

In the above photograph, two unknown gentlemen paddle their boat westward down the main thoroughfare of Howard Street shortly after Hurricane Dora swept through Suwannee County. The awning on the building to the right testifies to the height of the floodwaters. On the left side of the photograph is Cheek Drugstore, a long-serving local business that is now Cheek and Scott Drugstore and is located on US Highway 129. To its right is Fleet's Store, a business that served the community for many decades. In the photograph below, an unidentified man and three women paddle their way farther west along the same street. (Both, SCCC.)

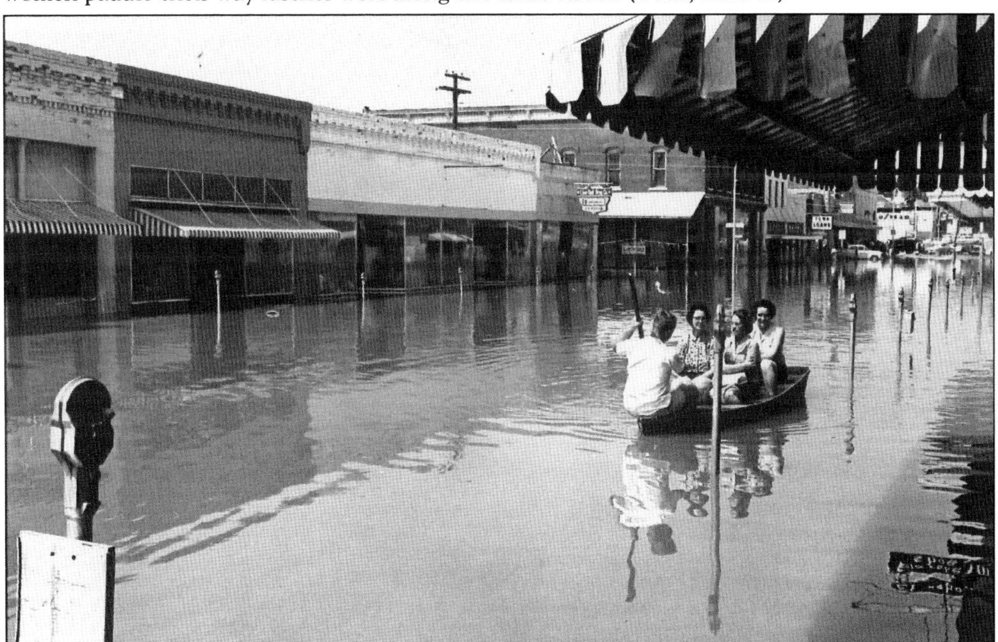

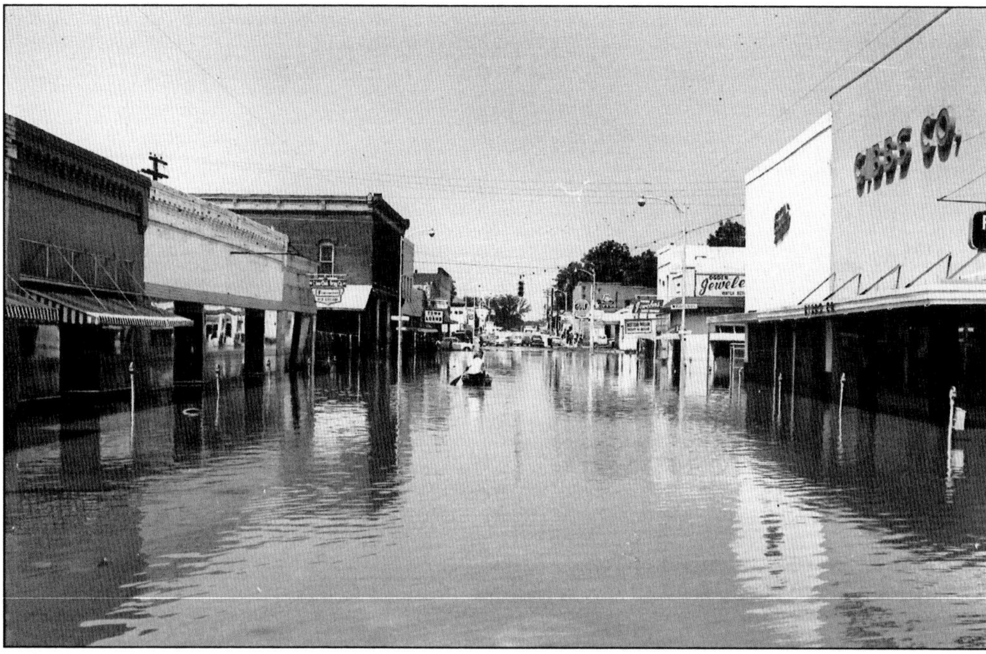

Taken near the same vantage point as the two photographs on the page before but from the middle of the street, this angle gives a better view of the amount of flooding that had occurred on the main thoroughfare of Howard Street during Hurricane Dora. In the right foreground stand Gibbs Company Store and Eagle's Store with part of their lower floors flooded. These two buildings would survive Dora only to be destroyed by arson that also destroyed the offices of the *Suwannee Democrat* and several smaller stores in 1995. Now, the land upon which they sat is the location of Millennium Park. (Both, SCCC.)

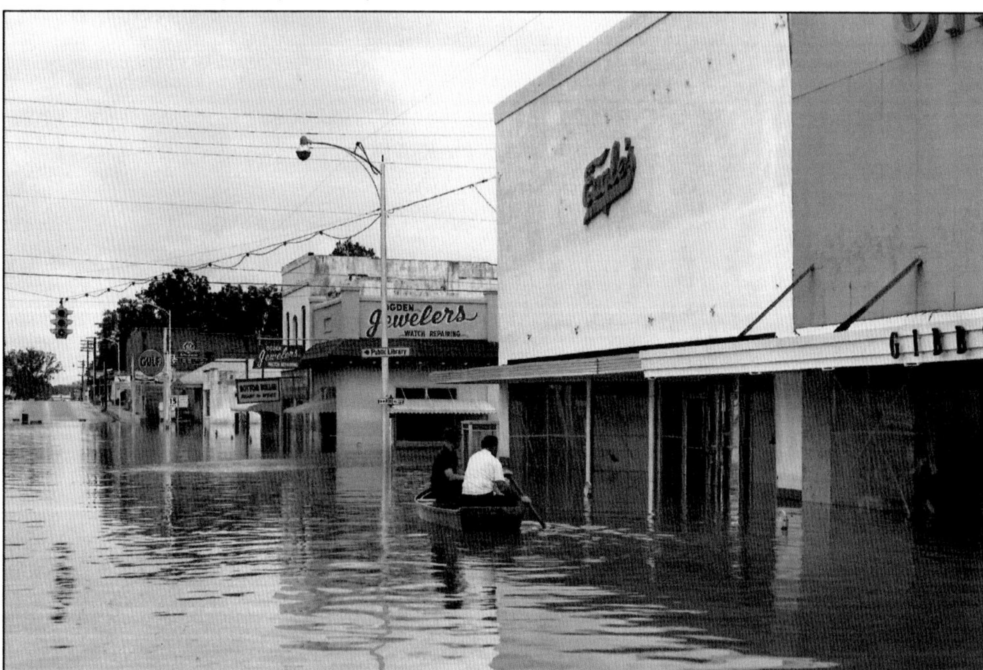

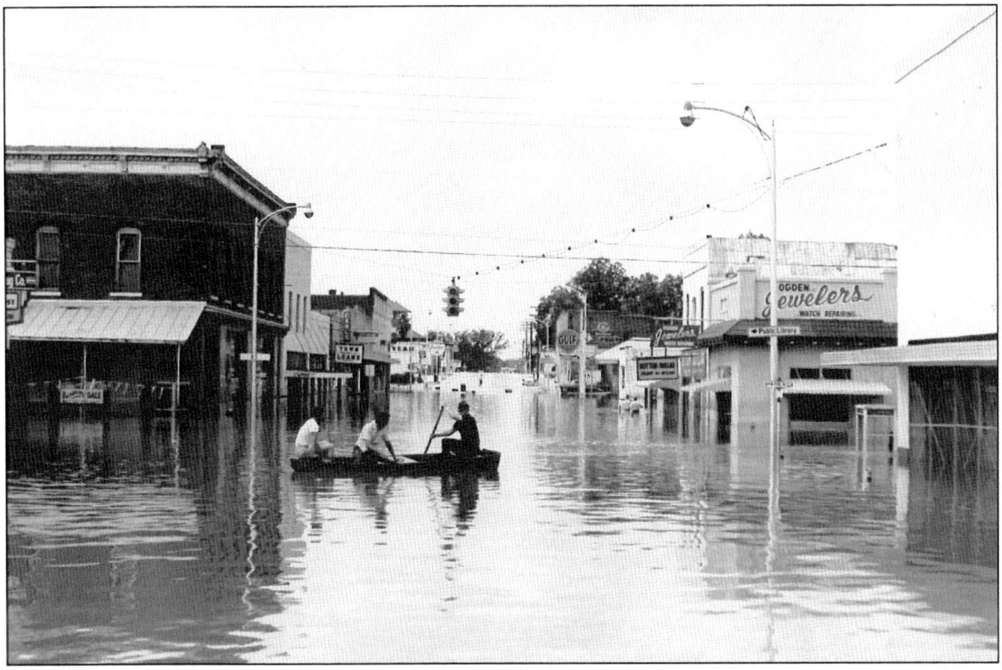

Moving westward along Howard Street, these two photographs show the intersection of Pine Avenue and Howard Street in some detail. Ogden Jewelers on the right was replaced by Morrison's Cleaners, which served the community for several decades before closing up in the first decade of the 21st century. An antique shop now operates in the building. The two-story, dark brick building on the left burned down in the late 1900s and was replaced by a park honoring Suwannee County's many veterans. In the center background, Howard Street can be seen rising out of the waters as it goes over one of Live Oak's small hills. (Both, SCCC.)

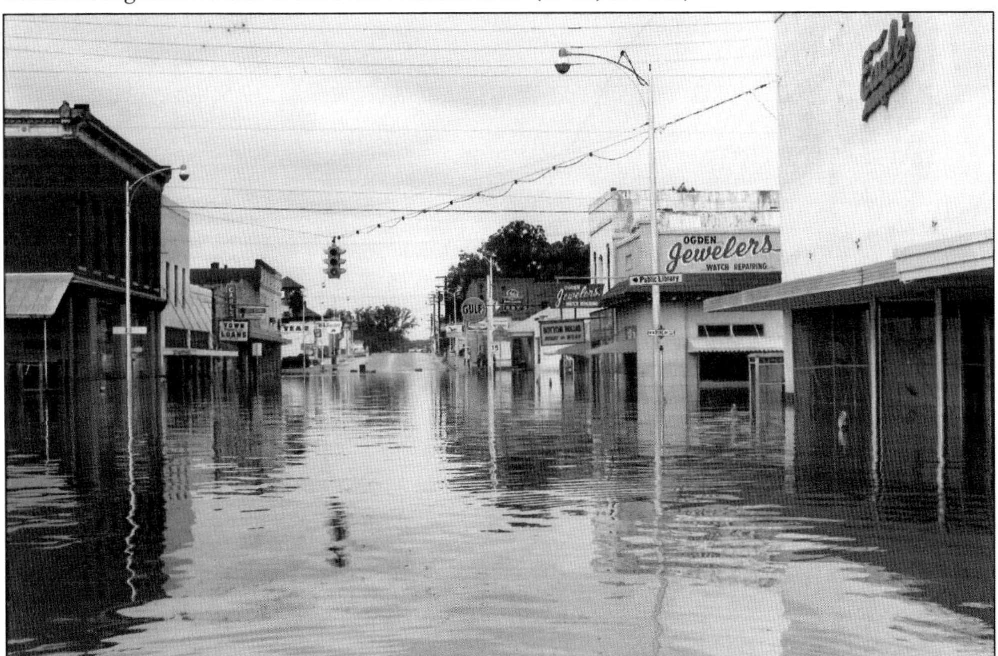

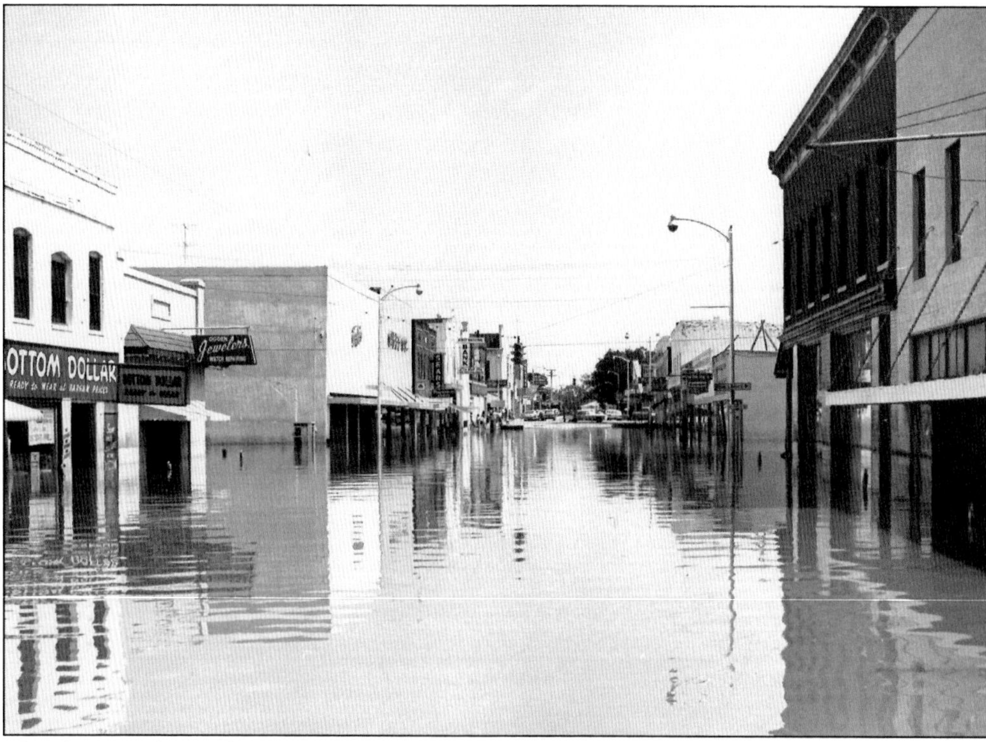

The photographs on this page show the flooding on West Howard Street, looking to the east. In the picture above, the Bottom Dollar bargain store is in the foreground at left, adjoining Ogden Jewelers. Bottom Dollar, long gone, has recently been replaced by a local specialty sewing business. Today, this district is the home of several community activities that use Millennium Park (where the buildings in the left background are) and Veterans' Park (where the dark building on the right is). In the picture below, Gibbs Company and the Sears store stand in front of the First National Bank and other businesses. The Gibbs building was burned down by arson in 1995, while the Sears store continues to operate today as J. Sherman Frier and Associates, Surveyors. (Both, SCCC.)

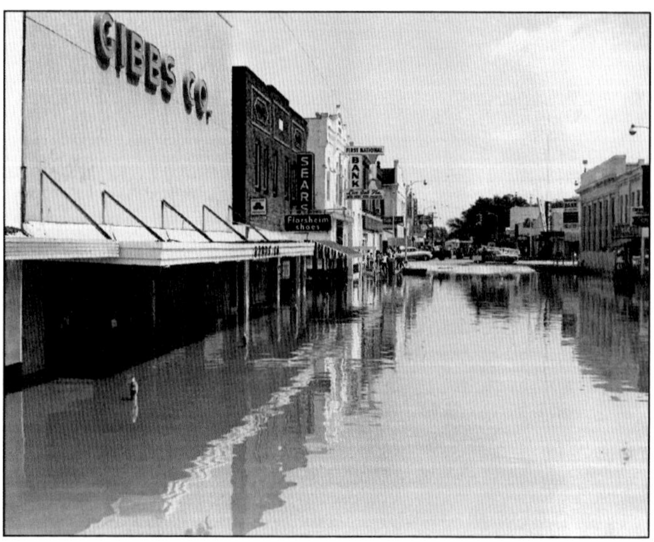

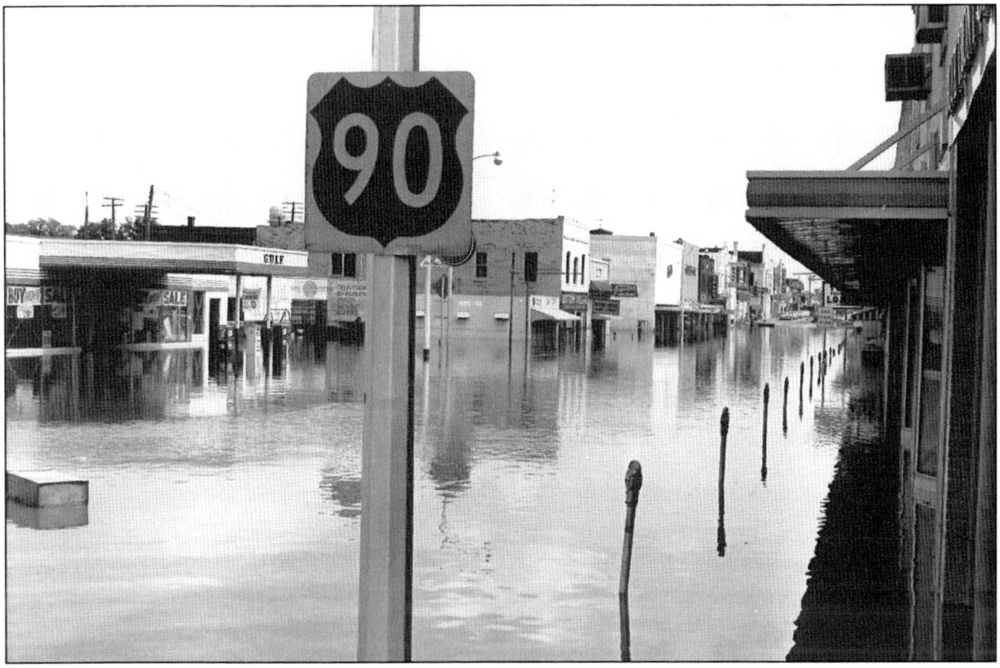

These photographs show West Howard Street, looking east. In the picture above, a US Highway 90 sign features prominently in the center foreground. In this period before the Interstate Highway System was completed, US Highway 90 was the main east-west thoroughfare through the northern part of the state; traffic had to be rerouted until the waters subsided. On the left side of the picture is Kirby's Gulf Station; it later became Howell's Office Supplies until it burned down in the first decade of the 21st century. In the picture below, the waters have begun to subside, and business owners are busy trying to salvage what they can. The car backed up to the Liberty National office stands in stark contrast to the motorboat moving less than 100 feet behind it. (Both, SCCC.)

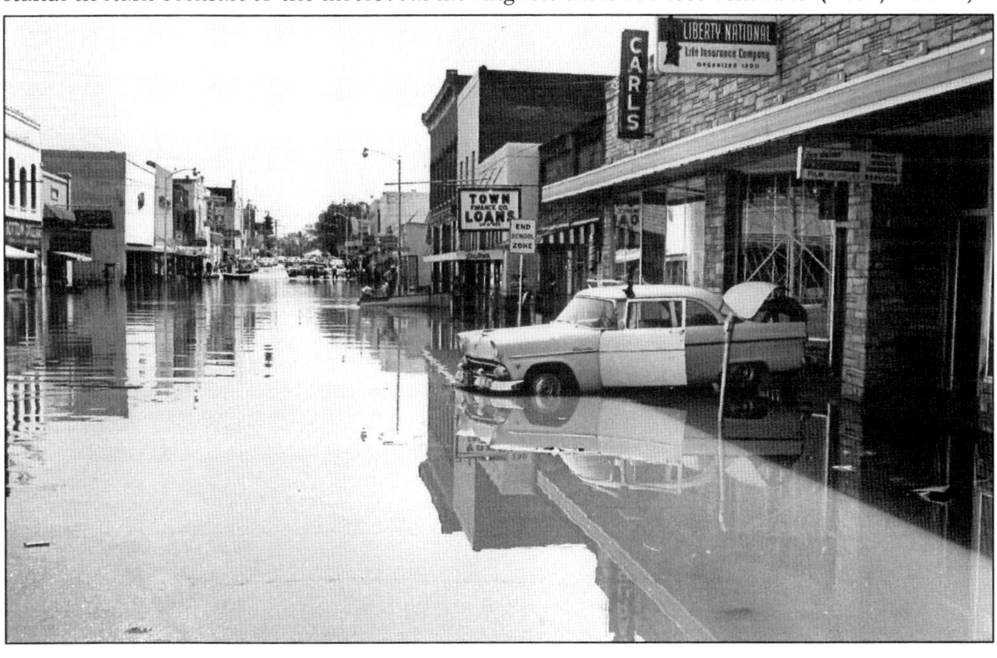

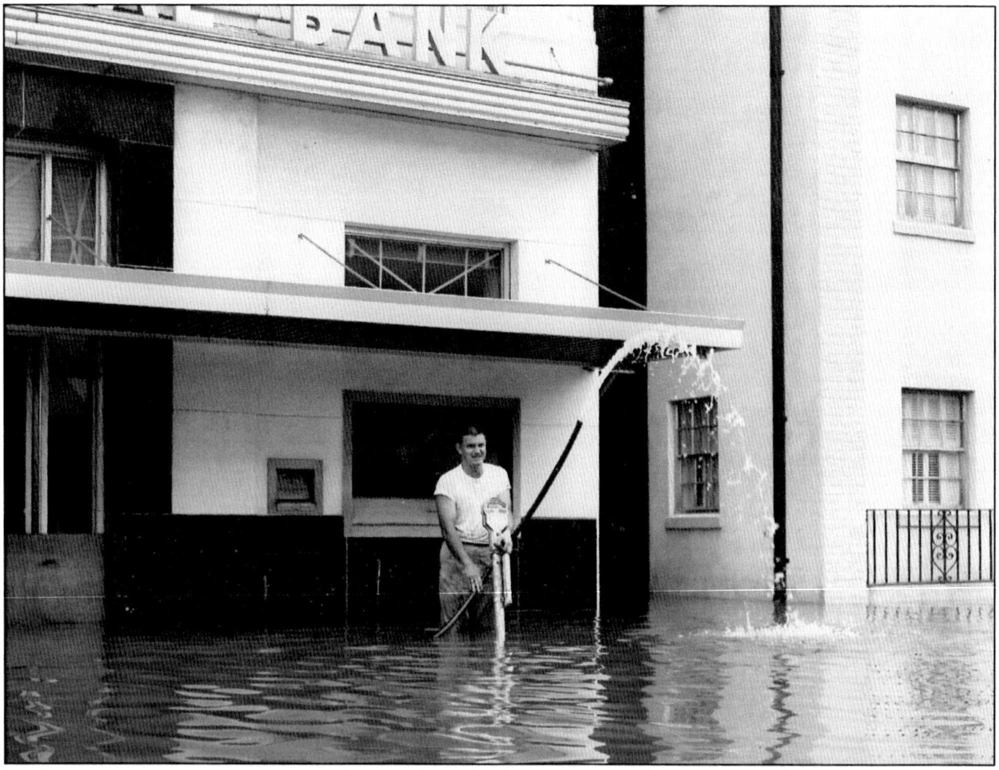

In these two pictures, readers can get a sense of the flood damage incurred by downtown Live Oak during Hurricane Dora. In the photograph above, water is being directed out of the First National Bank on West Howard Street. Notice that several days after the flooding, the floodwaters are still knee-high. In the photograph below, a local is seen standing in front of the bank's vault door, pointing to the high-water mark inside the building. As a result of this flood, First National Bank purchased property on higher ground across from the courthouse and constructed a new building in 1966; it stands today as Bank of America and has never flooded. (Both, SCCC.)

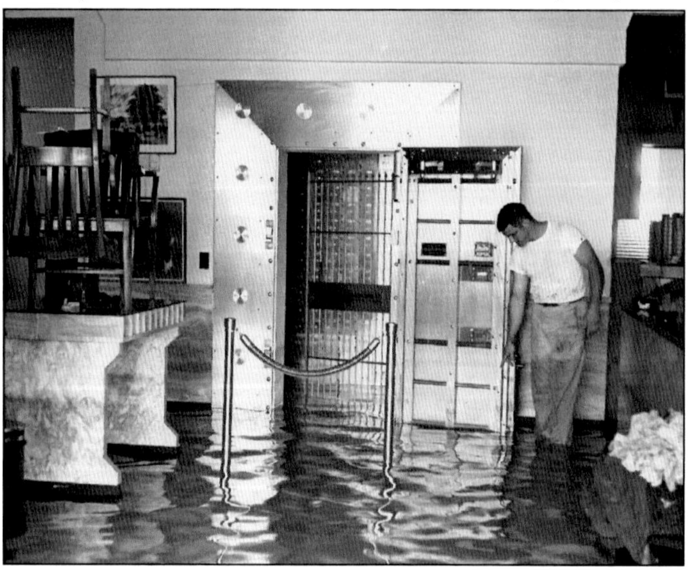

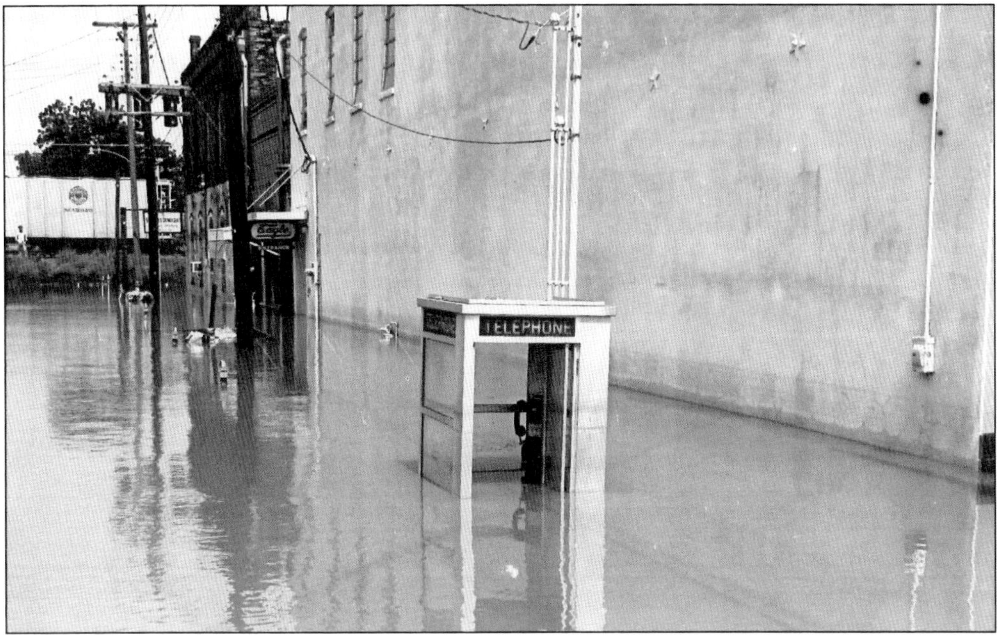

These two pictures show some of the flooding on Pine Avenue, running perpendicular to Howard Street, one block west of its main intersection with Ohio Avenue. In the picture above, a telephone booth stands half-flooded beside Eagle's. In the background center, the offices of the *Suwannee Democrat* show signs of flooding as well. These businesses would survive Dora only to be burned down in 1995; the loss of the *Suwannee Democrat* office was particularly unfortunate, because nearly a century of priceless newspapers were lost. In the picture below, the one-story Suwannee River Regional Library and two-story health department behind the courthouse show flood damage. (Both, SCCC.)

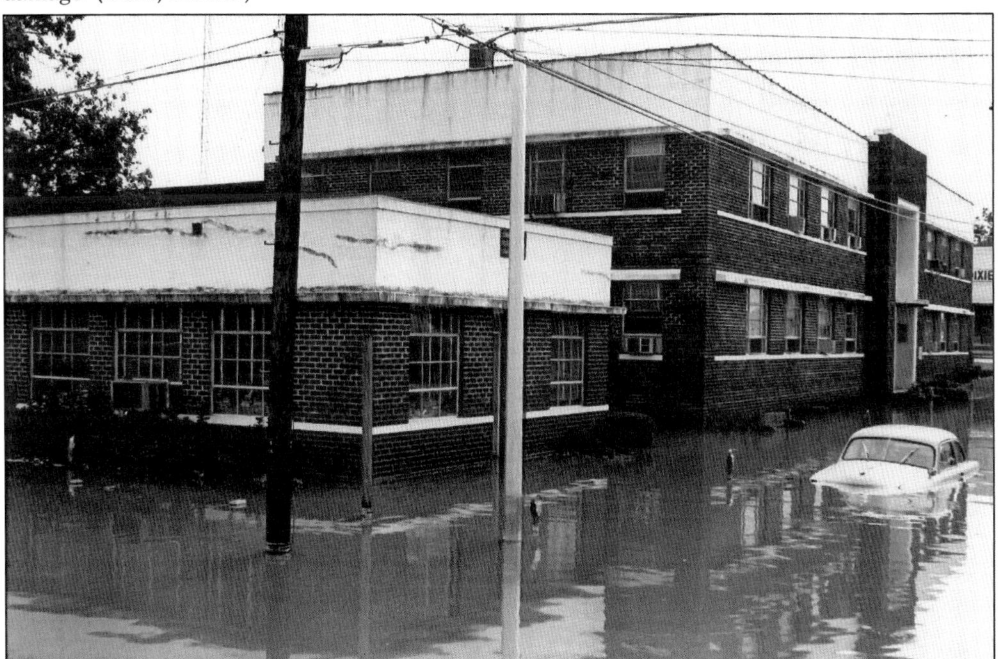

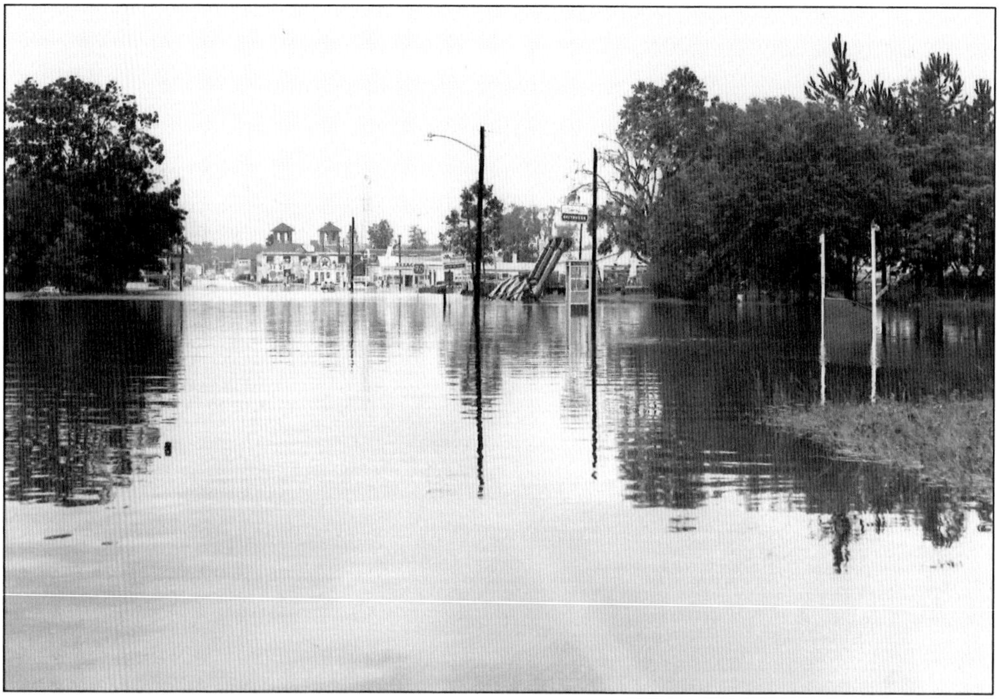

The photograph above catalogs devastation to the western side of Live Oak, looking east toward downtown. The twin bell towers of the old First Baptist Church rise in the center background with gas stations, farm implements, and the Greyhound bus station flooded in a line toward the camera. In the photograph below, part of north Live Oak is shown, looking south toward downtown. US Highway 129 lies flooded below many feet of water, as only the tops of houses poke out in the center of the picture. In the distant left background are the bell tower of the Second Advent Christian Church and city hall. Despite being flooded, the house shown on the right (behind the highway sign) remains occupied today. (Both, SCCC.)

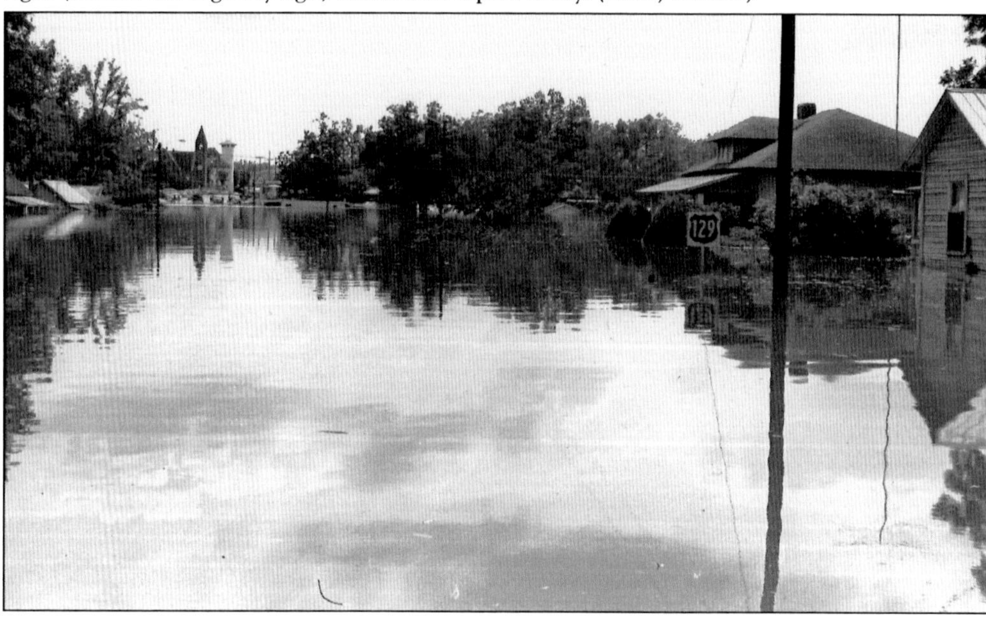

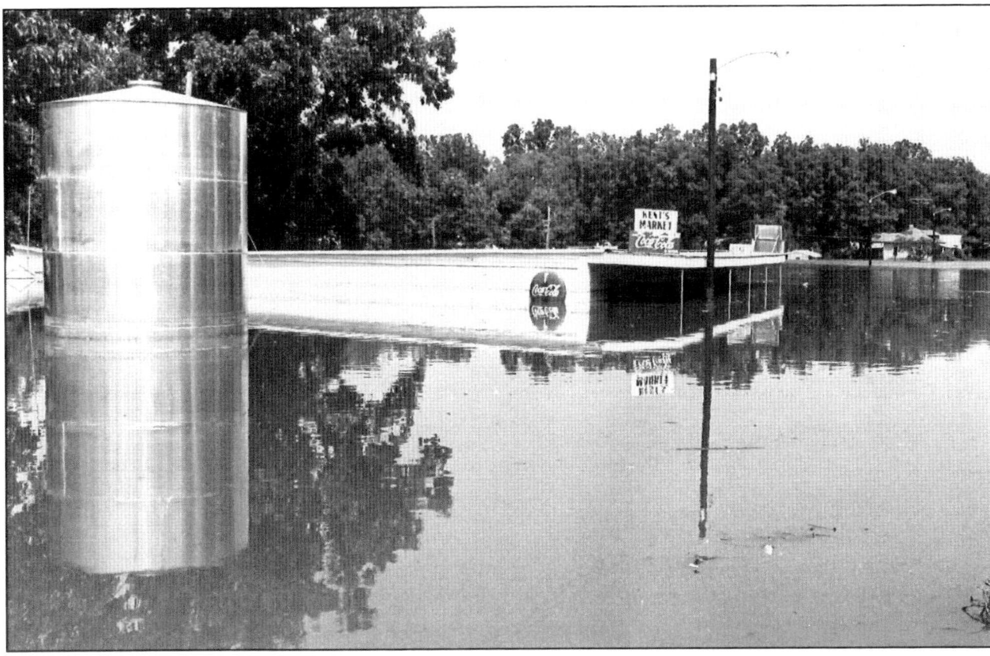

These two photographs show some of the heavier flooding on US Highway 129, just north of downtown Live Oak. In the picture above, looking north, Kent's Market still lies nearly covered by floodwaters several days after Hurricane Dora barreled through the county. The picture below was taken from the same vantage point as the picture above but looking west. Local residents use a motorboat to view the devastation along US Highway 129 and adjoining streets. The flooding here was exacerbated because it was, and still is, a natural low point between two hills. Although Kent's Market has long been out of business, the structure still stands today. (Both, SCCC.)

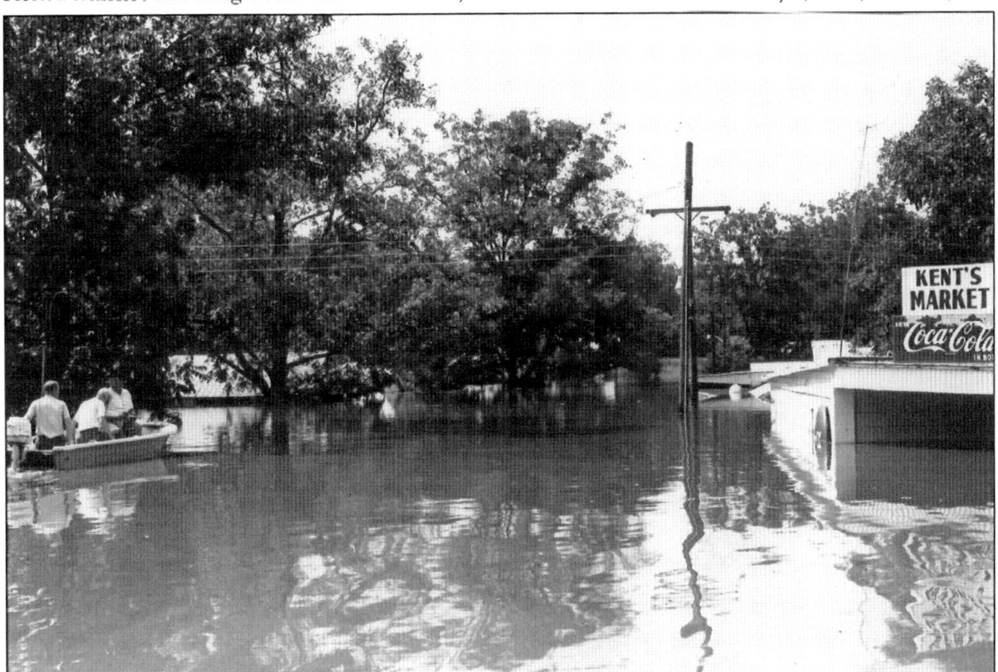

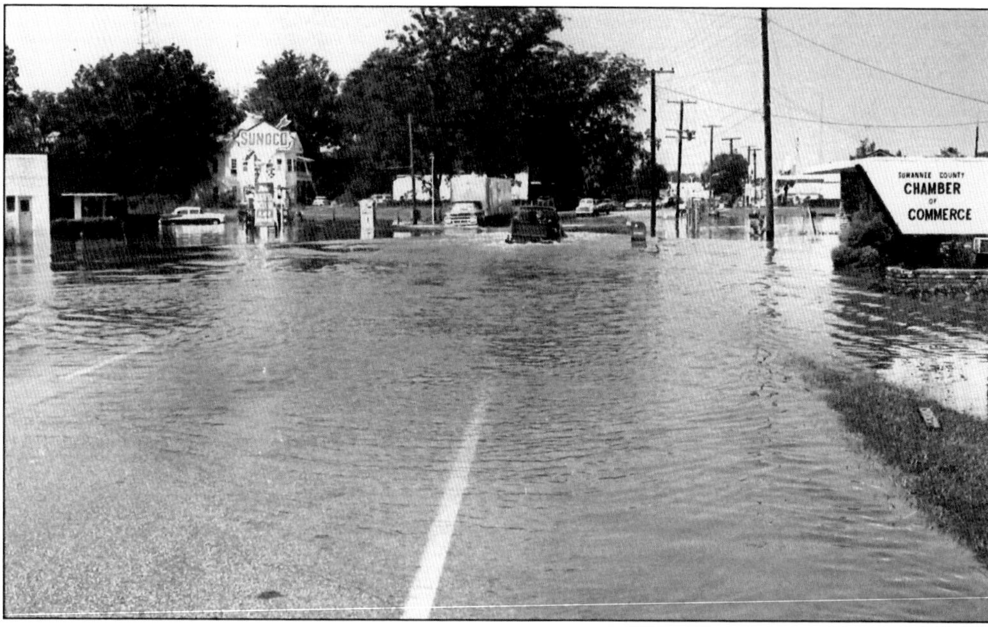

The photograph above shows some of the devastation on the east side of town along Howard Street, looking west into downtown Live Oak. A new city hall would be built in the 1970s in the background center, where the large trees are located in this picture. In the picture below, Florida governor Farris Bryant discusses the flood situation with Maj. Gen. Louie C. Wadsworth of the Florida National Guard. Wadsworth was a native of Suwannee County and had been a former company commander of the Live Oak National Guard unit. In honor of his services to Suwannee County, the new Live Oak armory had been named the Louie Wadsworth National Guard Armory in 1958; it continues to serve the community today. (Both, SCCC.)

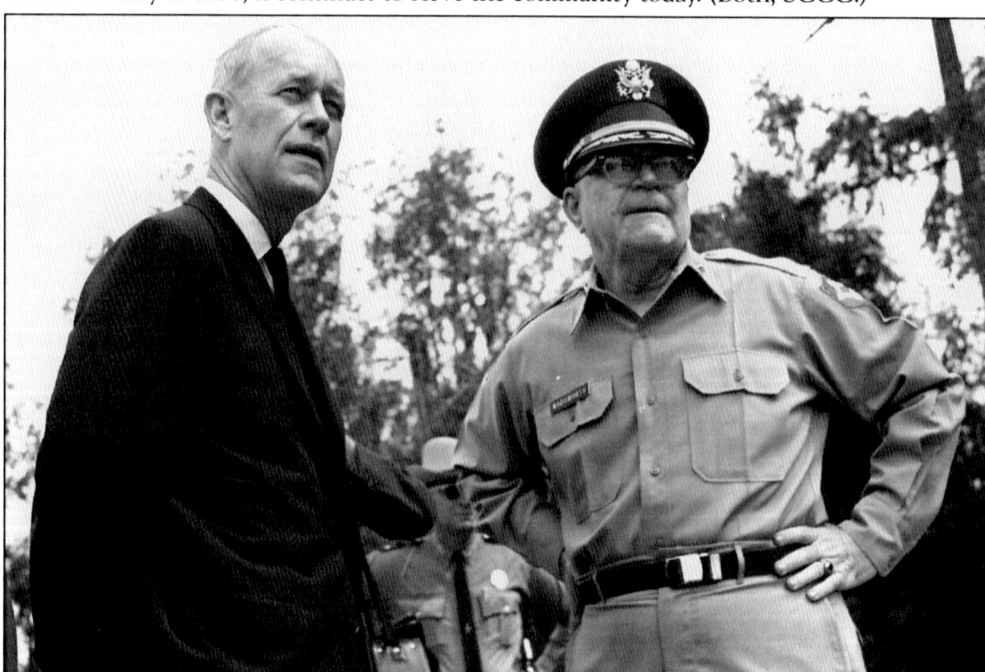

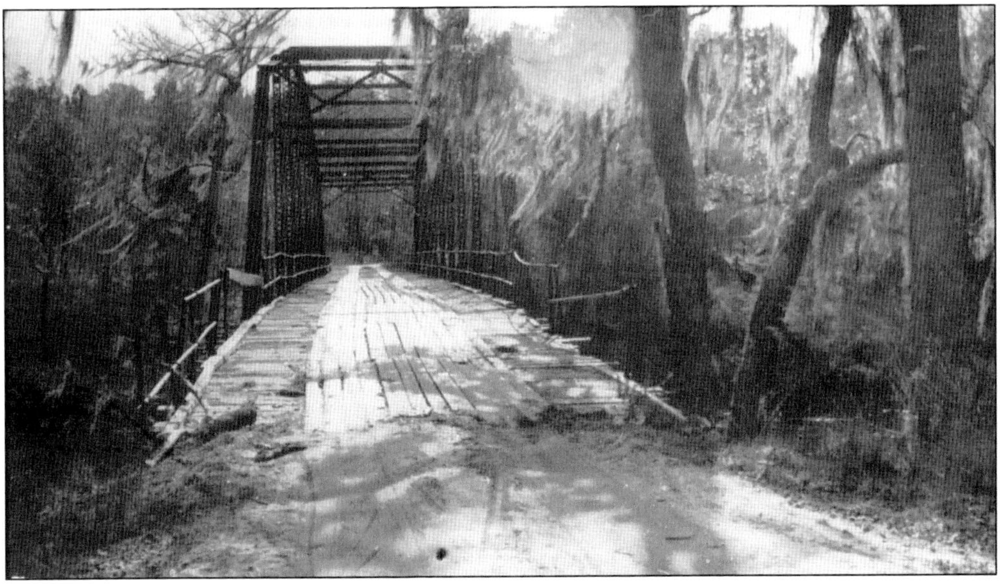

Sadly, some disasters in Suwannee County's history could have been avoided. The fact that the Suwannee River spans three sides of the county has proven to be a hindrance at times, as has the fact that Suwannee County is a rural county with limited funding. The picture above shows the old Nobles Ferry Bridge on January 19, 1952; it had been constructed in the early years of the 20th century, when automobiles first became common. By the middle of the century, the bridge was in need of replacement but soldiered on long after it was not safe for use. Notice the wooden planks laid lengthways along the bridge. The picture below shows part of the floor of the same bridge, explaining the reason for the extra planks. It is a wonder folks continued to use the rickety bridge!

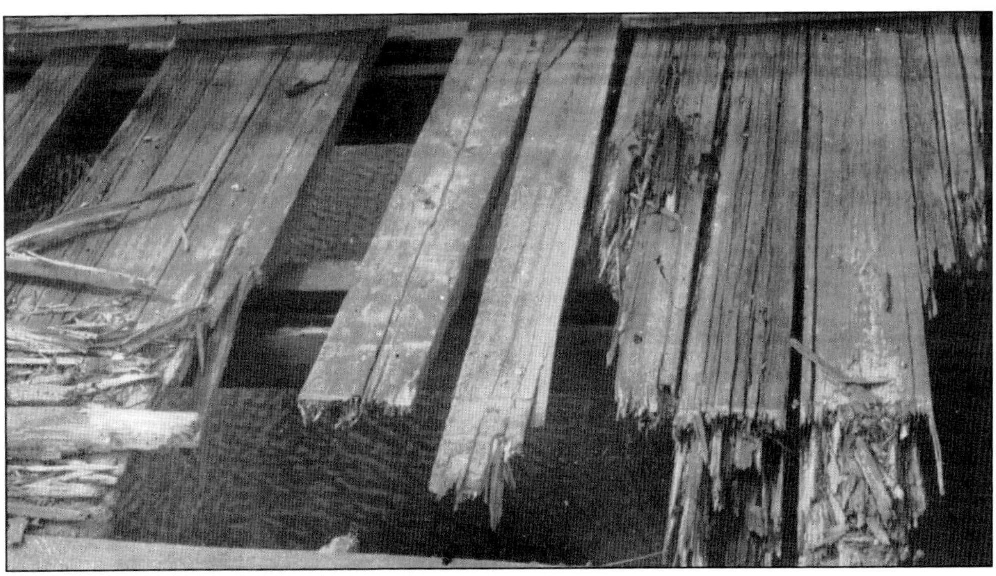

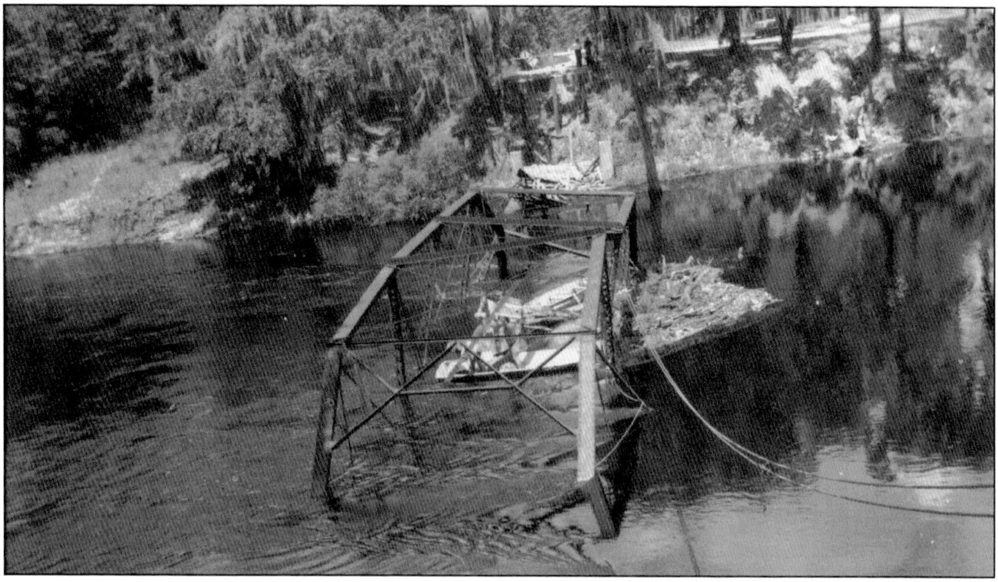

To the horror of onlookers, the Nobles Ferry Bridge collapsed on September 5, 1969, as a truck attempted to cross the old, weakened structure. The metal frame could no longer take the weight of such a large vehicle and crashed into the Suwannee River below, cutting off access to Hamilton County from this route for months. The pictures on this page show the Nobles Ferry Bridge shortly after it collapsed. Debris and even a couple of boats have built up around the remains of the structure. Fortunately, the bridge would be replaced by a modern structure, which continues in use today to link Suwannee and Hamilton Counties along the old Nobles Ferry Road.

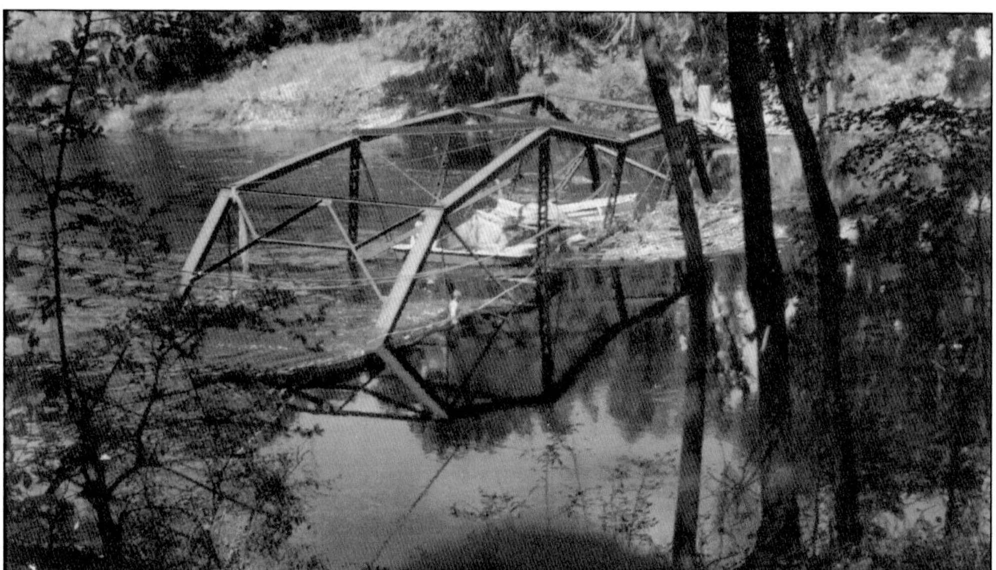

Six

Changing Times

The 1950s and 1960s was a period of great change for Suwannee County, as it was for the entire nation. The civil rights movement was in full swing, culminating in the desegregation of the South. The United States became embroiled in the Vietnam conflict during this same period, and many of Suwannee County's men went off to war. Social equality was a hot-button topic, with the 1952 murder of white Dr. Clifford LeRoy Adams, prominent physician and recently elected state legislator, by Ruby McCollum, an African American woman of high standing, taking center stage for part of this time.

Hurricane Dora, mentioned in the previous chapter, did much to change the landscape of Suwannee County and Live Oak in particular. As with other disasters, Suwannee County recovered from Hurricane Dora, although some of the historic homes and businesses that had been built at the beginning of the 20th century were torn down because of flood damage. Some buildings that had escaped Hurricane Dora fell victim to progress, being torn down and replaced by modern homes and businesses. Other buildings, such as the courthouse, were more fortunate, and renovations and additions have allowed its old charm to continue to serve as a landmark in the community.

Today, Suwannee County continues as an agrarian community with various industries dotting the landscape. Many people are multigenerational Suwannee Countians, but others are drawn to the area for its relaxed atmosphere and conservative values.

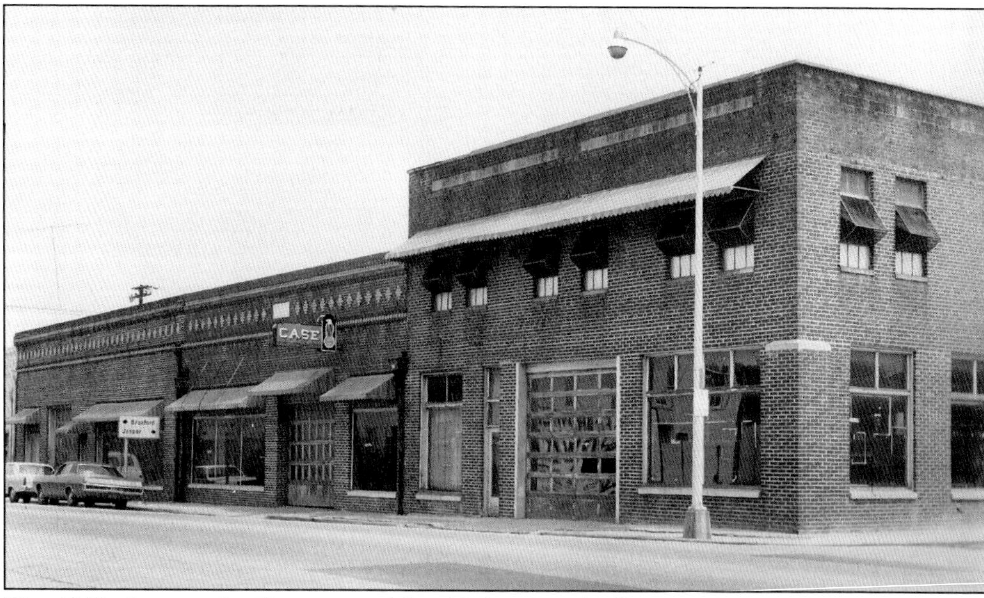

This 1960s photograph offers a view of the old abandoned Allison Ford Dealership. The one-story portion of the building was eventually torn down, but the two-story structure on the right was later bought and remodeled by the Poole Realty Agency, which continues to use it today. This photograph is a good comparison to the one on page 42. (SCCC.)

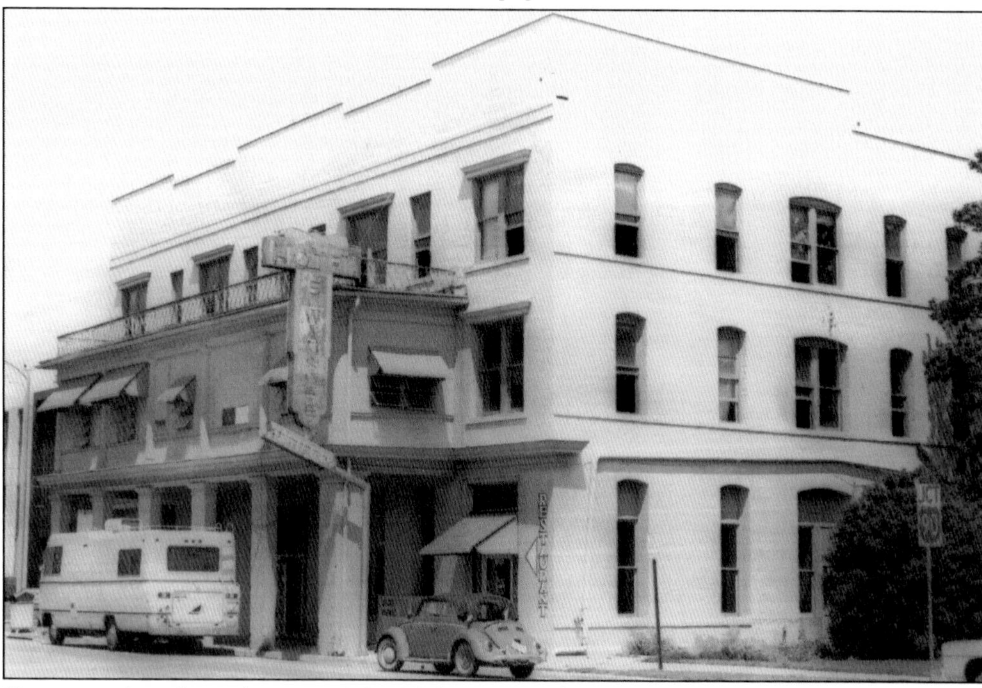

Constructed in the early years of the 20th century, the Suwannee Hotel epitomized the high status of Live Oak at the time. Used as a luxurious stop for railroad travelers, its fame was carried throughout Florida and beyond. Unfortunately, by the middle of the century, the hotel had lost much of its grandeur. This photograph, taken around 1965, shows the Suwannee Hotel in its last years.

The Suwannee River Regional Library System is the oldest regional rural library system in the state of Florida, having been established in 1958. In 1948, a one-story structure had been built behind the courthouse to replace an old house originally used as a library (seen on page 71). In 1966, a two-story addition was constructed. The photograph on the right shows the one-story portion in 1966, while the lower photograph shows the newly completed two-story addition the same year. Both portions were torn down in 2001, along with the old jail behind them, because of possible subsurface movement; the space is now used for courthouse parking. (Both, SCCC.)

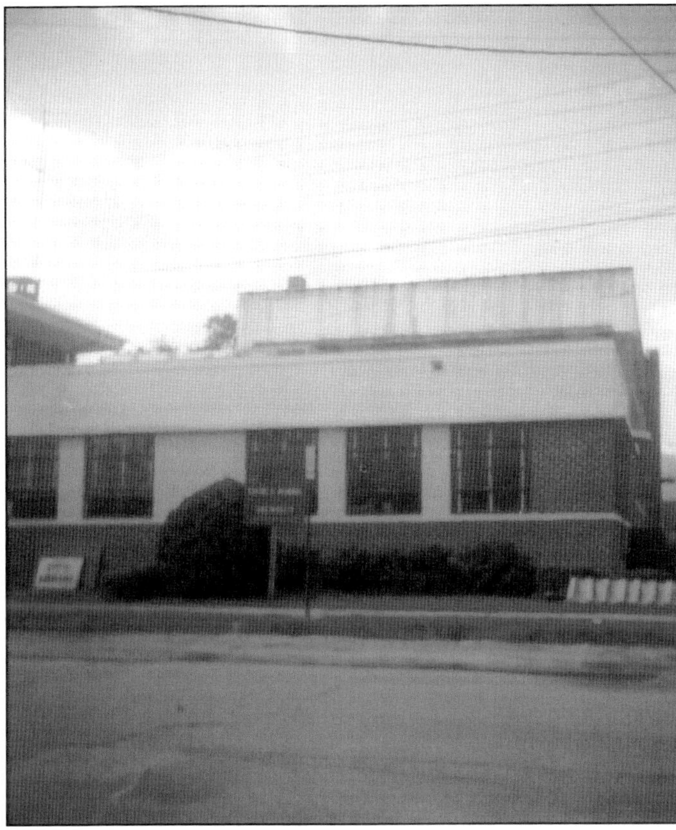

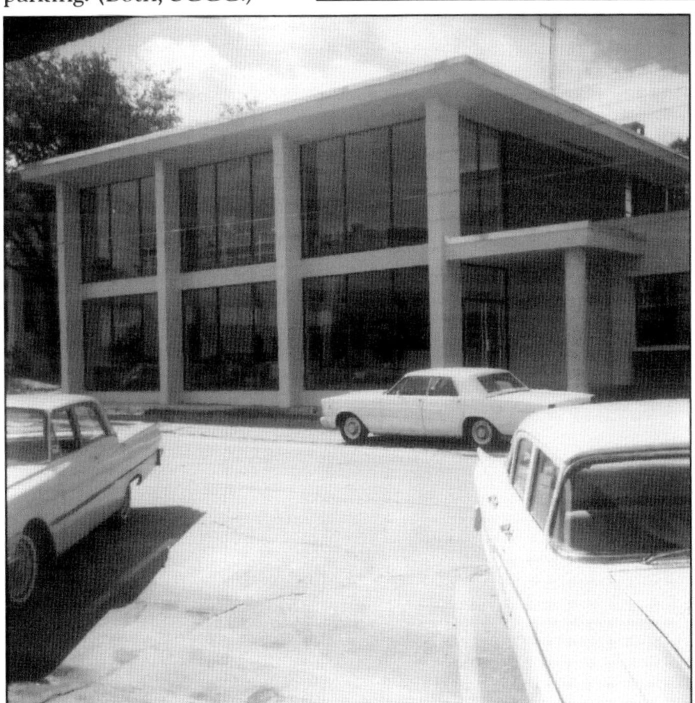

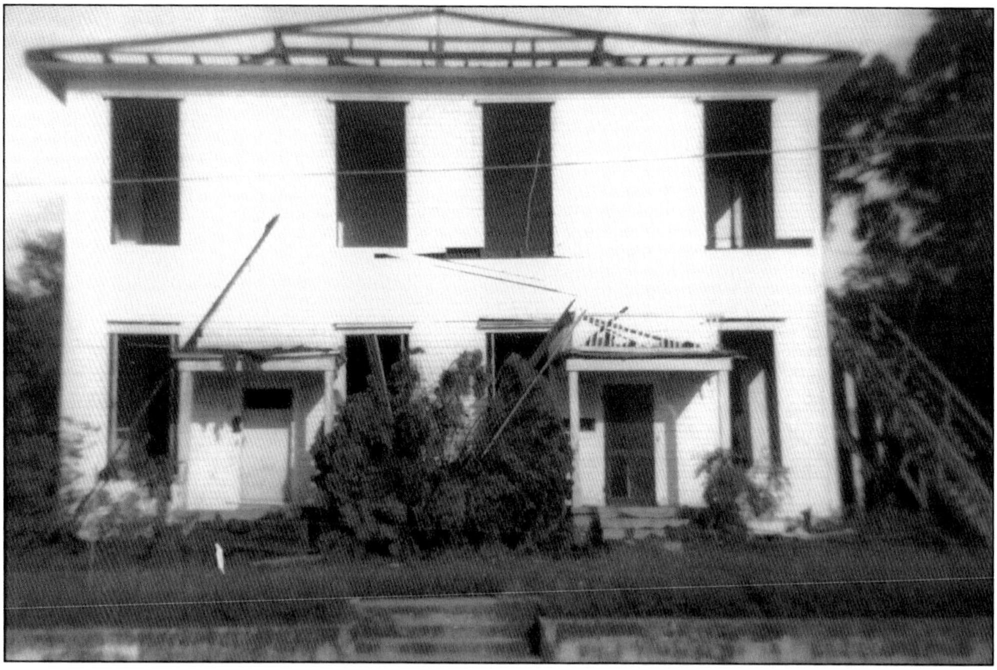

Among the victims of progress during the last 40 years of the 20th century was the old courthouse. Originally built in 1873–1874, it had been moved across Wilbur Street when the new brick courthouse was constructed in 1904. Thereafter, it had served as an apartment complex. By 1966, the building was old and in need of repairs or replacement. In a move that angers historians today, the old courthouse was torn down and replaced by a parking lot. These two photographs, taken from different views, show the old courthouse in 1966; notes on the back indicate that repairs were being made after storm damage, but it is more likely that this was demolition work.

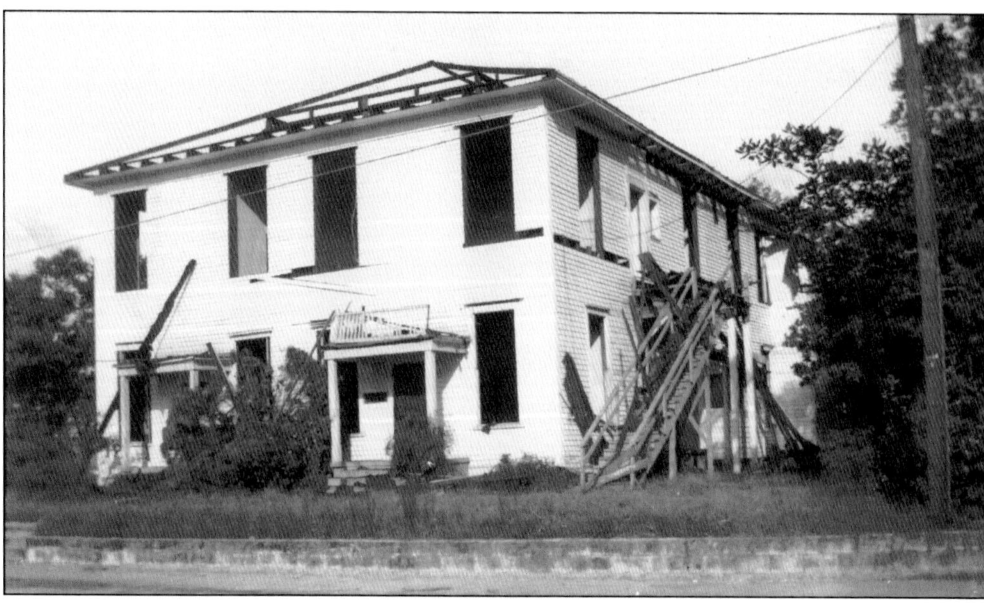

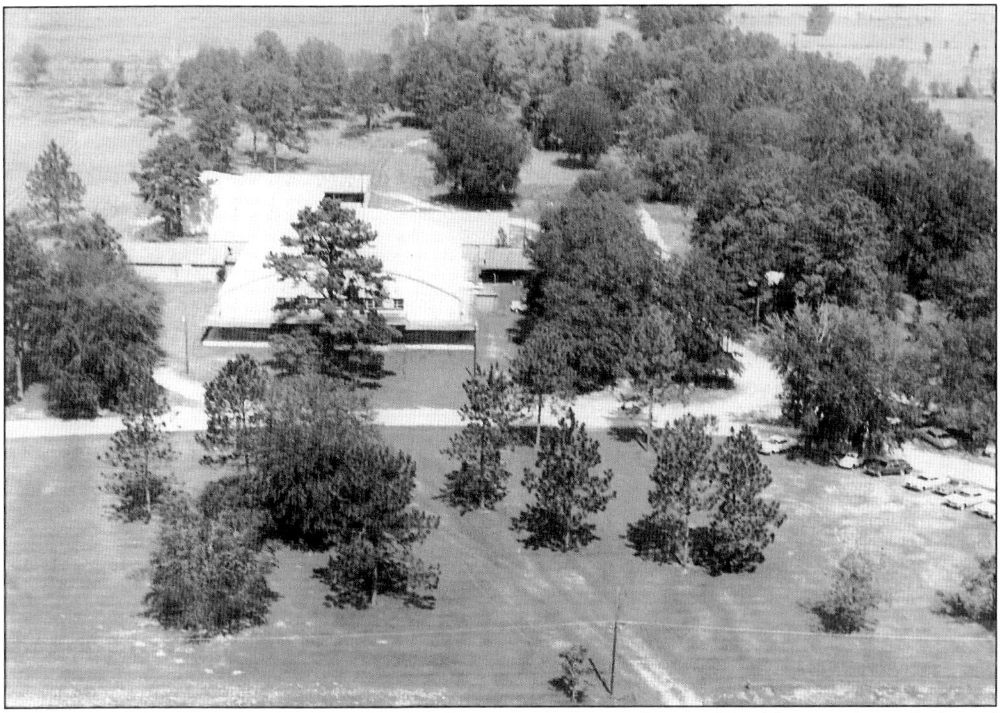

The last 50 years of the 20th century saw the construction of several buildings in Live Oak and beyond. In the above 1960s aerial picture, looking north, the Suwannee County Coliseum rises among farmland on the western outskirts of town. Constructed in 1955 on Newbern Road (County Road 136), the coliseum has been renovated and expanded and continues to serve the community in a variety of capacities today. In the below photograph, taken at the same time, the Louie C. Wadsworth Armory stands in the right foreground with the coliseum and accompanying buildings beyond it. The armory continues to serve the local 269th Engineering Detachment today. Dozens of homes, a new hospital, and other features now dot this landscape as well. (Both, SCCC.)

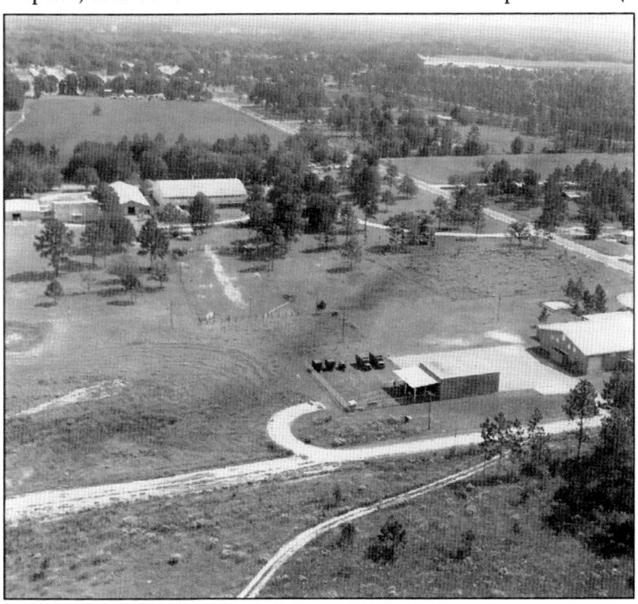

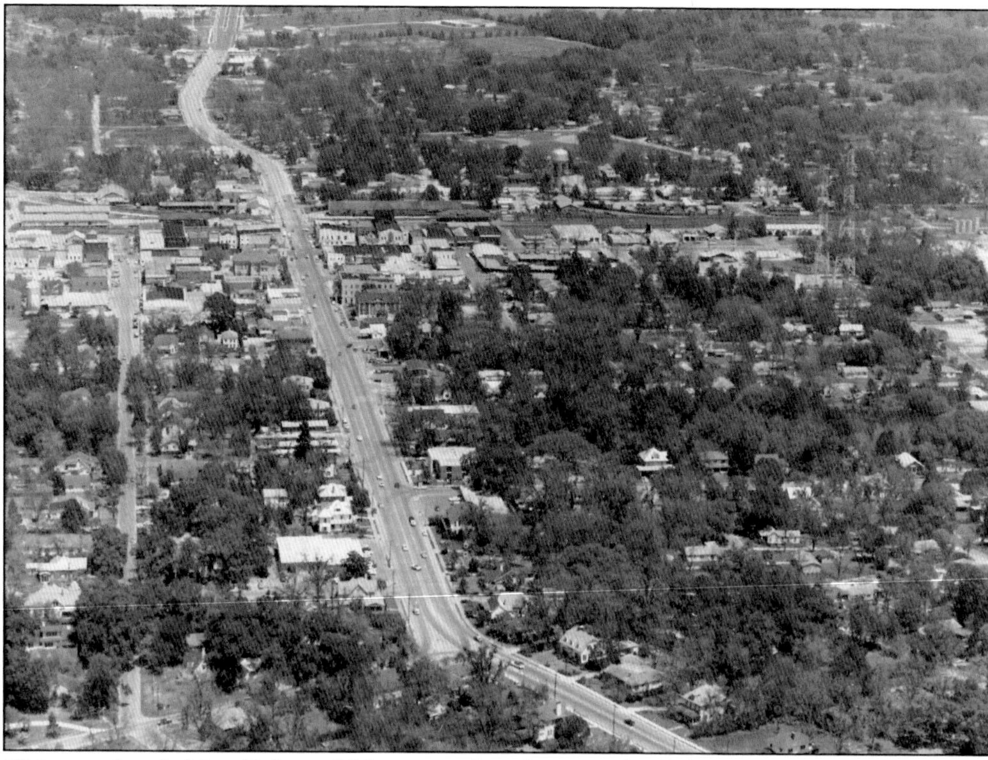

Citizens of early Live Oak would be amazed at the growth of their city today. In these two photographs, taken around 1970, downtown Live Oak sprawls for several miles. In the photograph above, taken looking north, the downtown business district takes up the background, while farther south, numerous homes and businesses stand among the trees. Land at the bend of US Highway 129, at the bottom center, was considered "way out of town" 100 years ago, yet today, it is closer to the geographic center of the city. In the photograph below, the west side of the business district rises in the foreground, while the recently completed Interstate 10 is faintly visible in the background; at the time of this photograph, there are no gas stations or fast food restaurants there. (Both, SCCC.)

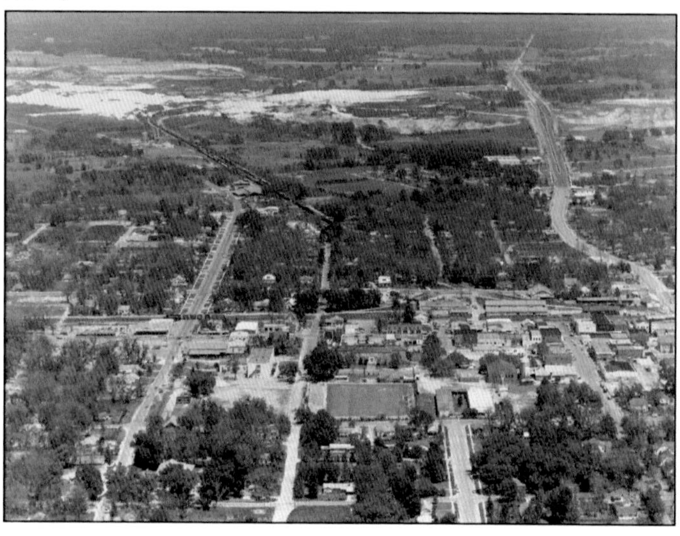

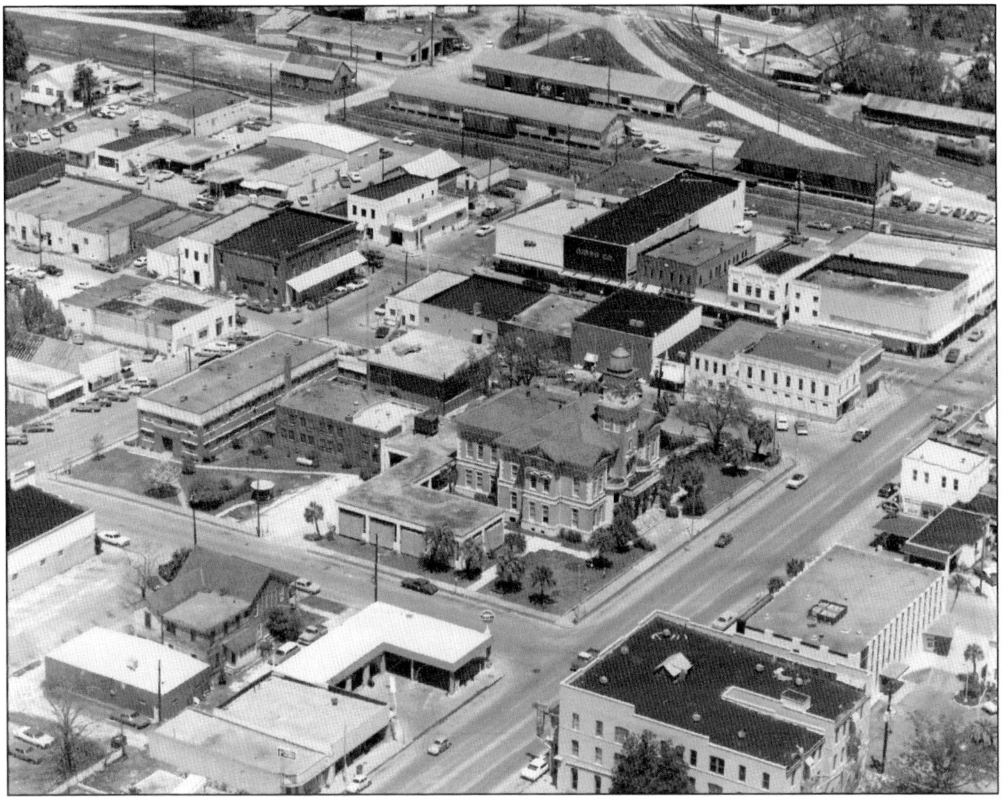

These two photographs were taken at the same time as those on the preceding page but are from a closer viewpoint. In the photograph above, the courthouse rises in the center of the view, with the 1964 courthouse addition connecting it to the old jail behind it; the library and health department (now property appraiser and tax collector's offices) complete the block. On the right-hand side of the picture across the street, the recently completed First National Bank is dwarfed by the three-story Suwannee Hotel in the right foreground. In the photograph below, a recently completed shopping mall on the eastern side of town occupies what only a few years prior had been pastures. (Both, SCCC.)

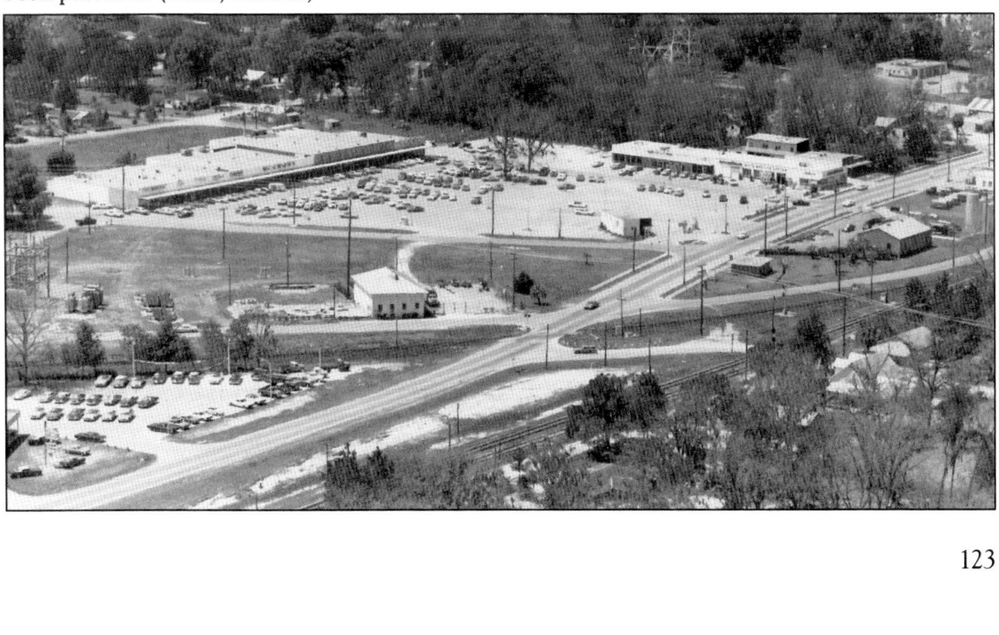

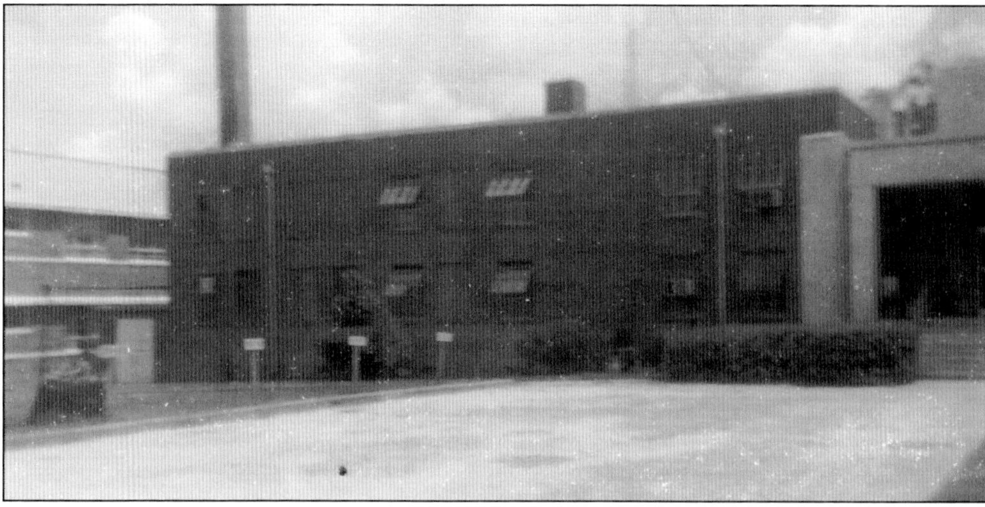

The Suwannee County Jail, constructed in 1938, housed many inmates during its 55-year history. This photograph shows the jail in 1971, by this time adjoining the courthouse through the 1964 courthouse addition. The jail would be torn down in 2001 after a new jail was constructed next to it.

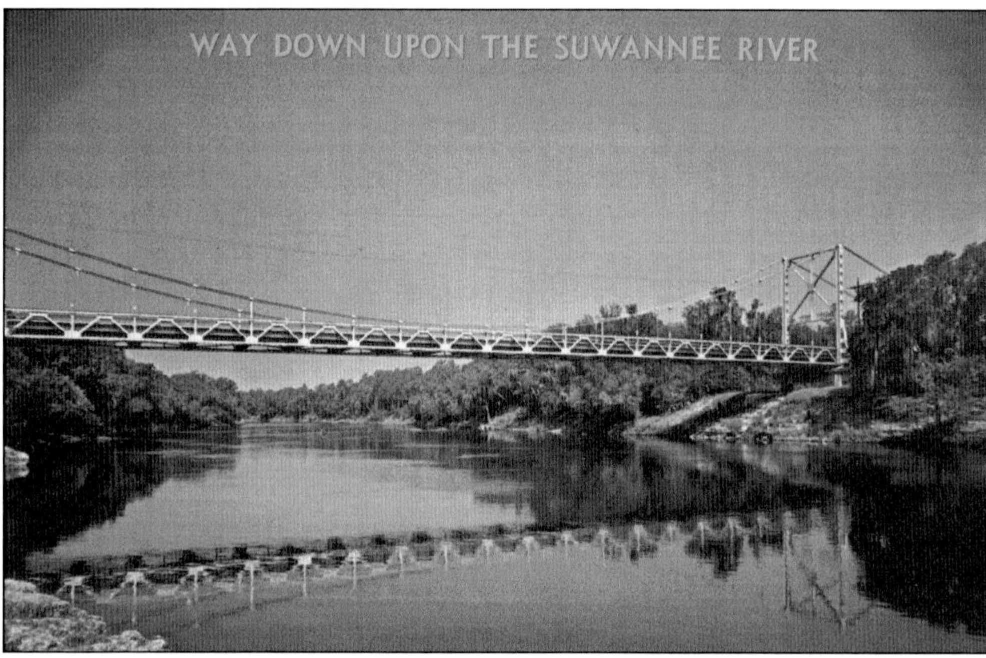

The Hal Adams Bridge, dedicated in 1947 as the first suspension bridge in Florida, is one of Suwannee County's more well-known bridges. Named after county and circuit judge Hal Adams, it continues to serve Suwannee County and neighboring Lafayette County today. This postcard shows the bridge in 1976; it looks practically the same today.

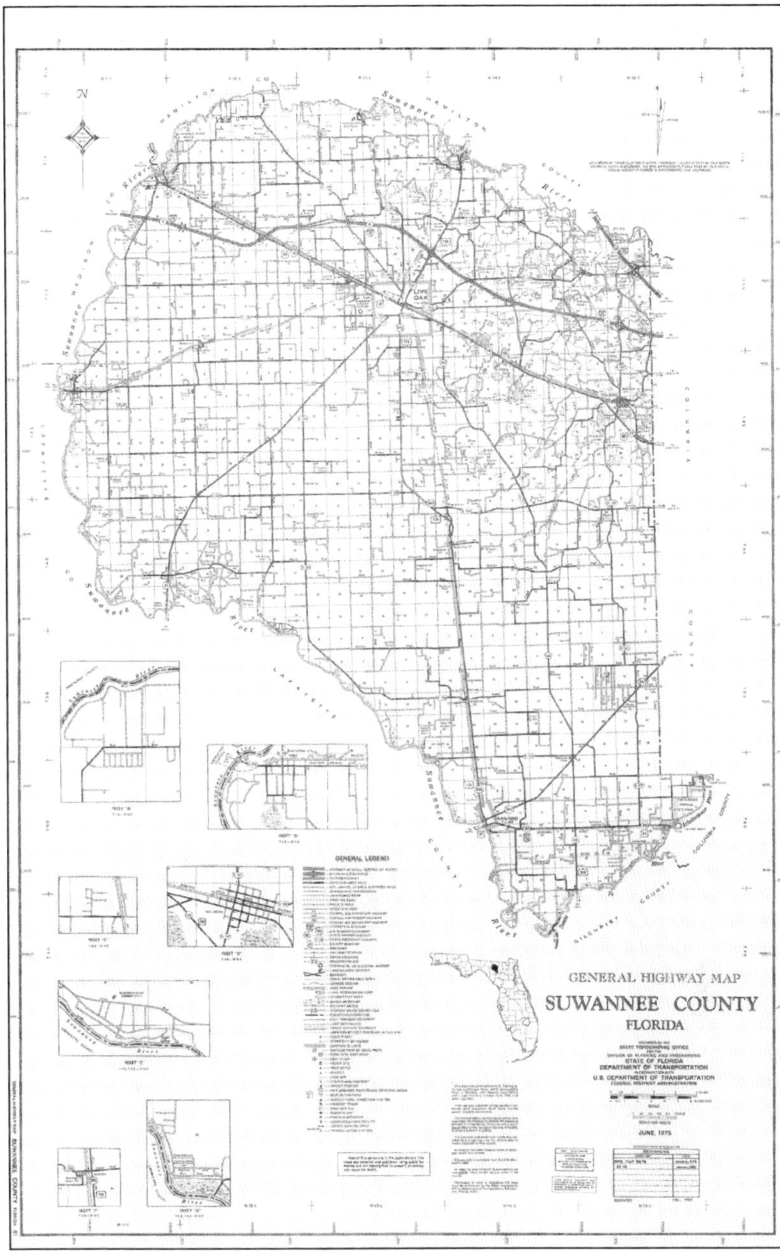

This 1975 map shows Suwannee County much as it still is today. As it has been for more than 100 years, Live Oak remains the hub of transportation services, with adequate access by railroad, state and local roads, and more recently, by Interstate 10, running just north of the downtown area. In the outlying areas, and joining Live Oak via state roads, are Wellborn to the east, Dowling Park to the west, and McAlpin, O'Brien, and Branford to the south. Interstate 75, a major north-south-running route into Florida, cuts through the northeastern part of the county. Numerous county roads, many of them still unpaved, allow access to the various farms, subdivisions, and homesteads throughout the county. Many of the churches that give Suwannee County its conservative values are marked, and a plethora of state and county parks, most revolving around the many springs, complete the map. (David Phinney.)

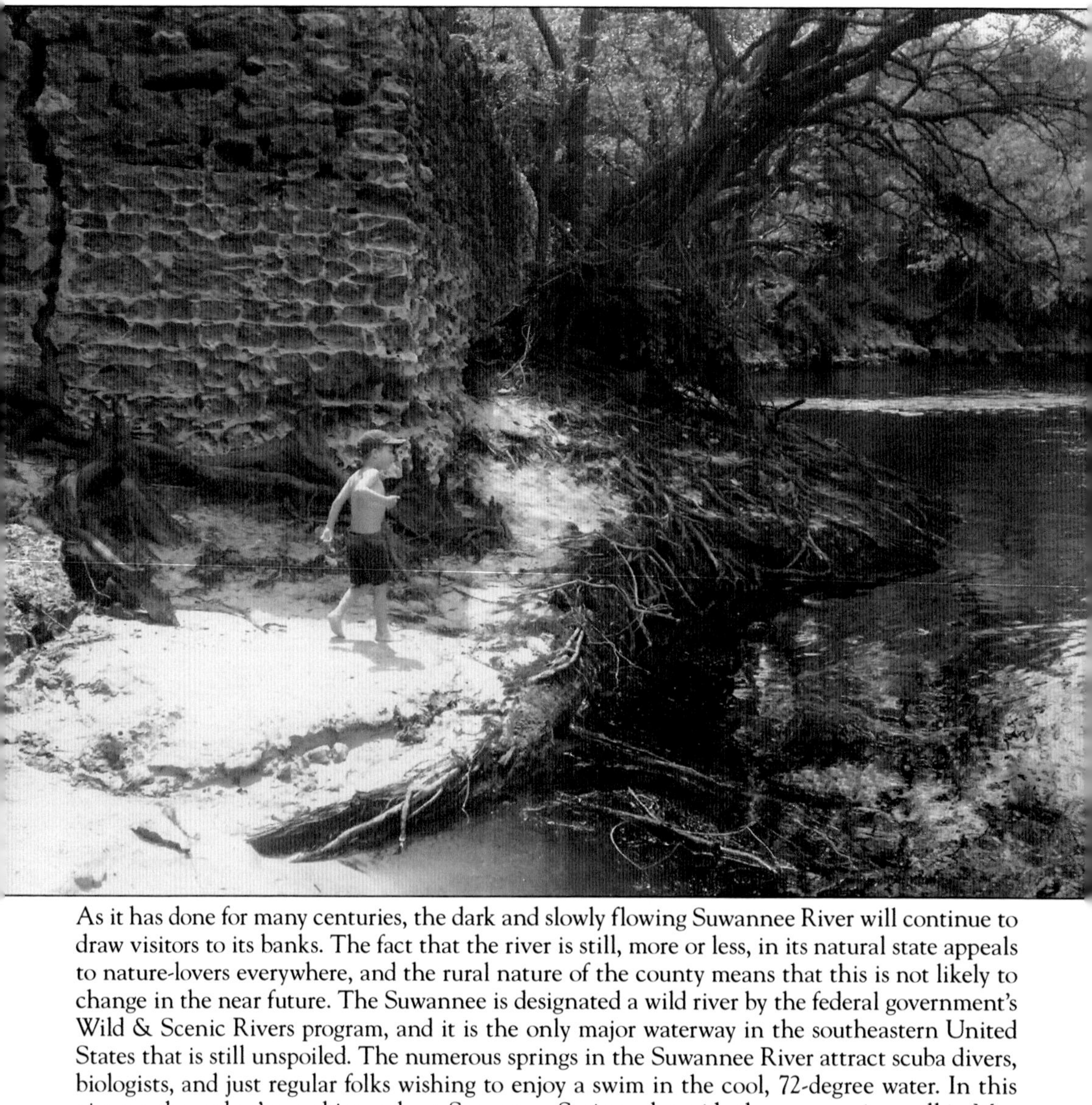

As it has done for many centuries, the dark and slowly flowing Suwannee River will continue to draw visitors to its banks. The fact that the river is still, more or less, in its natural state appeals to nature-lovers everywhere, and the rural nature of the county means that this is not likely to change in the near future. The Suwannee is designated a wild river by the federal government's Wild & Scenic Rivers program, and it is the only major waterway in the southeastern United States that is still unspoiled. The numerous springs in the Suwannee River attract scuba divers, biologists, and just regular folks wishing to enjoy a swim in the cool, 72-degree water. In this picture, the author's son skips rocks at Suwannee Springs alongside the stone spring wall in May 2008, much like others have been doing for well over 100 years. (Author.)

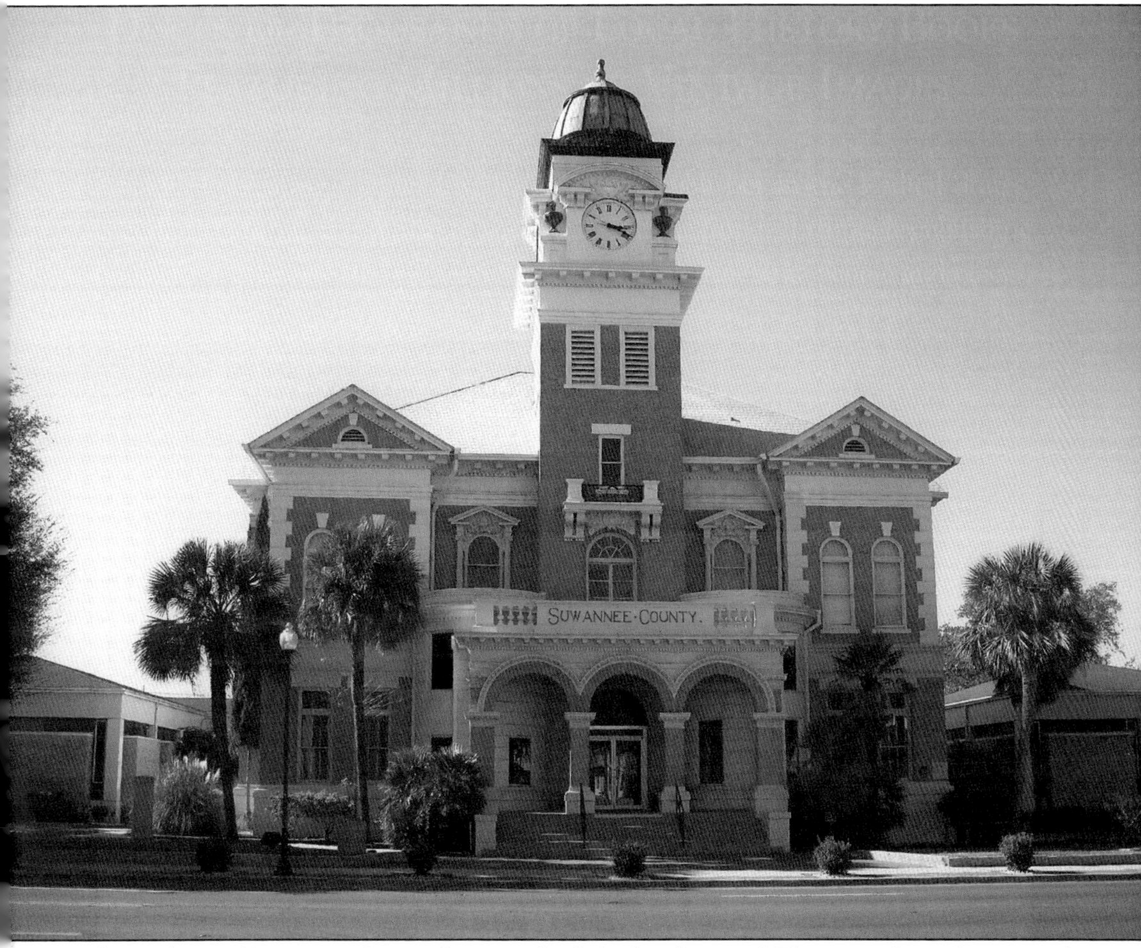

The residents of Suwannee County have much of which to be proud. Their courthouse has entered the second century of its service as part of an expanded government complex, comprising several buildings. It still rises above the landscape as the tallest building in the downtown area, with its crafted bell ringing out every hour as it has done since 1904. New businesses are appearing in Live Oak and the outlying areas of Suwannee County, although agriculture continues to be the predominant employer of residents. An abundance of historic events have occurred here since Suwannee County was created in 1858, many of which are documented in this book. Countless others have been lost to history. As Suwannee County has now entered the 21st century, citizens must reflect upon those who have come before them, those who have left their mark on this great community, and those who will continue to do so in the future. (SCCC.)